SUDAN:
State, Capital and Transformation

SUDAN

STATE, CAPITAL AND TRANSFORMATION

Edited by
TONY BARNETT and ABBAS ABDELKARIM

CROOM HELM
London • New York • Sydney

© 1988 T. Barnett and A. Abdelkarim
Croom Helm Ltd, Provident House, Burrell Row,
Beckenham, Kent, BR3 1AT

Croom Helm Australia, 44-50 Waterloo Road,
North Ryde, 2113, New South Wales

Published in the USA by
Croom Helm
in association with Methuen, Inc.
29 West 35th Street
New York, NY 10001

British Library Cataloguing in Publication Data

Sudan: state, capital and transformation.
    1. Sudan — Economic conditions
    I. Barnett, Tony. *1945*– II. Abdelkarim,
    Abbas
    330.9624'04   HC835
    ISBN 0-7099-5902-8

Library of Congress Cataloging-in-Publication Data

Sudan: state, capital, and transformation / [edited by] Tony Barnett
    and Abbas Abdelkarim.
        p.   cm.
    Papers presented at a seminar held at the School of Development
Studies, University of East Anglia, Norwich, England, in July 1984.
    ''Published in the USA . . . in association with Methuen, Inc.'' —
—Verso t.p.
    Includes index.
    ISBN 0-7099-5902-8
    1. Sudan — Economic policy — Congresses. 2. Sudan — Economic
conditions — Congresses. 3. Agriculture and state — Sudan-
-Congresses. 4. Agriculture — Economic aspects — Sudan — Congresses.
5. Debts, External — Sudan — Congresses. I. Barnett, Tony.
II. Abdelkarim, Abbas, 1950–   . III. University of East Anglia.
School of Development Studies.
HC835.S83534   1988   87-27575
338.9624—dc 19

Printed and bound in Great Britain by
Biddles Ltd, Guildford and King's Lynn

Contents

Preface

Many people have helped in the production of this book. The families and households of all the contributors have played some part. We would like to thank them. The School of Development Studies at the University of East Anglia provided finance and accommodation for the seminar at which these papers were first presented, as well as for the typing and editing of the manuscript. Two members of the School, John Cameron and John Harriss, acted as discussants for some of the sessions, and, as always, made valuable contributions.

Tony Barnett would like to thank two of the contributors, Abbas Abdelkarim and Abdalla Mohammed Elhassan, who spent four and five years respectively at the School of Development Studies exploring the problem of agrarian and rural transition in the Sudan, and in the process probably taught their thesis supervisor more than he taught them.

Very sincere thanks also to Samia Mahjoub and to Sarah Knights.

Readers should note that we have used the standard forms of Arabic words for common words, and the form provided by contributors where unusual words are concerned. The commonly used Sudanese unit of area, the feddan, is equal to 0.42 hectares or 1.038 acres.

Tony Barnett, Norwich, England.
Abbas Abdelkarim, Hawalli, Kuwait.

Introduction:
the Sudanese Crişis and the Future

Tony Barnett

The analysis of long-term scenarios should not divert our attention from the harsh reality of the moment. In 1984, for a number of reasons the rehabilitation programme came off-track. The new financial crisis is so severe that it cannot be solved with the traditional economic packages and debt reschedulings. The country has no creditworthiness except for the most concessional forms of aid and, in fact, cannot even afford the new terms of the IMF facilities. The time is pressing to find new solutions and establish an orderly process to address this crisis. In the absence of both strong economic measures and very generous aid, the true alternative scenario is one whereby Sudan's balance of payments and debt problems would result in a sharp and chaotic downward movement of the economy at great cost to the Sudanese people.

(World Bank 1985: xix)

Sudan's debt crisis is apparently insoluble. It cannot and will not totally default on its debt repayments since this would end all foreign aid and alienate its most important allies. At the same time continual rescheduling cannot and will not resolve the long term crisis. All it does is to drain the country of foreign currency and thereby prevent any sustained economic recovery. Unlike industrialised countries such as the US or UK, Sudan is in no position to 'tighten its belt' – it requires an economic emergency feeding programme rather than a diet. The only long term solution to the economic crisis is for part of the debt burden to be lifted.

(Gurdon 1986: 32)

INTRODUCTION

In July 1984, a group of predominantly Sudanese scholars met at the School of Development Studies, University of East Anglia, Norwich, England. The title of the seminar was 'State, Capital and Transformation in the Sudan'.

At that time it was apparent that the Numeiry regime could not last much longer. With the introduction of a particularly oppressive form of shari'a law, the brutal execution of eighty year-old Ahmed Mohammed Taha for 'heresy' in February 1985, a mounting debt crisis, and widespread but at that time under-reported famine, the focus of the seminar was an attempt to make sense of the enormous changes which had taken place in Sudan since independence in 1956, and particularly since 1969, and to consider the possibilities for the future.

Many of the participants in the seminar were completing or had recently completed their doctoral theses. Coming from a range of social science disciplines, it was at times difficult to tell in which particular discipline they had been trained. They shared a common language in which the insights from social anthropology, sociology, economics and geography could easily be combined, and were combined in their common concern over the future of their country.

For many years the Sudan had been one of the two expatriate social anthropologists' playgrounds (the other to my mind being Papua New Guinea), but now Sudanese scholars were taking control of their research and trying to use it to make sense of the historic processes at work in their society. This was the substance of the seminar and is the substance of this book.

Sudan is a predominantly agricultural country. Thus much of what was discussed had to do directly or indirectly with agrarian policy and the changes occurring in rural society. In common with many other countries of the Third World, Sudan was facing a crisis, but in this case, with mounting debts, civil war and famine, combined with a government trying ever more desperate strategies to remain in power, the crisis was fast turning into a tragedy of massive proportions, which at the time of writing seems to have little prospect of resolution as the very sombre quotations above suggest. While the famine in Ethiopia received widespread publicity, the authorities in Sudan were attempting to hide its first clear manifestations in the west of the country. The first famine refugees from the western provinces were beginning to arrive in Khartoum and the Gezira, and were shipped back to their home areas so as to remove visual evidence of the problem from the national capital.

The famine which by late 1985 and early 1986 engulfed half the population, was not a natural event. Although the precise conditions which transform any particular drought into a famine are still only partially understood (Sen 1981; Babiker 1985; Hulme and Trilsbach 1986; Barnett 1986), it has become increasingly apparent that to understand famine it is necessary to look at it in a very broad perspective and to understand the various ways in which human agency creates the conditions in which a drought becomes a famine. In short, to perceive famines as a problem of distribution which reflect the relative power of different social groups in the struggle over available resources. In this collection, we are provided with a range of detailed studies of many aspects of this struggle as it is taking place while Sudan undergoes its transformation to capitalism.

To state the case broadly, and thus to do violence to the disagreements and subtleties within this book, the Sudan has undergone two broad processes. During the colonial period, its agricultural development was designed to serve the requirements of the United Kingdom. Cotton monocropping took precedence over most other forms of agricultural change. In the post independence period, and particularly in the fifteen years of Numeiry's rule, a class of merchants, traders and commission men took almost exclusive control of social and political power, and thus of the state, for its own ends. This class, focusing on its own needs for accumulation and conspicuous consumption, and amply encouraged by the United States, and to a lesser extent the United Kingdom, for their strategic and commercial purposes, moved development policy in a direction which led to the neglect of the subsistence needs of the rural areas and rural populations. The impact of these policies was not uniform – some areas and some populations were needed to provide labour for profitable investment projects. Others, particularly in the south and west, experienced both exploitation and neglect, in this case overlaid by a patina of racism. It is noteworthy that the two regional investment projects on which central government spent most time, energy and money in the later years of the Numeiry period were oil exploration and the Jonglei Canal Project in the south — both of which can be perceived as ways of transferring natural resources, oil and water, from the south to the north (Johnson 1986: 47)

It became apparent as the discussions proceeded, that if anything was to be achieved after the departure of Numeiry, a clear analysis had to be made of how the Sudanese tragedy had been brought about. The papers in this book provide an outline for such an understanding.

INTRODUCTION

THE SHAPE OF THE CRISIS

The focus of any understanding of the present crisis must be on rural and agricultural policy, its roots and its effects. In some earlier research (Barnett 1975 and 1977), I emphasised the external causation of socio-economic transformation in the Sudan. This was in the main an adequate account, given that the Gezira Scheme, central to the country's economic performance, was a colonial construct. However, it is now apparent that the main focus of research today and for some time to come must be on the details of internal processes and their relationship to external changes and conditions. Of particular importance, is an attempt to understand the relationship between different sources of investment capital, policy assumptions current in government, and the forms of agricultural production which are planned and implemented. At a theoretical level, such research engages directly with classical debates about the role and development of agriculture (Lenin 1967; Banaji 1976; Chayanov 1966), as well as with broader discussions of social differentiation and the nature of the peasantry in the Third World (Bernstein 1977). These issues are discussed explicitly in the contributions by Elhassan and Abdelkarim.

However, this is not the whole story. The collection is entitled Sudan: State, Capital and Transformation, a recognition that the state is a major actor, that its policies express the interests of different factions of capital, both national and international, and that the form of society and economy which will determine the lives of most Sudanese in the last decade of the twentieth century and into the twenty-first century is now being struggled over in many arenas, which range through forms of labour contract, changes in land tenure, the organisation of the labour process, interpretations of popular Islam, to the introduction of Islamic law and banking and the shape of agricultural policy. In this struggle, the form and legitimacy of the Sudanese state and of Sudanese identity itself are in question. A recent observer of the situation in the south has described one outcome of such a struggle, a de facto breakdown of the state and of civil society, saying that "There is no longer a liberation struggle in south Sudan. It has now become a series of uncontrollable and catastrophic inter-tribal food wars" (Cater 1986).

In the early 1970s, the Sudanese government and also many of the governments of the Gulf states, notably those of Saudi Arabia and Kuwait, saw the country as the potential grain basket of the Arab world – a path out of the dependence by the Gulf states on imported food supplies, notably from the United States. Such a strategy would have been of some geopolitical importance, enabling in particular Saudi Arabia to play a more independent role in regional and world affairs. Within the Sudan, this

4

policy would have entailed a change in agricultural strategy, away from a long-term emphasis on the production and export of cotton, gum arabic and groundnuts, towards greatly increased food production, geographically more widely distributed, but even so, still predominantly for export. This expansion and change of direction was envisaged as taking the form of large projects, under the management either of government corporations or of various types of agribusiness entity. An important internal political pressure for increased geographical dispersion of these projects was a quest for a solution to the political problem of the south, and ultimately over the legitimacy of the state itself and the nature of "Sudanese" identity (see Doornbos in this collection). With the ending of the civil war in the South, in 1972, and the suppression of some other regional movements, the government in Khartoum made attempts to ensure that development investment was seen to be more evenly spread throughout the country. There were some very real achievements, in particular in the development of Sudan's infrastructure and in food production, the country becoming self-sufficient in basic foods such as sorghum during the mid-1970s.

These policies required a massive boom in public investment, funded by western and Arab money. Between 1972/73 and 1973/74, public investment rose by fifty percent in real terms (World Bank 1985: 2), and doubled in real terms by the end of the next year. This programme took place within the framework of the Five Year Plan, 1970/71-1974/75, which was later extended to 1976/77. This inflow of funds pushed economic growth up to around nine percent per year (World Bank 1985: 2; Gurdon 1986: 23). But much of it fed into private consumption, and, inevitably inflation also began to rise. The increase in world oil prices in 1973 added to the inflationary pressure. By 1976, the first problems began to appear. There was a sharp fall in foreign aid, but despite this, the government continued with its expansionary policies, attempting to finance the shortfall from domestic borrowing. With a low level of domestic savings, another twist was added to the inflationary spiral, and resulted in a depletion of foreign reserves. These developments, combined with management problems in the parastatals, as well as an artificially high exchange rate, quickly led to a falling-off of the growth rate. The exchange rate policy, which under-priced imported consumer goods, benefited those social groups which were already benefiting from the generous commissions and contracts spilling over from the high level of public sector investment.

Thus the period from 1969-83 was different from the preceding post-independence years. In particular, it marked a break in the relative balance of civilian and military rule in the Sudan. There was a disjunction in the political and socio-economic spheres, with a complete change of emphasis and orientation, away from some kind of, albeit uneasy, social consensus in which big-landowners, tribal leaders, religious leaders, major merchants and urban notables ensured the stability of the state (Niblock 1986: 35).

It is possible to divide this period into three distinct blocks. The first, from 1969 to 1971, covering the early years of the Numeiry regime, with its widespread nationalisations and flirtations with socialist rhetoric, stands out as a very distinct phase because a new coalition of social forces came to play a decisive role in the economy and the society. The polarisation and intensification of the struggle within the new coalition — including "workers, tenants and national capitalists" — over future paths of development was very pronounced. This coalition did not hold together for very long. Early in 1971, the conservative Mahdist forces rose against the apparently socialist government. This rising was put down with some brutality, and the Mahdists were seriously weakened. The continuing struggle for state power came to a dramatic conclusion following the defeat of the 19 July 1972 military movement led by left-wing members of the Free Officers' Organisation which had initiated the May 1969 coup d'etat. The subsequent execution of the leaders of the 19 July movement, completed the destruction of opposition forces, and opened the way for the state to be effectively taken over by the class of merchant capitalists, in alliance with the army and sections of the civil service, which had up to that time played an important, but never uncontested, role in Sudanese society.

The period from 1972-1976 witnessed sharp departures from the declared "socialist oriented" policies of the preceding period. This was a time of transition. On the one hand, it coincided with a process of consolidation of the political hegemony of the bureaucratic bourgeoisie, reorientation of the regime's policies and the adoption of its new socio-economic programme, the Interim Programme of Action, promulgated in 1972. This process of reorientation, reformulation and preparation of a "more conducive atmosphere" for foreign investment involved denationalisation and deconfiscation, suppression of trades unions, new investment acts, and was a preparation for the next period. This was characterised by an "open door policy", in which merchant capital was to take clear control of the state (see Gadkarim in this collection).

The emphasis of the period from 1976-1983 was on a development strategy in which foreign capital played a major role. In examining the Sudanese version of the Egyptian *infitah* policy, we have to take account of the complex interaction of both internal and external forces which contributed to the policy in the first place. In general terms, we are here concerned with the impact of the 1973 oil price rise and the need for recycling of OPEC surpluses both regionally and internationally, and in particular in relation to the Sudan, within an ideology of Afro-Arab Cooperation and a pan-Arab strategy. The latter was, as noted previously, directly related to the food strategy of the major Arab oil exporters, in which the Sudan figured as the most important partner. From 1978, however, a new phase was discernible within the open door policy. Direct and indirect reshaping and reorientation of the policies, programmes and plans were a result of pressures from multinational donors and investors through the combined effort of the IMF and the IBRD (Hussein in this collection).

Internally there was a continuing need at the political level for an accommodation between merchant capital, productive capital and foreign capital. This took various forms: privatisation, dismantling of state monopolies over certain areas of foreign trade and the financial sector, streamlining of the incentive structure in all sectors of the economy.

Such a brief attempt to periodise events has its limitations. Development plans and strategies are overlapping, discontinuous and even contradictory. This reflects the state's responses to the formation and reformation of political alliances, the internal structure of these alliances, the intensity of social contradictions, and, of course, international pressures. Despite these limitations, the method is useful for demonstrating clearly the general form of state policy over the whole period, and there is substantial agreement on this view of what happened (Gurdon 1986; Niblock 1986; Gadkarim in this collection). As demonstrated in a number of contributions to this collection, the outstanding feature at every level, from remote parts of Darfur (Doornbos) to large rainfed schemes in Kordofan (Elhassan), is the control of state policy by merchant capital, a process which has been documented in some detail elsewhere by Elhassan (1985) and Abdelkarim (1985). Although by 1983, this influence had weakened and Numeiry and his personal allies stood very much alone (Niblock 1986), it is the combination of this control with external factors, such as the effects of the oil price rise, the politics of oil supplies from Saudi Arabia, and above all the indebtedness resulting from the earlier massive investment policy, which is the major explanation of the current Sudanese tragedy. Suggestions for a way out of such a pit cannot be provided by a book like this. It can only come about as a result of the struggle of the Sudanese people against their exploitation and poverty, a struggle which takes many forms - the wage bargain of the labourers in Gedaref market place, the civil war in the south, and even the struggle by the Sudanese contributors to this book independently to understand the origins of the present situation.

THEMES

In the first paper in this collection, Taisier Mohammed Mahmoud Ali, analyses agricultural policy as the key to understanding the nature of the Sudanese state. He argues that state intervention in agricultural production extends beyond the mere allocation of resources, to a direct involvement in, and regulation of economic development and production. The state is analysed as an arena of class struggle in which the fundamental divisions, conflicts, compromises and forms of domination in society are worked out. It has generally functioned so as to perpetuate the reproduction of capitalist relations, and has taken on the form of a bourgeois state in which the fundamental contradiction is between labour and capital. He suggests that three broad periods can be identified in the development of agricultural policy. They are:

> 1956-1964: when there was horizontal expansion in government and private irrigation schemes combined with efforts to sustain and expand mechanised agriculture in the rainfed areas.
> 1964-1972: which saw extensive nationalisation of private schemes, encouragement of cooperatives and state farms and, in the final phase, an emphasis on rural development and self-help programmes.
> 1972 onwards: characterised by the development of joint ventures with foreign capital, management contracts with foreign firms and investors, intensive mechanisation, feverish attempts to involve international agribusiness and Arab capital.

Each of these stages in the development of agrarian policy signalled a rearrangement of political power within the ruling class and shifts in the balance of power among class fractions. However, there was also a high degree of continuity, involving a rearrangement of the relations between fractions of the dominant class. Apparently "new" policies are seen as having been expressions of the balance of political power between these fractions.

Hassan Gadkarim takes up another aspect of this question in his discussion of the state's attitudes to foreign private investment. Through a detailed analysis of legislation and of policy decisions, the divergence between state policy and practice in this area is exposed. He argues that the period from independence until 1969 can be seen as characterised by:

i) efforts to expand investment, mainly from domestic savings and loans from foreign governments and international organisations. At this time little foreign private capital participation was envisaged.
ii) concentration on investments in agriculture, which left the industrial sector (with the exception of some public sector factories established in the early 1960s) for the private sector.
iii) a dual policy of export promotion and import substitution, although in the end the underlying direction was export-oriented agriculture dependent on cotton.

Although the Numeiry regime began with an attitude hostile to private capital (both foreign and local), it soon reversed its position. Indeed, special attempts were made to attract foreign investment. The degree of change is exemplified by the supposed role of Lonrho in helping the Numeiry regime regain power in 1972. From this time onwards, there was increasing involvement of private capital in the Sudanese economy, and in particular of Arab investment. This strategy envisaged large inflows of foreign capital, mainly from Arab countries. The process continues up to the present, and, Hassan suggests, has at the very least, hindered the role of domestic savings and investment.

In the following paper, Hussein examines an important aspect of public foreign investment, taking up the now familiar question of the impact of the "conditionality" attaching to IMF loans in relation to the Sudanese case. By and large, the IMF imposes devaluation supported by anti-inflationary policies and the liberalisation of trade.

In correcting payment deficits, the IMF devaluation model attaches great importance to the mechanisms of relative prices, income distribution and real money balances. Serious doubt is cast in this case study on the appropriateness of the IMF diagnosis of balance of payments disequilibrium and the effectiveness of its policy prescriptions for the Sudan, policy prescriptions largely repeated again in the 1985 World Bank proposals (World Bank 1985). Nur al Din's objection is that the IMF diagnosis does not attempt to distinguish the underlying causes of payments deficits from their effects. Owing to its adverse effects on the terms of trade, and the low price and income elasticities of demand for imports, devaluation cannot contribute to an improvement in the balance of payments situation. He concludes that devaluation led to loss of foreign exchange earnings per unit of domestic input and also to a deterioration in profitability. It certainly did not stimulate increased production for export.

On the basis of this analysis, the paper concludes that "The Fund's role as an instrument to advance and protect the political and economic interests of some rich nations, its partiality and bias, are logical outcomes of the power structures within the fund".

In a note written hurriedly, and literally on the eve of the 1985 coup, Brown provides some background on the final round of economic austerity measures imposed by the Numeiry regime, and suggests that they constituted the end of a long process whereby the USA had attempted to maintain the Numeiry regime in power.

He attempts to shed light on the circumstances in which this particular policy package was formulated and implemented. In doing this, he also tries to illustrate the lengths to which the donor community, led by the government of the United States, was prepared to go in its efforts to avert, or at least forestall, the social and political manifestations of the deepening economic crisis. It is also argued that this last rescue operation differed from those of previous years in one important respect, perhaps signalling what was to have been the start of a new phase in the International Monetary Fund's relations with the authorities of Sudan, and which also brought out into the open the direct involvement of the US government in persuading the international donor community to commit the extraordinary levels of foreign aid that had been necessary to maintain some semblance of stability in an otherwise explosive environment.

The details of the transactions between the Sudanese authorities and the IMF in the twelve months prior to the downfall of Numeiry, raise a number of important questions. These concern both an understanding of the role of the international donor community in ousting the Numeiry government as well as the difficult task of formulating and financing a programme of economic reconstruction.

Brown says that while it is true that the Sudan will remain dependent on substantial external funding for some time to come, it can in fact bargain on the terms of this dependence from a position of relative strength in view of the West's fears of the alternatives to agreement with it.

The second part of the book presents a number of case studies. These deal with various aspects of the changes and shifts in policy discussed in the first part. Lako's contribution looks at the effects of one of the major proposed projects, the Jonglei Canal, on the people of the area, and in particular on the Dinka. It is the first paper in which we hear the voice of rural Sudanese expressing their views as to the effects of government policy on their lives. It is fitting that the first paper in this section should express the views of an important Southern group in view of the state of war between north and south, and the history of suspicion and distrust between the two. However, the aim of this paper is to present the views of the Government as well as those of the Dinka people. To this end, an analysis of government thinking about the Dinka subsistence, semi-nomadic economy is presented. This is followed by a consideration of the attitudes of the Dinka towards the scheme. Finally, some comments are made on the form and substance of the debate between Government and Dinka in the light of recent developments.

In particular, this paper looks at the differences in attitude among the Dinka in relation to the development of social differentiation, a subject which has received some consideration in studies of Northern communities, but which is under-researched as far as the south of the country is concerned.

The paper concludes that government views, attitudes and intentions have completely ignored the fact that Dinka society is now characterised by differences in wealth and capital endowments. Not only is Dinka society non-egalitarian, but it is likely to become more pronouncedly so with the development of the Jonglei project. The majority of the Dinka people are likely to gain little from the project.

Paul Doornbos's paper, dealing with developments in the west of the country, examines a question which is quite central to our concerns, the nature and construction of "Sudanese" identity. In a country as large, diverse and replete with social contradictions as the Sudan, state legitimacy is problematic. In this careful analysis, Doornbos shows the clear links between Sudanese identity, popular Islam, and the ideological hegemony of the merchant class, a link of some importance when we remember the rise to dominance of the merchant class during the Numeiry period and the introduction of shari'a law by that regime, as well as the strong showing made by Islamic forces in the 1986 election and the refusal of the new government of Saddiq al Mahdi to repeal shari'a.

Doornbos says that the introduction of shari'a law and its application to everyone present on Sudanese soil regardless of region or religion, cast doubt on the country's claim to act as a bridge between the Arab and the Black African world and to seek unity in diversity. In

11

fact, he suggests, trends towards furthering a more Islamic lifestyle and national identity have been going on for a long time, both formally and informally. Formal measures have included prohibition of alcohol in many provinces, as well as a ban on forms of gambling. There has also been government support for Islamic banking, insurance and missionary activities.

This paper looks at the informal spread of a more Arab-Islamic lifestyle in Western Darfur. Over a period of five years, the author has witnessed the virtual disappearance of traditional dancing, and a growing polarisation within the local community. The source of the polarisation has been disagreement over the proper way to live as a Muslim. The different ethnic groups of the area have lost much of their specific ethnic identity. This process represents the conversion from what is considered an increasingly irrelevant, narrow ethnic ethos and worldview to a new, prestigious and powerful ideology and practice. This trend, while splitting local communities, strengthens certain types of class and national identifications, and forms an important part of the process whereby the Islamic/merchant ideology becomes identified with the very legitimacy of the state.

Richard Brown and Elfatih Shaaeldin take up another important aspect of this Islamisation — the spread of Islamic banking. Since the formation of OPEC and the first rise in oil prices, Middle Eastern finance capital, and in particular the banks, has played an increasingly important economic and political role. This has not been restricted to the Middle East, but has affected the international financial system. Associated with this development there has been a revival, indeed a considerable upsurge, of Islamic banking practices in the region. Islamic banks are spreading throughout the Middle East, and some are being established in the non-Muslim west.

In Sudan the first bank of this type, the Faisal Islamic Bank (FIB) began operations in May 1978. This chapter has two purposes. It traces the origins, principles, performance and practices of the bank. It then goes on to analyse and interpret the significance of the FIB in the broader context of the role of banking capital in relation to its two counterparts – merchant and industrial capital. The main point of departure for the discussion is that the past and future activities and performance of the bank cannot be analysed or assessed purely in terms of Islamic principles and ideology. The underlying thrust of bank policy is to check foreign cultural domination of Muslim countries, with the longer term intention of eradicating Muslim feelings of inferiority vis-a-vis the West. In addition, the authors suggest that the Islamic banking system operates in the interests of particular fractions of capital.

The next two papers in the book examine processes of class formation and class struggle in rural Sudan. Abbas Abdelkarim discusses
some aspects of commoditisation and transformation. He begins by
looking at commoditisation of the means of production and consumption and the role of circulation capital. He argues that increased
dependence on the market to obtain the means of production has been
characteristic of many farming communities during this century. He
identifies two main forces in this process – the introduction of water
pumps and of tractors. These innovations have not merely involved the
introduction of a higher level of forces of production. Their use has
also expanded as a result of quantitative changes in the process of
primitive capital accumulation. Their introduction has contributed to
the deepening of this process, tractorisation in particular has caused
fundamental changes both in the level of forces of the production and
in the nature of class structure.

The role of trade and finance has also been important. Household
producers are in general increasingly dependent on the market to meet
their subsistence needs. As a result of government policies, agricultural products exchange on unequal terms with internally produced
goods, thus household producers enter into unequal exchange when
purchasing internally produced commodities. Given these increasingly unfavourable terms of exchange, the more the household producers depend on the market for subsistence, the greater the pressure
towards commoditisation. The more the households need to cashcrop
and/or sell their labour power to supplement their previous production,
so they face increased pressure towards commoditisation in the credit
market.

Abdelkarim argues that circulation capital feeds the commoditisation process in a number of ways. It enlarges the circle of needs of the
household producers, it leads to deterioration of the conditions of
exchange, it breaks up the peasant household, ultimately leading to a
capitalist reorganisation of production relations.

Having dealt with the general processes of commoditisation,
Abdelkarim turns to the transformation of labour organisation and the
commoditisation of labour power. He looks at a number of case studies
— Gedaref, the Gezira, Dar Kabbabish, Dongola, Western Savannah
and the Dinka region.

Finally, he examines the commoditisation of land. He argues that
the state has been the main force behind this. He observes that there is
a strong relationship between the two processes of commoditisation -
of land and of labour. Where there is a distinct landless class, and where
there is a predominance of wage labour, the commoditisation of labour

13

has reached its highest level. Where an initial step towards land
alienation has been taken (as in the Gezira) and where the state has
hindered the process of commoditisation of land and labour, a process
of decommoditisation has begun (Barnett and Abdelkarim 1987).
However, he mentions that as in the case of other social relationships,
a positive relation between the two processes of commoditisation can
only be described as a tendency. At any specific place or time, a number
of other variables may intervene.

In a related study, Abdalla Mohammed Elhassan focuses on the
effects of the expansion of money-commodity relations, and more
specifically large-scale mechanised farming, on the Nuba peasant
farmers of the Western Savannah in South Kordofan. Using data from
a study of four villages, the chapter shows how, prior to the establishment of mechanised large-scale farms, land was abundantly available.
Expansion of capitalist farming has led not only to land confiscation
and reduction of the land area available to the villages, but also to a
reduction of the available forest areas which played an important part
in the subsistence activities of the people. Equally, the development of
the mechanised schemes has made it possible for a small segment of the
better-off peasants to hire tractors and also those workers who have
been "freed" as a result of the expansion of the schemes.

Three forms of labour organisation are available to the peasants of
the Western Savannah — their own household labour, wage labour and
traditional voluntary labour gangs. The combination of these different
forms differs in different production units. However, there is a clear
trend towards larger landholding employing wage labour. As yet, there
is no landless class, but what is clear is that the smaller the land available
to the household, the more likely are household members to sell their
labour on the local labour market.

Elhassan argues that dependence on the market, either in buying or
selling labour, has become essential for the reproduction of the peasant
households. For some relatively well-off households, involvement in
non-farming activities such as craftwork, has become crucial for
household survival. For some of the better-off households involvement
in these off-farm activities is a stage in a process of accumulation and
investment in agriculture. For others, off-farm activities are necessary
in order to supplement their inadequate agricultural production.

The expansion of money-commodity relations, and especially the
expansion of large-scale mechanised farming, has led to a process of
differentiation among the peasantry of the Western Savannah. While
for the present this is not very pronounced, the study predicts that the
same sort of land pressures and changes in the social structure which

have occurred in two of the villages closest to the new, extensive farms will in time affect the other two villages, as rainfed capitalist farming expands. This indicates clearly that processes of differentiation are in train in the rural Sudan, leading to the development of a rural bourgeoisie and proletariat.

In his chapter dealing with the urban sector, Ibrahim examines aspects of rural-urban relations in a manner which connects directly with the concerns of the two preceding papers. He considers the emergence and expansion of the urban wage labour market, emphasising the connection between that market and the more general processes of peripheral capitalism. He looks closely at the "intra-urban" processes underlying the operation of the urban wage market, concentrating on the colonial period, but with the clear implication, taken up elsewhere (Ibrahim 1985), that these processes continue into the present.

The central point which he raises is that, from their inception, urban wage labour markets have been underpinned by the processes of what he terms "peripheral capitalist urbanism". This term is meant to characterise that pattern of urban life whose primary objective is the fulfilment of the requirements of capital accumulation in a colonial trade economy created by the internationalisation of the capitalist mode of production. This results in conditions where small producers are unable to develop their forces of production, and means that they cannot initiate and sustain viable accumulation which might lead to mechanisation, because of the monopsonistic position of the commercial bourgeoisie and petty-bourgeoisie (Ibrahim 1980; O'Brien 1980).

He argues that, given the centrality of agricultural production in the process of peripheral capital accumulation, it is hardly surprising that during both the colonial and post-colonial periods, serious attempts have been made by government to conserve and sustain (as opposed to 'develop') domestic production. But, although the colonial administration attempted to to conserve the domestic form of agricultural production, its incorporation into the circuit of capital, through subordination to merchant capital, has in the long run resulted in proletarianisation (if only seasonally) of increasing numbers of small producers. Given the virtual absence of alternative arenas for the extraction of surplus value, the main refuge for the partially proletarianised peasants and pastoralists is wage employment in both the large irrigated and rainfed schemes. It is only recently, with the escalation of the economic crisis and the decline in the real earnings of small producers, that increasing numbers of wage labour migrants have turned towards urban centres in search of income-generating opportunities.

Having developed this point, Ibrahim goes on to suggest that the

15

processes of urbanism and urbanisation in contemporary Sudan, which originate in the colonial period, are founded on the requirements of the colonial trade economy. Thus, the main processes underlying Sudanese urbanisation since the turn of the century have been administration and commerce, maintaining primary export production and capital accumulation. Such a pattern of urbanisation not only presupposes the conservation of domestic agricultural production, but also requires a substantial urban wage labour force. The emergence of such an urban wage labour force in the contemporary Sudan, however, hardly relates to the basic activities underlying the rise and growth of urban areas. Rather, it is the consequence, on the one hand, of the acceleration of proletarianisation in the rural areas and, on the other, of the increase in opportunities in the so-called "urban informal sector". This last, moreover, is closely related to the rapid urban population growth which is not so much natural increase as a consequence of the increase in the numbers of civil servants, professionals and members of the different fractions of the bourgeoisie and their dependents. These latter categories are the elements that control the larger part of the surpluses created in the countryside and transferred to the urban areas, especially to Greater Khartoum. In this connection, it is the writer's central contention that the increase in the size of the urban wage–labour force in recent years reflects the hope by many migrants of gaining access to a share in the surplus by providing various services to those who control that surplus. These processes and structures, grounded in the colonial era, have not altered fundamentally in the post-colonial period.

Thus, we see the same themes appearing and reappearing at every level in this collection. The dominance of merchant capital, the development of differentiation in the rural areas, the relation between the Nile Valley and the rest of the country, the conflict of interests between the Sudan and its creditors and, fundamentally, the questions of who is to control the state, on what terms, and in whose interests?

REFERENCES

Abdelkarim, A. (1985) "Primitive Capital Accumulation in the Sudan", unpublished Ph.D. thesis, University of East Anglia.

Babiker, M., "Agricultural Production and Environmental Change in Western Kordofan, Sudan", unpublished paper presented to the conference on The Human Factor in Ecological Change: case histories from the 19th and 20th centuries, Nuffield College, Oxford July 8 1985.

Banaji, J. (1976) *The Agrarian Question* (by Karl Kautsky): translation and summary of selected parts, *Economy and society*, vol. 4, no. 1, pp. 1-49.

Barnett, T., The Gezira Scheme: production of cotton and the reproduction of underdevelopment, in Oxaal, Barnett and Booth 1975.

Barnett, T. (1977) *The Gezira Scheme: an Illusion of development*, Frank Cass and Co., London.

Barnett, T., Socio-economic processes of drought and famine in Eritrea and Sudan, unpublished paper presented at conference on Problems and Prospects in the Sahel, at the Institute of Terrestrial Ecology, Grange- over-Sands, Cumbria, May 28-29 1986.

Barnett, T., and Abdelkarim, A. (1987) *Sudan: The Gezira Scheme and Capitalist Transformation in Agriculture*, Frank Cass and Co., London.

Bernstein, H. (1977) Notes on capital and the peasantry, *Review of African Political Economy*, vol. 10, pp. 60-73.

Cater, N., "When food is a deadly weapon", *Guardian*, London, August 8, 1986.

Chayanov, A.V. (1966) *The theory of peasant economy*, edited by D. Thorner, Richard D. Irwin, Illinois, 1966.

Elhassan, A.M. (1985) "The state and the development of capitalism in the Sudan", unpublished Ph.D. thesis, University of East Anglia.

Gurdon, C., "The economy of Sudan and recent strains", in Woodward 1986.

Hulme, M. & Trilsbach, A., "Rainfall trends and rural changes in Sudan since Nimeiri: some thoughts on the relationship between environmental changes and political control", in Woodward 1986.

Ibrahim, I.E., unpublished note prepared for the seminar State, Capital and Transformation in the Sudan, University of East Anglia, Norwich, 1984.

Ibrahim, S.E. (1980) *Beyond underdevelopment: structural constraints on the development of the productive forces among the Jok Gor*, Sudan, African Savannah Studies, Bergen Occasional Papers in Social Anthropology, no, 22, The University Printer, Bergen.

Ibrahim, S.E. (1985) "Peripheral urbanism in the Sudan: explorations in the political economy of the urban wage-labour market in Greater Khartoum", unpublished Ph.D. thesis, University of Hull.

International Bank for Reconstruction and Development (1985) *Prospects for rehabilitation of the Sudanese economy*, three volumes, Report no. 5496-SU, Washington.

Johnson, D., "North-South Issues", in Woodward 1986.

Lenin, V.I. (1967) *The development of capitalism in Russia*, Progress Publishers, Moscow.

Niblock, T., "The background to the change of government in 1984", in Woodward 1986.

O'Brien, J. (1980) "Agricultural labour and development in the Sudan", unpublished Ph.D. thesis, University of Connecticut.

Oxaal, I., Barnett, T. and Booth, D. (eds) (1977) *Beyond the sociology of Development*, Routledge and Kegan Paul, London.

Sen, A. (1984) *Poverty and famines: an essay on entitlement and deprivation*, Clarendon Press, Oxford.

Woodward, P. (ed.) (1986) *The Sudan after Nimeiri*, Centre of Near Eastern and Middle Eastern Studies, School of Oriental and African Studies, University of London.

2

The State and Agricultural Policy: In Quest of a Framework for Analysis of Development Strategies

Taisier Mohammed Ahmed Ali

INTRODUCTION

The reasons for proposing an analysis of agricultural policies as the key to understanding the Sudan's socio-economic and political conditions are simple but forceful. In the Sudan, agriculture engages over 85% of the labour force, contributing about 40% to Gross Domestic Project, provides more than 90% of the country's hard currency earnings and accounts for over 90% of the exports (Ministry of National Planning 1977).

Even the industrial sector is primarily concerned with processing agricultural products. Thus, the output of this sector determines the performance of the whole economy. For this reason, policies directed toward the agricultural sector are of fundamental importance. Not only do they affect the everyday life of all Sudanese, but because of the overwhelming importance of agriculture, it is inconceivable that any government policy toward this sector could long continue if it did not reflect the power and interests of the dominant socio-economic forces. State intervention in Sudanese agricultural production is massive, extending far beyond the mere allocation of resources to the direct regulation and programming of economic development. Through licensing, export-import control, financial and other budgetary and planning policies, state organs govern land allocation, pricing, market-ing and financing of crop production as well as the quality, quantity and cost of farm implements, machinery and other inputs. In return, agriculture and its related operations furnish the national treasury with the greatest proportion of its income. During the early years of independence, this represented about 80% of central government

19

revenue (Department of Statistics 1960). Since then, the Sudanese state has continued to appropriate an increasing share of the surplus generated by agriculture and has deepened its management of the sector and its direct engagement in production, accumulation and consumption. Thus the Sudanese state is wedded to agriculture in a very catholic fashion.

National development initiative, particularly in agriculture, was focussed mainly on the regions surrounding the Gezira and along the banks of the two Niles and the main Nile. The outer regions were given attention only insofar as they provided agricultural output from which the state treasury, and thus the dominant social groups, benefited. Social services in the fields of health, education and general welfare have been concentrated in the urban areas around the capital, the sea port at Port Sudan, and around the large agricultural schemes. The inhabitants of regions remote from these have too often been left with minimum state support to fend off malnutrition and poverty. The difficulties of these communities have been aggravated further by the continuing migration of their young and able-bodied members in search of economic opportunities.

The population of the Sudan's southern provinces have faced even worse conditions than those in the north. Not only have they shared the deteriorating socio-economic fate of other rural areas, but they have been subjected to brute, and very often indiscriminate, state violence. As a result, during the years from 1956 to 1972, the very few agricultural schemes in existence underwent virtual collapse. Instability in the southern provinces provided successive regimes with a ready excuse to freeze and deny agricultural or any kind of development to the local population. In fact, for the seventeen years preceding the Addis Ababa Agreement, little or no effort was made to reach the local populace; instead the ruling class directed all its efforts towards military objectives and negotiations with political representatives of groups in the south with interests congruent to its own. As a consequence, state policies perpetuated violence and throttled any chance of development in the region.

This paper examines the evolution of agricultural development strategies while at the same time identifying those social groups whose interests were either served or sacrificed. Consequently, the emphasis is not on agricultural policies per se, but rather on the link between development strategies and the changes in the socio-economic structures and in turn on the dialectical relationship of these with politics.

Underlying this analysis is the assertion that state policies are not the work of an individual minister or a single specialised department of state. It is assumed that state policies do not automatically embody the common good. The state is not a divinely solid and unified institution to be revered, feared or hated for itself. Like other institutions, it is the product of socio-economic interactions among people engaged in living their lives within specific relations of production. States are special insofar as they tend to reflect or condense the fundamental divisions, conflicts, compromises and inequalities in a society. States in capitalist societies are deeply implicated in processes of capital accumulation and the establishment of political hegemony. Hence, in order to understand agricultural strategies, we need to know about the evolution of the state in the Sudan. This will enable us to capture the processes of growth, propagation and development of the various socio-economic and political forces.

From this perspective, the state in the Sudan has its particular institutional matrix, but the institution is not independent of social classes or of the conflicts between them. On the contrary, it is itself a product of conflicts, competing interests, negotiations and strivings for domination. In the case of the Sudan, application of this theoretical perspective is complicated by the fact that relations of production are in a state of transition from pre-capitalist to capitalist forms; thus class struggles and conflicts of interest reflect aspects of this transformation. The bureaucratic and coercive power of the state gives it a certain institutional autonomy, but its main source of power derives from the power of the classes and the class fractions which at any time constitute the dominant power bloc. The autonomy of the Sudanese state vis-a-vis Sudanese society has at times been heightened by the strength of external interests — particularly, at different times and in different degrees, those of Britain, Egypt and the United States.

While the existence of pre-capitalist relations adds to the complexity of analysing the state in the Sudan, it is still possible to uncover its essence, which is that the Sudanese bourgeoisie has consistently used the state sector to serve its needs as it accumulates and expands its capital.

The post-colonial state has generally functioned in such a way as to perpetuate and further the reproduction of capitalist production relations, so much so that the capitalist mode of production is now the driving force in contemporary Sudanese society. Therefore, the state in the Sudan — despite local specificities — has all the hallmarks of a bourgeois state. While for many decades in the past, the primary contradiction was within and between fragments of the dominant class, each attempting to exploit sectarian or ethnic sentiments to further its interests, the fundamental contradiction which has gradually evolved is

21

that between labour and capital.

The aim of this paper is not solely to provide a description of agricultural or economic strategies. The objective here is to analyse the formulation as well as the consequences of such policies. It is not only what those policies were which concerns us, but essentially why and how they came into being. In other words, to understand the 'real' meaning and purpose of the agricultural strategies, we need to examine the dynamics of this profoundly complex configuration of interests.

ON AGRICULTURAL STRATEGIES

If we examine the agricultural strategies adopted by successive Sudanese regimes, we can identify certain shifts in their professed policies. The fact that these shifts have not been revealed in previous analyses, reveals shortcomings in the literature. One major reason for these shortcomings is that changes in economic policies have been attributed almost entirely to changes in regimes or in cabinet portfolios. The present paper presents a very different perspective.

In the first place, declared policies have to be seen as expressions of political biasses arising from existing power structures and property relations. Linkages between political biasses and economic strategies are not transitory or accidental. Both are anchored in class interests. But we know that social conditions and relations among socio-economic groups are in constant flux, and that they carry within them the seeds of new social alliances and conflicts of interests.

PERIODISATION

The changes in Sudanese agriculture that this paper identifies can be delineated as follows:

> 1956-64 Horizontal expansion in government irrigation schemes, e.g. the Managil Extension to the Gezira Scheme and the Khashm al Girba scheme; expansion of mechanised agriculture in rainfed areas.
> 1964-72 Nationalisation of the private schemes; encouragement of the cooperatives and state farms; later a strong emphasis on rural development and self-help programmes.
> 1972+ Joint ventures with foreign capital; management contracts with foreign firms and investors; intensive mechanisation; attempts to involve international agribusiness and Arab capital.

Certain basic facts about Sudanese politics must be emphasised. First, the ruling parties and the dominant political strata of the early independence years failed to produce any clearly defined programmes. Secondly, decisions were invariably taken by fractions of the ruling class and were imposed from above, with minimal grass-roots participation. Third, the bureaucracy remained locked into practices and attitudes which had been laid down by the structure of the colonial administration.

Nonetheless, since the shifts described earlier resulted not from clearly articulated plans but were essentially reactions to various cross-pressures within the state, the policy shifts often appeared as irresolute and wavering policy drifts. Sudanese agriculture, as with the whole national economy throughout the 1960s, seems to have been experiencing a process of rumination rather than of transformation — chewing again what has already been chewed once. This metaphor sums up agricultural policy during the early post-colonial period. Obsolete practices have lingered or reappeared at later dates. Total and complete change rarely took place, either in economic policies or in agricultural strategies. Attempts at radical change were effectively contained by the dominant social groups who benefited from the structures passed down by the colonial rulers.

The policies adopted by the first parliamentary government of 1956 continued without noticeable interruption despite the military takeover in 1958. The popular movement which restored civilian rule in 1964 exerted new pressures on the ruling class to implement progressive socio-economic policies. The military coup d'etat of 1969 was but one reflection of the continued strife among various forces in Sudanese society. The year 1972 was a political watershed in that it marked the beginning of a new power arrangement realised by a faction of the petty-bourgeoisie which was reflected in policies towards the agricultural sector.

What is consistent throughout the history of agricultural development over the past thirty years is that policy was always in harmony with the interests of the dominant class. A major contention of this paper is that changes in agricultural policies always signalled a re-arrangement of political power within the ruling class and shifts in the balance of power among class fractions. For that reason, changes in agricultural strategy were never fundamental; they invariably represented a new articulation of the changed composition of, and interests within, the dominant class. No wonder, then, that these shifts did not lead to a reduction in income differentials. Nor did they alleviate the abject poverty of the majority of Sudanese. In 1976, the International Labour Organisation reported that:

> ...living conditions and the way of production for millions of people in the Sudan are not very different from what they were at the end of the last century (ILO 1976: 11).

THE COLONIAL STATE AND AGRICULTURE

In the Sudan, state involvement in agricultural operations has a long history. Both the Turco-Egyptian government and the Mahdist state exercised control over land use as well as output and distribution of the product. But it was the sixty year Anglo-Egyptian Condominium which overwhelmingly shaped the present economy in general, and agriculture in particular. Condominium rule was essentially British rule, Egypt itself being a protectorate of the British Crown. It should be of no surprise then that the policies formulated by the colonial administrators were designed to suit the interests of the imperial power. It was because of the grand strategic interests of Britannia that the Sudan was first occupied and this remained an important factor governing the nature of the colonial state throughout its span of six decades.

If Britain's acquisition of colonial territories was generally motivated by economic interests such as hunger for raw materials and the securing of markets, then the case of the Sudan is an exception from the general pattern. The conquest of the Sudan was engineered mainly in response to the threat posed by the Mahdist state and its attempts to destabilise Egypt. Such a situation jeopardised Britain's hold over the Suez Canal, essential to its trade routes to the Far East.

It would be erroneous to suggest that the military character of the condominium administration was created solely by regional strategic and security imperatives. In addition, the threat of nationalist opposition and Mahdist fervour did not end with the defeat of organised Mahdist resistance. Rather, "hardly a year... passed [following] the reoccupation without the need for a punitive expedition" (MacMichael 1954: 107).

Militarism was not the only characteristic which differentiated the Sudan's colonial administration from that of other British colonies. The Governor-General commanded the unquestioning loyalty of his British staff without the intervention of any department in London, and was delegated full authority by the Foreign Office. In this fashion extensive state control of the economy took root in the administration of the country. Not only was statism entrenched during the colonial period, but together with its accompanying tendency, militarism, it continued to plague the post-colonial state.

However, neither an understanding of statism nor of militarism can adequately explain the full range of forces which shaped state policies. Such an understanding requires consideration of the class basis of the decision-makers. A study of the colonial administration indicates that:

> Some of the members of the Sudan Political Service were sons of the country gentry, and the remainder were generally the offspring of their collateral branches...None came from either the working class or even the managerial groups (Collins 1972: 301).

The socio-economic background of the British officials was to a large extent responsible for the conservative social and economic policies of the condominium regime. This conservatism was further strengthened by concern for the unstable state of internal security. As a result, the colonial state delicately nurtured the traditional leaders and hereditary rulers of Sudanese society. As a result, economic policy was excessively conservative. Even the colonial state's most prized achievement, the massive Gezira irrigation scheme, was not the result of an independent bold initiative by the Sudan Political Service. Rather, it was brought about by the concerted effort of several interested parties (including private enterprise) which only materialised after more than a quarter of a century of colonial rule.

The Sudan, like the majority of African and Asian countries, experienced rapid social and economic transformation as a direct result of colonial rule. The condominium regime expanded the infrastructural base of the economy through the construction of a new sea port at Port Sudan, linked by railway to the crop–producing areas. This was accompanied by expansion of some of those areas, particularly in the Tokar delta. Gradually, the Sudan was given the task of supplying British markets with cotton and some other primary products. At the same time, the national market became the exclusive domain for British products. These processes accelerated integration into the money economy, and signalled the most important phase in the penetration of the capitalist mode of production.

Colonial rule accelerated structural change. A major catalyst in this process was the implantation of a capitalist sector geared towards exclusive production of primary products for export. From the establishment of the Gezira Scheme in 1924, the state emerged as a large capitalist entrepreneur, investing in infrastructure and in production and the hire of wage labour. Simultaneously, local petty commodity production was discouraged by foreign imports; national industry, limited as it was, suffered.

Export-oriented agricultural production was stimulated. Even subsistence production was drawn into the money economy, and small-scale agricultural and pastoral activities were brought into the export market through the mediation of an expanding fraction of the bourgeois and petty-bourgeois class, the small brokers and rural traders. Colonial rule in the Sudan reshaped, redirected and reoriented previously existing processes of change and development. Admittedly, these indigenous processes were not highly advanced and their evolution was slow; still, the pre-colonial development process was self-sustained and was in harmony with and parallel to the level of productive forces of its time.

The pattern of colonial development was preceded by the establishment of administrative, judicial and technological institutions to serve, protect and propagate the new order. The bureaucracy and the legal code, not to mention military might, ensured the stability of colonial rule. Apart from its taxation weapons, the colonial state extracted surplus at the level of exchange through monopoly control over the marketing of primary commodities, a form of indirect taxation. In addition, a direct assault was launched at the level of production through control of landownership. In the first year of the condominium, a land ordinance was passed, making all land the property of the colonial state unless private ownership could be proved (Martin 1921: 353).

Such policies, together wih the expansion of the economic infrastructure, the existence of an autocratic administration eager to expand foreign export-import oriented operations, a private sector dominated by expatriates, were all important factors for the reorientation of national productive resources along channels servicing foreign trade and the requirements of the new markets.

The traditional leaders and hereditary rulers were quick to take advantage of the opportunities opened up by the British conquest. They ensured that their sons learned English and secured positions in the civil or military bureaucracies or in commercial enterprises. Traditional merchants became underlings of the foreign import-export houses, and their trading activities within the country became largely oriented to collecting exportable materials and distributing imported goods. Colonial agricultural policies favoured the traditional civil and religious leaders, offering great opportunities for rural traders and grain handlers to realise profits well above normal by imposing rack-rents on the peasants and lending money at usurious and at times astronomical rates of interest (Awad 1973). The Sudan at this time was experiencing a build-up of productive forces directly organised around the production and marketing of agricultural exports. Thus there was a growth of incomes gained from and dependent upon these exports.

From the early days of the condominium, foreign capital began to perceive an Eldorado in the enormous areas of uncultivated land. Yet the conservative economic policies of the colonial state, coupled with the previously noted class ideology of its British personnel, were suspicious of foreign private enterprise, and thus very few concessions were granted. The Sudan Experimental Plantations Syndicate (SPS), which later managed the Gezira Scheme, was the first of many foreign investors to operate in the country. Formed in 1904, the enterprise was the brainchild of an American agriculturalist, who in partnership with some London merchants planned to bring black Americans to the Sudan as settlers. At about the same time and parallel to these moves, the London based British Cotton Growers Association (BCGA) was formed in 1902 with the aim of promoting cotton cultivation in the colonies. The BCGA was pushed to the centre of the stage by the failure of the American and Egyptian long staple cotton crops in 1909.

A longer term cause of Britain's concern was that Egyptian cotton production had levelled off for a decade with no additional cultivable land remaining. Equally significant as a source of concern over the supply of raw cotton for the British spinning and weaving industry, was the need to guard against supply shortages and consequent rises in price, since '...an increase of 2 1/2 d per lb on the world's cotton crop would be equivalent to a sum of sterling pounds 100 million' (Martin 1921: 338-9). Thus, when the BCGA publicised news of the Sudan's potential, it relieved the anxiety of British capital concerning the supply of cotton, which showed heightened interest in the Sudan's cotton. For this reason the BCGA acquired shares in the Sudan Experimental Plantations Syndicate.

Involvement of the BCGA with the Syndicate gave the latter greater leverage vis-a-vis the colonial state, which recognised the Syndicate's potential as a lobby for industrial capital and the pressure which the BCGA could exercise on the British Government. Ironically, the efforts of the BCGA and the SPS to conclude a management agreement for the Gezira Scheme with the Sudan Government took much longer than that which was needed to achieve the more difficult task of obtaining a British Government loan for the construction of the irrigation system. Much of this delay was symptomatic of the previously remarked economic conservatism of the members of the Sudan Political Service, and their anxiety at possibly losing control of the affairs of the country.

Not all of the colonial policies connected with the agricultural sector

27

were the result of external pressures. One far-reaching decision that was inspired by domestic considerations dealt with the granting of licences for private pump irrigation. Briefly stated, the official aim of this policy was to encourage large-scale production of cotton along the Nile. The immediate significance of these developments lay in the fact that they were used by the colonial state to create an economic base for its supporters. After more than two decades in the Sudan, the British finally discovered allies in the leaders of northern indigenous political institutions. This traditional leadership possessed the potential to fulfill certain tasks. First, this leadership was to provide the bulwark against nationalist ideas which might threaten the established order; second, the native administration would serve as a relatively inexpensive system of indirect rule.

Following the inauguration of this system, the British began to issue licences for the private pump schemes on the Nile. Many tribal and religious leaders obtained the largest of these schemes. The list of those granted permits for private schemes included the most prominent traditional leaders, the pillars of Sudan's religious aristocracy. These included the three main sectarian leaders who were knighted by the British and later sponsored the country's largest political parties, the Umma, the People's Democratic Party and the National Unionist Party. In short then, private pump schemes were used as prizes to win the support of indigenous leaders so as both to reward their compliance and strengthen their dominant social position.

Sudanese businessmen, together with foreign finance capital, were also deeply involved in these schemes. Their participation added an economic significance to the previously noted political role of this form of capitalist development. Most of the finance for these schemes came from foreign commercial banks with branches in the Sudan (particularly Barclays DCO) as well as foreign capitalists operating in the country. In general, the banks shunned direct investment of this type because of its long term nature. The common practice was for them to provide the capital for agents, who would later deal with the scheme owners. A result of this type of operation was the rise of a group of Sudanese financiers, many of whom were themselves landowners.

The Nile Pumps Control Ordinance which governed these schemes allowed for ten to fifteen years ownership, but emphasised the financial ability of applicants. The spirit and practice of the ordinance, as indeed the whole evolution of the private pumps policy, reveals the economic leitmotif of the colonial state. This was to ensure the production of more cotton at the lowest possible price. As a result, it was essential to keep operating expenses to a minimum. The relationship between licensees and tenants was governed by rules which discriminated against the latter (Ali 1983).

Hence, the first half of this century witnessed not only the birth and expansion of gravity irrigation, but also the growth of private pump schemes. The number of the latter rose from 13 in 1904, to 244 by 1939. By 1954, the total had risen to 1,331. In the Gezira, the initial pilot projects in 1915 covered 21,600 feddans; by 1930 these had increased to 240,000 feddans, and in the 1950s the cropped area had expanded to nearly one million feddans.

A third variety of agricultural activity which existed among rural communities in the savannah regions was rainfed cultivation. In these areas, and in the absence of access to cash crop markets, production based on the accumulated experience of the farmers was almost entirely geared towards subsistence crops. Agricultural activity was supplemented by herding, hunting and charcoal burning. Some members of these communities, in locations close to irrigated areas, were at times attracted to the seasonal labour market for cotton operations. On the whole, however, the colonial state almost totally ignored the rainfed regions and their inhabitants.

The outbreak of World War II, and the supply needs of the Allied forces in Africa, attracted the attention of the colonial state to the potential of rainfed cultivation. In an effort to create a grain surplus, the government promoted the extension of shifting cultivation, and in addition experimented with mechanised farming operations — mainly in the Eastern Sudan. Thus in the short period between 1944 and 1946, the area of mechanised rainfed agriculture in Gedaref increased from 12,000 to 21,000 feddans. Following that expansion, some 340,000 feddans were expropriated from the nomadic Shukriyya people. From this time, rainfed mechanised farming increased steadily and was left exclusively to private operators. During the early period, 1948/9, plot sizes averaged about 30 feddans; a few years later, these increased to 240 feddans. But it was not until the early 1960s that this form of agricultural activity experienced an explosive expansion. By then the pattern of operation which had emerged was very lucrative for the leaseholders, and a key element in the overall process of capital accumulation.

Plots of 1,000 feddans were leased for very nominal charges, and the government surveyed, tested and prepared the land at its own expense. Moreover, the state imported agricultural equipment and offered it on easy terms to farm owners, most of whom were merchants or civilian or military bureaucrats. The traditional farmers were forced either to seek land further away from their villages, or to hire themselves out as wage labourers, while the nomadic tribes, deprived of their traditional grazing grounds, were forced to drive their herds over longer distances, with great inconvenience and loss of livestock.

Such were the colonial state's activities in the three main areas of Sudanese agricultural production. A feature of these activities had been the introduction of intensive capitalist production relations and the marginalisation of the traditional farmers.

THE POST–COLONIAL STATE AND AGRICULTURE

The Anglo-Egyptian Condominium government, up to the time of World War II, made no provision for long range public investment in, or development of, the Sudan's agricultural resources. The main thrust of colonial economic efforts centred on the development of "growth enclaves" in irrigated agriculture. These were mainly for cotton production. Apart from this, the state made some allocation for basic infrastructure expenditure and a few limited social services, but all the time maintaining a tight grip on fiscal stability. Following World War II, a Development Priorities Committee composed of top civil servants was formed to chart a long range plan. This committee introduced a five–year "development programme" for the period 1946-51, and later a second plan covering the years 1951-56. The real significance of the committee was that it acted as an incubator for the ideas of the economic overlords of the post–colonial state.

From independence in 1956, which coincided with the end of the second five–year colonial development programme, until 1961, long range planning was discontinued (Abdelwahab 1976). Instead, the regimes of the period relied on an annual amalgam of unconnected projects, presented under the rubric of "New Schemes Programmes". The main objectives of these was to expand irrigated agriculture and to produce more cotton. In reality, most of the projects were anything but new. Many of the schemes were leftovers from the colonial era, while a few were dictated by the pressures of political expediency. Independence did not bring about qualitative changes in the "ideology" or processes of development planning. The reasons for this were rooted in the nature of the independence movement, the past experience of the national bureaucracy, and the power relationships underlying the class equilibrium of the post–colonial state.

The yearly "New Schemes Programmes" continued until 1962, when the Ten Year Plan for National Economic and Social Development (TYP) was promulgated. In the meantime, the Sudan's first experiment with liberal democracy had collapsed and the reins of state power had fallen to the Army High Command in 1958. Six years later, the changed balance of socio-economic and political forces brought down the military and restored parliamentary rule. The new civilian government declared that it was abandoning the TYP a mere three years after its inception. In fact, the break with the plan was not complete. Throughout the second period of political rule (1964-1969), the TYP remained the only frame of reference which was used to set the objectives and evaluate the results of annual development plans introduced by the civilian governments.

The annual plans produced during this second parliamentary period bore a striking resemblance in spirit and form to the budgetary projections of the Development Priorities Committee of the colonial state. Also, and at a higher level of generality, none of the long term development plans was even formulated during periods of civilian rule; all such plans were introduced by military governments. Even then, none of these plans survived for the projected period of time. Thus one year after the military takeover of 1969, a Five Year Social and Economic Development Plan was designed. This plan was shortly thereafter replaced by the mercurial Interim Action Programmes, which only continued for about three years.

In 1977, and with unusual publicity, a Six Year Plan was introduced to realise the Sudan's agricultural potential as a regional "breadbasket" and a "world granary". By 1980, however, as a result of devaluations of the Sudanese pound, reductions in public spending and the freezing of new investments, the Six Year plan had been effectively abandoned. Instead, a three–year General Stabilisation Programme, approved by the IMF and prescribing that institution's harsh panaceas for economic recovery, was followed with great zeal. At the same time, contracts were signed with foreign companies for the management and rehabilitation of public sector agricultural projects. Unable to escape the shadow of looming economic disaster in late 1981 and 1982, the Sudan, once again with the blessing of the IMF, substituted its Plan for Economic Retrenchment for the Stabilisation Programme. This led to further devaluations, contraction of government expenditure and the withdrawal of state subsidies which had been aimed at maintaining low prices for basic commodities.

THE CLASS BASIS OF AGRICULTURAL POLICY

Development plans and and other economic policies are but the subject of analysis. They are not self-explanatory. Their design and use

31

depends on the interests they are meant to serve. In other words, planning policy cannot be divorced from the overall political situation produced by particular class relationships. These class relationships are reflected in the state.

In the Sudan, state policies remained virtually unchanged for many years after independence. The economic plans of the post–colonial state maintained the same old pattern of appropriating the surplus derived from the subordination of the peasantry. This situation has meant a continuous inability to shake off the the plague of authoritarian statism and all that it entailed in terms of an erosion of real forms of democratic participation and basic human rights. The pattern of class dominance changed very little. Democratic forms were needed by the assertive bourgeoisie only during the transition to independence; thereafter, democratic trappings were an inconvenience to be abandoned as the state apparatus reverted to its oppressive colonial character.

In the Sudan, the state can be characterised as the state of a marginalised, dependent and peripheral social formation. The most obvious evidence of this condition is the country's present relationship with international capital. More than a quarter of a century since political independence, the country remains dependent on the production of low profit primary commodities (mainly cotton) and is a net importer of foodstuffs (wheat) as well as of all finished goods, from machinery to textiles.

During the two decades preceding independence, certain indigenous social groups stood out in terms of their economic power and their social prestige. Towering over the national scene were the sectarian leaders, wielding immense spiritual control over the majority of the people. This power and the blind following which supported it, particularly in the rural areas, allowed these leaders to extract a huge surplus from the massive agricultural operations which the colonial state had helped them to establish. The expansion of capitalist economic activities also enhanced opportunities for accumulation by Sudanese landlords engaged in cotton production. At the early stages of these developments, the operations of Sudanese engaged in finance and trade were circumscribed by foreign capital and expatriate traders. But over time these groups were accommodated in the network of capitalist accumulation. The rise of indigenous capitalism and its expansion required certain technical advice and services which segments of the educated state functionaries were recruited to provide. In this manner then, the religious aristocracy, indigenous capitalists engaged in agriculture, finance and commerce, together with elements of the educated Sudanese, came to constitute the power bloc which won independence and dominated the post-colonial state until the late 1960s.

The colonial state did not claim to have local roots, and was eager to avoid the possible, but extremely expensive reliance on outright force. A marriage of convenience took place between the state and the traditional dignitaries, who mediated the state's legitimacy and subordination of the peasantry. The reward was opportunity for capital accumulation.

Early consorts of the state were the religious leadership who from the outset were accorded recognition that Islamic Laws as interpreted by the government's Council of Ulema would be safeguarded and implemented. A second, and at times more favoured, spouse of the colonial state was the traditional leadership of tribal chiefs who were given judicial as well as taxation powers.

Without the active support of these two groups, the imperial construct would have failed to exert the social control necessary for its operation. Mindful of Mahdist persecution and incapable of challenging the representatives of foreign capital, the merchants accepted for many years their subordinate role and restricted operations, attempting to make the most of whatever opportunities were offered by the colonial system. It was from this constellation of merchants, religious and tribal leaders that an indigenous bourgeoisie eventually emerged.

From its early formative days, this bourgeoisie has been a highly fragmented class. It was divided by internal contradictions emanating from their different modes of capital accumulation and economic activity. Those involved in agriculture were, on the whole, interested in expanding cotton production, and consequently were dependent on the international bourgeoisie and their agents who controlled credit facilities, major import operations and access to foreign markets. Originally, finance companies were family concerns, formed during the early years of British rule. Over time, these became the base of a small but economically influential financial bourgeoisie. This fraction, together with the larger segment of the incipient agricultural bourgeoisie, shared a general interest with the British and was antagonistic towards Egypt. Egypt, because of its need for Nile water, was opposed to the expansion of irrigated agriculture in Sudan and thus to any expanded accumulation by these fractions of the bourgeoisie.

The expanding operations of the colonial government necessitated the appointment of more technical and administrative cadres. The employment of Sudanese by the state served two objectives. First it reduced government expenses. Second, this policy was thought to help pacify the population — Sudanese administrators acting as a buffer.

For these reasons, the educational system was expanded and improved to provide functionaries for minor posts in the administration and the cotton projects. Over a period of time, the aspirations of segments of the educated paralleled those of the rest of the bourgeoisie. They wanted to free Sudanese capitalism from domestic and foreign control in order to be able to play a leading role and thus enter the ranks of the ruling class. This view is supported by the political behaviour of these educated people towards the populace, and their attempts to attain constitutional changes without allowing the masses to strengthen their capacity for independent action and organisation on the economic and political levels.

This "incipient bourgeoisie in the state" was in favour of the capitalist mode of production; they were basically hostile towards those they viewed as responsible for the obstruction of capitalist growth — the colonial system, the tribal chiefs and the expatriate functionaries occupying high positions in government (Hamad 1980). Their position in society was but an outgrowth of the material changes engendered by colonial rule. Their outlook was shaped by the ideological rag-and-bone shop which emerged from the fusion of capitalist, feudal and pseudosocialist currents of thought (Ibrahim 1978). In more than one case they have been unable to make distinctions among the logical bases of these ideologies, a weakness which for decades bred an incoherence in programmes, and confusion and vaccilation in the practice of their political parties. This general ideological weakness coupled with the absence of any other group possessing a clear national programme, allowed the more resourceful indigenous state functionaries to take command of the nationalist movement.

The development of Sudanese dependent capitalism, conditioned by the dictates of the colonial state, and confined to areas in which it was tolerated by foreign businessmen and their companies, was not such as to offer great expectations to the state functionaries. In addition, the majority of the educated did not possess the qualifications for the upper levels of the private sector. Their qualities did not involve specialised skills or administrative and technical ability, but consisted primarily of family connections, ties to the religious aristocracy and good relations with foreign merchants operating in the country.

Yet, some Sudanese bureaucrats realised that they stood to gain from the expansion of national capitalism, and accordingly sought closer ties with leaders of religious sects who were large landowners or were involved in the finance, ginning and marketing of cotton. This relationship was not defined by a legal contract, but it was based on a network of complex mutual benefits. The religious aristocracy utilised the technical and administrative know-how and English language proficiency of this group, some of whom were lawyers, agriculturalists and engineers. Their capabilities were put to use in the expansion and organisation of the aristocracy's economic concerns and their dealings with the colonial state. These bureaucrats, in turn, gained social status, but most importantly, economic rewards. Economic benefits often took the form of partnerships in business operations, acquisition of agricultural land or real estate at nominal prices, or, on certain occasions, direct financial support. The pattern of economic rewards set this particular group of bureaucrats apart from other government employees. Some of the latter did indeed have ties with the religious aristocracy but they were of an entirely religious and spiritual nature. Motivated as they were by existential sentiments, their rewards were likewise spiritual.

This developing set of economic interests, which intensified over time, had eventually mediated the assimilation of such bureaucrats into the ranks of the bourgeoisie and began to operate political parties. Clearly the pattern suggested here does not imply that every educated person who was absorbed into the state automatically became a member of the bourgeoisie. Although state salaries ensured a relatively high income for functionaries, this cannot in itself be considered the basis for membership of the bourgeoisie. Those who did achieve that status later became the leaders of the nationalist movement. These leaders, offspring of Sudanese traditionalism and Anglo-Saxon conservatism, together with the religious sectarian leaders, dominated the independence movement. The educated leaders never entertained any idea of structural transformation or radical change in Sudanese society. Such notions were out of time with the training they acquired while serving the colonial agencies of repression — the police, army and local government — as well as with their education. As future developments showed, in reality their call for freedom and self determination was for the freedom of the bourgeoisie to accumulate and to grow. They disguised narrow class interest in the rhetoric of nationalist sentimentality and national interest.

Much of the change that has taken place over the past twenty five years has resulted from the contest for hegemony within this dominant power bloc, as well as from the struggles between that bloc and other social forces. These struggles, and the ensuing contest in society, were simultaneously manifested within the state, and were expressed through changes in economic policy and agricultural strategy. The separating of state, society and the struggle between classes may be convenient for an easy, formal analysis, but it is profoundly misleading.

Neither the bourgeoisie in the state, nor any other class or fraction,

35

succeeded in retaining indefinite ascendancy over the entire power bloc. In fact, frequent changes in the structure and distribution of power within the ruling bloc, and the unabated and unceasing quest for hegemony therein, characterised the post-colonial state and prevented the dominant social forces from achieving any enduring or stable equilibrium of class alliances. This situation in turn bred vaccilation in state policy as a whole, and in agricultural strategy in particular. Persistent strife within the power bloc and the intensification of the unresolved contradictions which fuelled it, deepened the weakness of the dominant bloc and forced certain of its elements to seek new allies. The cumulative effects of these developments coincided, at certain definite historic points, with a growth in the strength and organisation of the dominated social forces, and thereby presented opportunities to restructure the ruling bloc as a whole. Such strife and the resultant changes in the balance of social forces precipitated shifts in agricultural policies. It is in this manner that the above discussion attempts to propose a more general framework for the study of development strategies.

REFERENCES

Abdelwahab, A.A. (1976) "Development planning in the Sudan", in Elhassan, A.M. (ed.), *An introduction to the Sudan economy*, Khartoum University Press, Khartoum.

Ali, T.M. (1983) "Jouda: peasant unrest", *Review of African Political Economy*, No. 26, pp. 4-14.

Awad, M.H. (1973) "Min mashakil al-rif al-Sudani" (Problems of the rural Sudan), *Bulletin of Sudanese Studies*, Vol. 4, No. 1, pp. 148-164.

Collins, R. (1972) "The Sudan political service: a portrait of the imperialists", *African Affairs*, Vol. 71.

Department of Statistics (1960) *The national income of the Sudan: 1955/6*, Khartoum.

Martin, P.M. (1921) *The Sudan in evolution*, Constable and Co., London.

Hamad, M.H. (1980) *Al-Sudan: al Mazag al tarikhy wa affag al mustagabal* (The Sudan: the historic crisis and the future horizon), Dar al Khalymah, Beirut.

Ibrahim, H. (1978) "Moulahazat hawl al tarkieb al fikry lil bourgowazia al Soudania" (Notes on the ideological composition of the Sudanese bourgeoisie), *Affag Arabia*, No. 10, pp. 65-71.

International Labour Office (1976) *Growth, employment and equity: a comprehensive strategy for the Sudan*, Geneva.

MacMichael, H. (1954) *The Sudan*, Ernest Benn, London.

Ministry of National Planning (1977) *The six year plan of economic and social development: 1977/8-1982/3*, Vol. 1, Khartoum.

3

Sudanese Government Attitudes Towards Foreign Investment — Theory and Practice

Hassan Gad Karim

THE PERIOD 1956-69

The attitudes of Sudanese governments towards foreign investment have to be understood within an historical perspective.

Until 1956, the government was in no need of additional finance for its relatively small investment programme. In part this was because of the availability of funds accumulated during the period of the Second World War. After independence, the government resorted to foreign borrowing because of the expansion in services and the decline in export prices.

In 1955/6, the Economy and Finance Minister advocated and emphasised the need to accumulate sufficient foreign reserves, and to pursue an "honest" financial policy in order to gain the trust of foreign donors and investors (Government of Sudan 1956a).

In 1956, the government issued the hastily, and vaguely, drafted Approved Enterprises Act (Government of Sudan 1956b). This act was typical of such legislation in a newly independent country. It reflected recognition of a need for foreign resources to assist in development as well as the nationalistic feelings that such foreign involvement might evoke.

The Ten Year Plan of Economic and Social Development, 1961/2-1970/1, proposed "a considerable increase of exports and of import substitution" (Government of Sudan 1960: 40). In other words, the adoption of an import substitution strategy combined with increased exports. Behind this lay the government's fear of a heavy demand on its foreign exchange holdings, as a result of the development programme which was aimed at increasing exports.

In addition, the Ten Year Plan envisaged the external financing of investments totalling £S149.5 million — 26% of total investment. It

37

could be argued that a new stage of the development effort was commencing, involving some dependence on foreign resources, but based in the main on the horizontal expansion of large scale state agricultural projects. Prior to the Ten Year Plan, development programmes (with the exception of the Gezira Scheme) were less ambitious, and were financed by budget surpluses (£S113 million in the period 1951/2-1960/1). Neither was the foreign reserve position a major concern at this time. Indeed, it was at a peak of £S60 million at the beginning of the plan period.

It is noticeable that private foreign investment, at about £S22 million, was a small proportion of estimated total investment (Government of Sudan 1960: 22). It made up about 4% of total investment, and less than 15% of estimated foreign investment. According to the Ten Year Plan, this estimate was "modest". However, such a view was unrealistic for, during the period 1956-60, the inflow of private capital averaged £S0.7 million and capital repatriation averaged £S0.5 million (Government of Sudan 1960: 75).

There was, in fact, little in government policies to support the "optimistic" estimate. This is so because (i) the 1956 Act was not changed to attract more private investment, (ii) the official records and documents of that time do not reflect any understanding of foreign direct investment (FDI), the Ten Year Plan treating FDI as an inflow of capital, ignoring its other components such as technology and management, (iii) this item was treated all along as a residual, sometimes classified among "other", and subject to no systematic analysis. This having been said, it should be added that when the Abboud Regime (1958-64) was overthrown and replaced by a civilian government, the Ten Year Plan was abandoned, although it remained a policy guide.

The Abboud regime was overthrown by a revolution. Both before and after the revolution, nationalisation and land reform were issues of public concern. This government was characterised by a series of weak political coalitions, frequent changes of government and widespread labour strikes. Such an atmosphere was not attractive for FDI; indeed there was considerable pressure on government from local capital to pursue policies which might adversely affect foreign investors. For example, textile imports from Egypt were authorised and consequently the American-Sudanese Textile Factory lost its monopoly position and began to incur losses. There were also counter pressures on the government to favour foreign investors. For example, West German (Government of Sudan 1972: 65) investors alleged that the 1956 Act was vague and inadequate; they demanded more details and guarantees, and complained that concessions were delayed, or if granted were interrupted.

In 1967, the Organisation and Promotion of Industrial Investment Act was issued. The Act constituted admission of the shortcomings of the 1956 Act. However, more than a decade had elapsed since the 1956 Act, and from experience it had become apparent that in spite of the concessions which it gave to industry, many industrial enterprises were faced with a number of problems and impediments, either in the initial implementation stage or after they had started operating (Republic of Sudan 1967: 1).

Concessions given in the 1967 Act were more attractive and generous than in that of 1956. They included:

i) exemption from payment of Business Profit Tax for a period of five years, and if the capital of an enterprise exceeded £S1 million, then tax was to be levied at half the appropriate rate for five years;
ii) depreciation during the first five years was to be calculated at double or triple the rate in force;
iii) exemption from custom duties was allowed on machinery and spare parts, and there were to be reductions in respect of raw materials;
iv) land was to be available at reduced prices.

In addition to these provisions,

the Minister may, with the consent of the Council of Ministers, grant any special concessions not specified in the preceding subsection to an enterprise established in an area considered by the Council as being an area which falls within the traditional sector of the national economy (Republic of Sudan 1967: 11).

The apparent intention of this clause was to discourage the concentration of industry in the central area of the Sudan. However, the precise details of the concessions available under this provision were not detailed, leaving a wide area of discretion to the Minister.

Furthermore, the 1967 Act embodied a new condition for granting concessions, namely that enterprises would "employ directly or indirectly a large number of Sudanese employees and will train them to replace foreigners serving in the enterprise" (Republic of Sudan 1967: 10). Other typical conditions were that enterprises should help in expanding exports, in assisting and expanding import substitution, increasing national income, establishing new industries, and for industries considered to be of defensive or strategic importance, that they should be concerned to establish new industries using local raw materials. The fulfilment of any of these conditions was supposed to

39

secure some or all of the concessions outlined above.

The definition of terms such as "defence", "strategic importance" and "new industries" was left unclear. In addition, the 1967 Act did not concern itself with indirect employment and indirect benefits or costs of the new enterprises. Like the 1956 Act, the 1967 Act did not discriminate against foreign investment or investors. No restrictions were imposed regarding the volume of capital to be invested or its participation with local capital. Thus, the Act assured wide industrial opportunities (using the country's potential natural and human resources) for both foreign and local investors. Guarantees were given regarding nationalisation and compensation. Article 14 stated:

> In case of acquisition by the Government of anything owned by the Enterprise due to an emergency or for strategic reasons, the Government shall be bound to pay just compensation abroad in the currency in which it was imported (Republic of Sudan 1967: 12).

What constituted "just compensation" was left unclear, as was the question of what authority or arbitrator was to decide on the "fairness" of any compensation.

The 1967 Act guaranteed profit repatriation as well as the repatriation of capital imported in case of liquidation. It also empowered the Minister to submit recommendations to other government bodies for issuing and renewal of residence permits for foreign employees and for the transfer of their personal savings. It is clear from the foregoing that the Government had entrusted the private sector— both foreign and local — with developing an industrial sector "within the framework of a balanced and integrated development", while reserving the development of the modern agricultural sector to the state.

The period from independence until 1969 may be characterised as follows:

i) the Government made efforts to expand investment, mainly from domestic savings, together with loans from government and international organisations. The role of foreign private investment was to be minimal;

ii) there was a pronounced tendency for the state to concentrate on agricultural investment, while leaving industrial investment to the private sector;

iii) policy during this period may be conceived as dual: export promotion and import substitution, but on the basis of an export-oriented agricultural policy founded on cotton exports.

THE NUMEIRY PERIOD 1969-85

In its first two years, the new regime adopted a radical stance, declaring its commitment to "Sudanese Socialism". An initial step towards socialist transformation and the freeing of the economy from foreign domination involved a broad programme of nationalisation and confiscation.

The new Government achieved a 51% shareholding in the Shell Oil Refinery, and in May 1970, all foreign banks and four British companies were nationalised. Compensation was offered in the form of 4% bonds repayable between 1980 and 1985. A whole series of takeovers soon followed. These affected both Sudanese and foreign-owned establishments, including the Sudan Portland Cement Co., Blue Nile Brewery, Bata Shoe Co., National Cash Register Co., and Pepsi Cola. All cotton marketing companies were nationalised and "standardised". Import companies were affected by the same measures. By the end of 1971 foreign investment in the Sudan had declined to negligible proportions. Terms like "building economic independence" and "freeing the economy from foreign domination" appeared frequently in statements of government policy.

Another step towards the transformation of the economy and the society was the formulation of the Five Year Plan of Economic and Social Development 1970/1-1974/5 (FYP). This was mainly drawn up by Russian advisors and was socialist in orientation. The public sector was seen as leading the process of development. The FYP aimed to promote productive cooperative societies which would constitute the basis for future socialist economic development. Even so, the private sector's participation was seen as a component of the plan, as a subordinate sector, but contributing in the region of £S170 million over the plan period.

Similar in some respects to the Ten Year Plan, the FYP had as major targets the expansion of exports and a favourable balance of trade, but within a new framework of foreign economic relations. Thus:

In the sphere of foreign economic relations, apart from foreign trade development, the plan specifies measures for furthering economic, scientific, technical and business relations with socialist, Arab and friendly countries. The concrete programme of economic relations envisages utilisation of capital investment loans of £S110 millions, as well as credits and technical assistance granted and rendered to the Sudan on favourable terms and conditions...The latest production techniques and know-how of industrially advanced countries should be introduced (Democratic Republic of Sudan, 1970: 17).

Foreign private investment was not mentioned in the document. The importance of technology was realised, but it was to come through the medium of technical assistance.

Such a hostile attitude towards both foreign and local private investment did not endure. A retreat from the initial radical position was soon apparent, manifesting itself in the reversal of confiscation measures and in efforts to create an investment climate favourable to foreign investors (Dunning 1982). Fresh attempts to attract foreign investment included:

i) new investment acts. There were a number of these, starting with the Development and Promotion of Industrial Investment Act of 1972, followed by three others in 1973, 1974 and 1976. These acts were consolidated in the 1980 Act and the creation of an Investment Bureau;

ii) after the abandonment of the Five Year Plan and the breach with the Soviet Union, there was a diplomatic and economic campaign in which the President undertook frequent foreign visits with a view to attracting foreign investment;

iii) special government departments were established to cater for foreign investors, and businessmen received special treatment, such as preferential access to the President and his aides.

Of some importance here is the role which Lonrho apparently played in helping Numeiry regain power after the communist-backed coup of 1971 (Cronje, Ling and Cronje 1976: 178-83). This had at least two implications. First, there was more forceful articulation of the interests of foreign business in changing the Sudan's political and economic strategy. Second, Lonrho was appointed by Sudan as sole agent for state purchases of capital and semi-capital goods in the UK. In addition, in 1972, Lonrho announced an agreement for a joint venture in the cultivation and processing of sugar. Thus it can be argued that Lonrho's involvement had at least a favourable psychological effect on more general foreign investment interests. Lonrho also assisted Sudan in negotiating a £UK10 million credit with Britain's Export Credit Guarantee Department, and in coming to an agreement with Britain over the compensation arrangements for British companies which had been nationalised in 1971/2.

Sudan's Treasury Minister declared agreements with Portland Cement and Sudan Mercantile concerning compensation, and negotiations with the rest of the nationalised enterprises were progressing (Legum 1971). These moves eased relations with the UK, and Numeiry visited that country early in 1973. Diplomatic relations with the US were resumed in 1972 (they had been broken off after the 1967 Arab-Israeli war). Relations with the conservative states of the Gulf improved as a result of the Government's new stance towards the eastern bloc and towards left groups within the Sudan.

Changes in government policy affected the implementation of the FYP in two respects. These were that while eastern bloc assistance was no longer available, there was no assurance of its replacement by assistance from the west.

In 1972, the Sudan Socialist Union amended the FYP by introducing a Five Year Interim Programme of Action. This was called the Extended Five Year Plan, to coincide with Numeiry's first period in office which ended in 1977. The Action Programme, which was incorporated into this, was meant to serve as a guide for development policy, and aimed at self-sufficiency in agriculture, basic industrial goods and improvement of the transport sector. Under this programme, the original plan investment target was increased.

Realising the need for private sources, both foreign and local, for such an ambitious programme, and in addition responding to the government's new political stance and worsening balance of payments situation, private investment was seen as a complementary source of investment. To facilitate this new direction, a series of acts was issued, the first of which was the Development and Promotion of Industrial Investment Act, 1972.

The 1972 Act specified that there was to be no discrimination between national and foreign enterprises or between public and private ones. To encourage foreign investment, this Act explicitly guaranteed extensive measures concerning profit transfer, capital repatriation and compensation in cases of nationalisation. As a reflection of the emerging tendency towards attracting Arab investment, the Act added another eligibility condition, that enterprises should be able to contribute to economic cooperation-operation with African and Arab countries.

All the provisions in the 1967 Act were retained in the 1972 Act. Moreover, the 1972 Act embodied a new provision to cover repayment of any customs duties paid by an enterpise for raw materials and packing materials used in exporting products. This demonstrates explicitly the favourable treatment of export-oriented enterprises. However, import substituting companies were not forgotten, as protection for local products was also granted. The succeeding Organisation and Encouragement of Investment in Economic Services Act of 1973 was passed with the objective of encouraging foreign and national capital so as to realise the overall development objectives. This act specified in particular the development of tourism, transportation and warehousing.

This specification of privileged subsectors seems to have stemmed from two factors. First, that Arab investors exhibited a preference for investing in such areas; secondly, government seems to have thought that private investment in these sub-sectors would provide the support services for its own public investment in large agricultural developments.

All the guarantees provided in the 1972 Act were retained in the 1973 Act. However, the former was repealed and replaced by the Development and Encouragement of Industrial Investment Act of 1974. This created the Advisory Committee for Industrial Development, which was supposed to advise on the overall purposes and implementation of the Act.

The 1974 Act resembled the preceding ones in most respects. It did, however, contain the most extensive, explicit and detailed guarantees against nationalisation and confiscation. These were of importance because the clear intention of the Act was to repair relations with those nations whose enterprises had been nationalised. In addition, the President once again undertook a programme of foreign visits in order to sell the Sudan to potential investors. In 1976 he visited the US, met American businessmen, and one outcome was the establishment of the Sudan-US Business Council. Delegations from corporations such as Tenco, Ford Motor Company, American Development Alternatives and Allis Chalmers visited Sudan in return. They showed interest in investing in fields such as agricultural machinery, fodder production, animal fattening and crop production. In order to facilitate these developments, the Ministry of Industry set up a special section to deal with investments by US firms.

Another important parallel development was the idea of the Sudan as the world's breadbasket, or more realistically, the breadbasket of the Arab world. Two main ingredients fed this direction of thought: the accumulation of Arab oil surpluses after the 1973 war, and the resulting search for investment opportunities, and the Sudan's rich agricultural land in close proximity to the oil-rich states of the Gulf.

The Development Perspective of the Sudan, 1976, spells out the base of the strategy as:

At the same time, the neighbouring Arab world looks to the Sudan as a focal point in the Arab economic integration plans, where the combination of financial resources of the Arab community, Western technology, and the agricultural resources of the Sudan could produce the food requirements of the community and agricultural raw materials for part of their industrialisation plan (Democratic Republic of Sudan 1976).

One source for this strategy is the ILO Report 1975 (ILO 1975), which assumes a clear comparative advantage for Sudanese agricultural and agro-industrial exports, and thus recommends an agricultural export- oriented programme. It says:

Looking to the future, Sudan has a clear comparative advantage in agricultural and agro-industrial exports. The potential for food grain and oil seed development, for sugar, cotton textiles and the processing of other primary outputs, may well be characterised as unique...It takes no great wisdom to see modern agriculture and modern agro-industry as the major engines of economic growth in Sudan for years to come (ILO 1975: 5-6).

This strategy envisaged large inflows of foreign capital, mainly from Arab countries. As the ILO report stated:

The cost of the investment contemplated in our strategy in the years 1975 to 1985 is estimated to amount to approximately £S3,500 million. It is understood that the programme being formulated by the Arab Fund, as a basis for Arab finance, suggests an investment of £S2,200 million over ten years in agricultural development and allied fields, out of which a sum of £S1,700 million would be provided by Arab capital and the remainder from local sources (ILO 1975: 9).

This policy assumed that Arab investment in the Sudan would be mutually beneficial, enabling the Sudanese economy to develop and the Arabs to invest productively for a time when the oil revenues began to diminish. In addition, the strategy was rationalised in the following terms:

Although world markets exist for almost all the agricultural products that Sudan exports, particular emphasis is likely to be placed on providing for the needs of neighbouring Arab countries which are importers of these commodities. Exports of vegetable oils, sugar, wheat and meat for instance could find a ready market in these countries (ILO 1975: 4).

The breadbasket strategy was basically an export-oriented agricultural policy dependent on foreign resources, with the modern sector as the major source of exportable surpluses. This policy differs in two particulars from preceding policies in the independence era. First, it emphasises food exports as well as cash crops—the Arab factor was, to our mind, the driving force for this emphasis. Second, it appeared to mark a response to the emergence of the Arabs as the potential major financiers of development in the South.

This strategy may be criticised on a number of grounds. It opts for a maximum export surplus irrespective of regional and social problems which might be created (such as labour migration and skewed income distribution). It may create developing 'enclaves' based on and related to world market rather than more local needs. It is likely to create problems associated with large scale, horizontal agricultural expansion, well known in Sudan following the Gezira example.

In order to implement this strategy, new legislation was necessary. The Promotion of Agricultural Investment Act 1976 was supposed to achieve self-sufficiency, export surplus, diversification of agricultural products, equitable regional distribution of agricultural development, and integration of animal and agricultural production and between agriculture and industry! This Act closely resembled that of 1974, but this time with respect to agricultural enterprises. It contained the same guarantees against nationalisation and for the transfer of profits.

The general policies and objectives which have been outlined above were codified in the Six Year Plan of Economic and Social Development 1977/8-1982/3. The Six Year Plan aimed at:

> developing industries as a complementary sector to agriculture, giving priority to agro-industries and import substitution ... improving the balance of payments by expansion of exports and import substitution (Democratic Republic of Sudan 1976: 31).

In contrast to the original five year plan, the six year plan (SYP) explicitly encouraged private foreign investment. Encouraging the private sector both foreign and local to play its role fully and effectively in development" (Democratic Republic of Sudan 1976: 31). £S1100 million of private sector investment was expected, half of which was to be from external sources.

The SYP was clearly concerned with private foreign investment:

> A well designed policy is needed to attract private foreign investment in strategic fields of the economy on well-defined terms and conditions. The agreement must cover the training requirements of the Sudanese in technical, administrative and managerial fields. A

portfolio of well-prepared bankable development projects must be ready to attract private foreign investment (Democratic Republic of Sudan 1976: 63).

However, it was thought that the existence of three distinct acts (the 1973 Act for Services, the 1974 Act for Industry, and the 1976 Act for Agriculture), with three different ministers empowered to guarantee concessions (in conjunction with various advisory committees and departments) had resulted in some administrative confusion. This overall lack of integration led to frustration among private investors. In an effort to rectify these shortcomings, an Encouragement of Investment Act 1980 was passed. It repealed all the preceding acts and established the Secretariat-General for Investment as a unified bureau to deal with private investors. This secretariat consisted of the Secretary-General, the Technical Secretary, and the Consultative Committee. All of these were supposed to work together so that:

> The Secretary-General shall undertake the preparatory work which consists of the technical studies prepared by the Technical Secretariat and of the recommendations issued by the Consultative Committee and of any other necessary substance or papers and he shall submit the same to the Ministerial Committee or the Minister, as the case may be, for the exercise of the powers conferred by this Act (Democratic Republic of Sudan 1980: 10).

In this context, "the Minister" meant the Minister of Finance and National Economy, who was entrusted with granting concessions. This appeared to concentrate all matters concerning private investment in his hands. The Ministerial Committee was established to frame general policy for encouragement of private investment and had no power (explicitly or implicitly) over the Minister.

The 1980 Act encouraged investment in agricultural, animal, mining, industrial, transport, tourism, storage and housing fields, without discriminating between national and foreign investment. It also guaranteed the usual privileges alluded to in the previous acts.

THE LEGISLATIVE HISTORY IN PERSPECTIVE

We can now look at this legislative history in perspective. Both export-promotion and import-substitution strategies have been tried in Less Developed Countries, usually as a response to balance of payments difficulties.

At first it was thought that Import Substitution was desirable because dependence on foreign trade made national planning difficult. As well as the problem of uncontrollable external factors, the terms of trade of many Less Developed Countries were unfavourable because of the price structure of many primary products.

As a response to this view, Import Substitution was encouraged and Export Substitution was discouraged, since primary products were faced with low elasticities of demand as well as competition from synthetics. Expansion of manufactured exports was more difficult because of the protective measures taken by Developed Countries against manufactures from Less Developed Countries, technological backwardness and the absence of economies of scale in LDCs. Thus, under conditions of unfavourable terms of trade, fluctuating prices, declining purchasing power of primary commodities, the more dependent a country was on exports, the more vulnerable its economy would become. Thus Import Substitution Strategy and Export Substitution Strategies were considered to be mutually exclusive.

The pattern of imports in LDCs, dominated by manufactured consumer and capital goods, pointed to the low level of industrial development. And, since industrialisation is one of the conventional measures of development, policy makers in LDCs opted for industrialisation. The easiest way to pursue this strategy seemed to be an Import Substitution Strategy to satisfy the internal market, save foreign exchange and help the balance of payments problem.

Large countries are considered to be more suited to an Import Substitution Strategy, and a general consensus seems to prevail that small countries are forced to adopt an Export Substitution Strategy in preference to an Import Substitution Strategy. Empirical studies such as those of Chenery (Chenery 1960; Chenery and Syrquin 1975) have established the existence of strong relationships between size of the country, resource endowment, level of income, and pattern of trade. A general conclusion of such studies is that large countries, with a few exceptions, have adopted more inward looking development policies because of the existence of a large internal market. In contrast, small countries have not been able to sustain satisfactory growth rates with import levels of less than 20% of GNP.

Sudan's policy in these respects has been primarily one of export promotion, although Import Substitution Strategy objectives have been declared. This is because "Import Substitution Strategy" has been used in a very narrow sense — curbing the import of certain commodities, particularly foodstuffs; there has been an absence of political will to support an inward looking development policy; the local market is small, and the established export-oriented economy would demand massive structural change in order to accommodate an Import Substitution Strategy.

Most of Sudan's imports are manufactured commodities. Thus an Import Substitution Strategy will be a manufacturing one. Lewis (Lewis 1968) argues that when manufacturing is the import sector and agriculture is the export sector, any Import Substitution Strategy utilising restrictions on trade will turn the terms of trade against agriculture. It could be argued that such restrictions are therefore by definition anti-Export Substitution Strategy, and for this reason it is difficult to see how the two could be applied simultaneously. The same logic could be applied if, as in the case of declared Sudanese government policy, import substitution is for specific agricultural products, since that will result in turning the terms of trade of those commodities against the export of agricultural products. This situation is even worse given that substitutability of inputs is more likely between agricultural products than between agricultural and manufactured products.

An Import Substitution Strategy has been criticised as leading to the expansion of production of consumer goods, as well as increasing income maldistribution, favouring those who work in the protected sectors. Khan (1963) studied four import competing industries and one export industry in Pakistan, and concluded that consumption liberalisation had taken place. He argued that the domestic absorption capacity had exceeded what would have been demanded had imports been allowed to enter. However, there are reasons to conclude that this does not seem to apply in the Sudan.

Against the possibility of an Import Substitution Strategy leading to bias against backward links (by depending on imported raw materials, intermediate and capital goods), Helleiner (1972) argues plausibly that this disadvantage may be overcome if the state is aware of the importance of linkages and interdependency within the economy, and thus takes action to establish these conditions.

In the Sudanese case, an Import Substitution Strategy was seriously adopted only twice: once when the Second World War erupted and disrupted international trade, and during the period 1969-71 when the state moved towards a socialist ideology.

In fact, however, the Sudan has usually followed an export-oriented policy, based on attempts to solve the balance of payments problem and save foreign exchange for development. In sum, the policy makers' approach seems to be founded on some notion of a "foreign exchange gap".

"Shortage of capital" is considered to be one of the most characteristic features of underdevelopment. The concept is used to explain problems of low productivity, unemployment and the underutilisation of natural resources. In addition, the balance of payments deficit, budget deficits and dependence on flows of foreign capital lead to the argument that shortage of capital is the major cause of underdevelopment and backwardness, and that any serious attempts to achieve development must contain some remedy for the assumed capital shortage.

Though capital shortage is an important problem, it is not the only or even the major cause of underdevelopment. The oil rich countries can be cited as the most obvious case. Availability of skilled labour, opportunities for profitable and productive investment, the capital absorptive capacity of the economy, all appear as very important factors in the equation.

The attitude of government in the Sudan has emphasised the importance of foreign capital inflows in achieving satisfactory rates of growth, and thus development. It is supposed that foreign inflows will help in the expansion of both investment and the imports necessary for this process, and hence accelerate the rate of growth. The two gap model which underlies this approach was developed (Chenery and Strout 1966; McKinnon 1964; Lal 1972) as a result of the interest shown by economists in devising an economic criterion for the allocation of foreign resources. It is used by Sudan — and many other LDCs — to project the aggregate requirements of both domestic savings and foreign capital. This view implicitly assumes that labour is abundant and of good quality, an unrealistic assumption which leads economists like Singer and Ansari (1978) to argue that there is no reason to limit the theory to two gaps, since some forms of aid, especially technical assistance, remove barriers other than those of foreign exchange shortages or of savings, for example, the availability of local skills.

The two gap approach suggests that in LDCs there exist two separate constraints on development and growth. First, the domestic savings constraint, and second, the foreign exchange constraint. This view suggests at least two functions for foreign inflows — to supplement and add to domestic savings and to add to the foreign exchange resources necessary for development. Critics of this view (Bruton 1969; Joshi 1970; Griffin and Enos 1970), and advocates (Chenery, Strout and Papanek 1972) alike, emphasise "aid" in their discussions of development financing, resource transfer and the foreign exchange constraints. A basic assumption in this essay is that the Sudanese government's policy has been based on a two gap analysis, emphasising the foreign exchange constraint, without distinguishing clearly between different types of resource.

The Sudanese government assumes that the foreign exchange gap is larger than the savings gap, meaning that the country suffers from a pure foreign exchange constraint, since in an ex post accounting sense, the two gaps must be equal. In essence, El Shibly and Thirlwall come to the same conclusion when they state:

> Thus, the existence of two gaps ex ante is quite possible, and they will only be equal by chance. Foreign inflows will thus be required to fill the dominant gap if the target rate of growth is to be achieved (El Shibly and Thirlwall 1981).

This view can be criticised because it is difficult to estimate within any reasonable degree of accuracy the existence of the dominant gap from historical data — which reflects definitional identities rather than behavioural patterns — and that the gaps can be identified only in an ex ante sense. Ex post they are of no significance.

Having said this, we can now proceed to examine the assumptions of the two gap approach and the validity of its critics as applied to the Sudanese case. There appear to be three key assumptions of the approach, these are discussed in turn.

i)The assumption of fixed relationships between capital and output, and the associated assumption that propensities to save and to import are constant.

El Shibly and Thirlwall estimated an historical incremental capital output ratio (ICOR) for the period 1960/61-1974/75 of 2.44, but in their estimates, they used an ICOR of 3 which had been assumed in government plans. However, they concluded that the historical ICOR was unlikely to prevail in the future. They said that an act of faith was necessary in order to maintain such a view. It can be remarked that an equal act of faith is required to assume a stable path for the economy and no change in the structure of investment.

The ratio of consumer goods in the import bill has not declined, and measures to decrease the import of these goods were not properly applied. The urban population constitutes a major actor in the politics of the country. This is especially so of the middle class and the elite. Thus any attempt to reduce the level of consumption will always entail political risks.

The policies which have been adopted are dependent on migrant workers' remittances. These are used to finance imports which are then made available to consumers via the commercial sector. To absorb consumers' anger at rising prices, a series of increases in the level of income took place during the Numeiry years. These changes indicate a rising rather than a constant propensity to consume.

ii) The assumption that any rise in the inflow of foreign resources will eventually lead to a higher level of investment and so of growth. It is not necessarily the case that foreign inflows will eventually lead to a higher rate of investment. Aid funds can be spent on non-productive consumption.

It has been argued that most LDC governments plan to maintain a specific rate of growth and thus estimate their capital requirements on this basis. Sudan is no exception. The capital required for development plans is estimated by adding domestic savings and foreign resources together.

The attitude of the Sudanese government supports our argument that the dependence on foreign resources has, at the least, not encouraged the tapping of potential sources of domestic savings. Government expenditure on conspicuous consumption can certainly be judged as "unnecessary". An additional potential for savings might be to curb the import of luxury goods.

It has to be pointed out that the focus on foreign exchange as a problem, externalises the problems, and diverts attention from possible internal solutions. Many internal policies can diminish the level of domestic savings. Poor performance in public sector agricultural schemes is one example, expenditure on "security" is another. While national security is an important issue, certain incidents during the latter years of the Numeiry regime were suggestive more of government inspired panics than of real threats to national security.

iii) That domestic and foreign resources can be substituted. This assumption depends on the specific country's endowment of resources and on its ability to utilise for production the proportion of output which is not consumed.

We can thus see that with the exception of a few intervals, Sudanese policy towards foreign investment has been based on a two gap theory. This has led to a long history of legislative action intended to facilitate the inflow of foreign capital. The long term effects of these inflows, as indicated by the present state of the economy, do not suggest that they represent a solution to the Sudan's problems.

REFERENCES

Bruton, H.J. (1969) "The two-gap approach to aid and development", *American Economic Review*, Vol. 59.

Chenery, H.B. (1960) "Patterns of industrial growth", *American Economic Journal*, No.50.

Chenery, H.B.and Strout, A.M. (1966) "Development alternatives in an open economy, *American Economic Review*, No. 56.

Chenery, H.B. Strout, A.M. and Papanek, G. (1972) "Effects of aid and resource transfer on savings and growth", *Economic Journal*, September.

Chenery, H.B. and Syrquin, T. (1975) *Patterns of development 1950-1970*, Oxford University Press, Oxford.

Cronje, S., Ling, M. and Cronje, G. (1976) *Lonrho: portrait of a multinational*, Penguin, London.

Democratic Republic of Sudan (1970) *Five year Plan of Economic and Social Development, 1970/71-74/75*, Khartoum.

Democratic Republic of Sudan (1976), *The Six Year Plan of Economic and Social Development, 1977/78- 1982/83, Khartoum*.

Democratic Republic of Sudan (1980), *The Encouragement of Investment Act, 1980*, Khartoum.

Dunning, J.H. (1982) "International Business in a Changing World Environment", *Banca Nazionale de Lavoro Quarterly Review*, No. 143, December, Rome.

El Shibly, M. and Thirlwall, P. (1981) "Dual-gap analysis for the Sudan", *World Development*, Vol. 9, No. 2.

Government of the Sudan (1956a) *The Budget*, Ministry of Commerce, Khartoum.

Government of Sudan (1956b) *The Approved Enterprises (Concessions) Act, 1956*, Khartoum.

Government of Sudan (1960) *The Ten Year Plan for Economic and Social Development 1961/62-1970/71*, Khartoum.

Government of Sudan (1972) *Industry and development*, Vol. 2, August 1972, Khartoum.

Griffin, K. and Enos, J. (1970) "Foreign assistance: objectives and consequences", *Economic development and cultural change*, Vol. 18, No.3.

Helleiner, G.K. (1972) *International trade and economic development*, Penguin Books, London.

International Labour Office (1975), *Growth, employment and equity; a comprehensive strategy for the Sudan* (two volumes), ILO/UNDP, Geneva.

Joshi, V. (1970) "Savings and foreign exchange constraints", in Streeten, P. (ed.), *Unfashionable Economics*, Weidenfield and Nicholson, London.

Khan, A.R. (1963) "Import substitution, export expansion and consumption liberalisation: A preliminary report, *Pakistan Development Review*, Summer, 1963.

Lal, D. (1972) "The foreign exchange bottleneck revisited: a geometric note", *Economic Development and Cultural Change*, Vol. 20, No.4.

Legum, C. (ed.) (1971) *Africa Contemporary Record: annual survey and documents*, Rex Collings, London.

Lewis, S.R. (1968) "Effects of trade policy on domestic relative prices 1951-64", *American Economic Journal*, No. 58.

Mckinnon, R.I. (1964) "Foreign exchange constraints on economic development and efficient aid allocation", *The Economic Journal*, Vol. 74.

Republic of Sudan (1967) *The Organisation and Promotion of Investment Act, 1967,* Khartoum.

Singer, H.W. and Ansar, J.A. (1978) *Rich and poor countries,* Allen and Unwin, London.

4

The IMF and Sudanese Economic Policy

Mohammed Nureldin Hussein

INTRODUCTION

IMF interventions are supposed to deal with economic crises. They usually have serious political and economic reverberations. This paper deals with the economic and political events surrounding the IMF intervention in the Sudan following the economic crisis of 1978. It provides an account of the devaluation debate between Sudanese and IMF officials prior to the IMF intervention. It examines the Fund's conditionality measures accompanying the 1978 Stand-by Arrangement, the 1979 Extended Arrangement, and the 1981 Second Stand-by Arrangement. In addition, some of the political and economic ramifications of the IMF programmes are considered.

BACKGROUND TO CRISIS

Speaking on Radio Omdurman on 25 May 1969, soon after taking power, General Numeiry announced that the history of the Sudan had been "a series of catastrophes" because too many parties had been in power. He asserted that the political parties had been "satellites of imperialism". Now it is time, he said, "to set out on the road of freedom and socialism".

In May 1970, the Revolutionary Council, together with the Cabinet, approved their first plan for social and economic development covering the five–year period 1970-75. This plan, designed by Russian and Sudanese experts, was supposed to lay the foundation for a strong socialist economy, free from foreign economic domination. It was said to "involve far-reaching political and economic consequences, especially for future generations" (Bank of Sudan 1970: 19). As we know, only the latter part of the statement turned out to be true. One year after the end of the plan period, Sudan faced its first foreign exchange crisis which called for intervention by the IMF.

THE DEVELOPMENT OF THE CRISIS

The Five Year Plan aimed at securing an annual increase of 7.6% in GDP, together with a 6.2% annual rise in per capita income. These targets were to be achieved through total investment of £S385 million over the plan period. The plan placed great emphasis on agricultural production, giving it 58.1% of total planned investment. 33.2% was allocated to industry, and the service sector was supposed to receive 8.7%.

Because of its socialist orientation, the plan assigned a leading role to the public sector, with total investment equal to £S215 million, or 55.8% of total investment expenditure. The remainder was left to the private sector. Moreover, 52% of total public expenditure was allocated to the directly productive sectors, such as agriculture and industry, while the bulk of private expenditure was allocated to housing.

The plan relied on internal resources to finance 48.8% of total public capital investment. This was supposed to come mainly from government surpluses. The remaining 51.2% was to be financed by borrowing from socialist countries. There was to be no deficit financing.

In a socialist spirit, and to strengthen the financial power needed to carry out the plan, the government undertook a series of nationalisation measures. During the first year of the plan, the Sudan concluded technical assistance and loan agreements totalling £S32 million with a number of socialist countries. These included loans from Soviet Union, East Germany, the Democratic Republic of Korea and the People's Republic of China. Repayment of these loans was to begin after the establishment of the projects, and was to be made through barter agreements for Sudanese goods (Bank of Sudan 1970: 88).

In the first year, only 73% of the year's plan was executed. The second year of the plan was interrupted by major political developments which not only changed the scope of the plan, but also the country's political direction.

In July 1971, Major Hashim Elatta (one of the original members of the Free Officers' Movement which had seized power in May 1969), with the tacit support of the Sudanese Communist Party, overthrew General Numeiry's government. The new regime lasted three days, and on June 22 Numeiry returned to power. Major Elatta and sixteen leaders of the movement were executed.

These developments gravely embarrassed the Russians who by then were deeply involved in the country's economic and political affairs. The Sudan's relations with the USSR and with the Soviet bloc deteriorated drastically and the country had to look to alternative sources to complete the remaining four years of the plan. The only possible candidates for such assistance were Western countries, pro-western Arab countries and western "international" institutions. However, in the light of the 1970 nationalisation and confiscation of foreign investments, aid from such sources seemed unlikely. Appreciating this, the government amended the nationalisation act and embarked on a series of denationalisations. The details of this legislation are discussed in Hassan Gad Karim's paper in this volume.

Following denationalisation measures, aid began to flow. In 1971, the Sudan received £S5.5 million from the Federal Republic of Germany for Sudan Railways; £S14.1 million from the PRC to build a Sudanese-Chinese Friendship palace and the Kassala-Port Sudan road; £S1 million from the UK to purchase irrigation pumps; and £S3.6 million from the American Commodity Credit Corporation to finance, together with the American Agency for International Development and the Government of Kuwait, the Rahad Agricultural Project.

The types of loan which were forthcoming were either tied by explicit stipulation as to where they could be spent, or tied to projects initiated by the lending sources, rather than projects initiated by the Sudanese Ministry of Planning. An example of one such project was the Kenana sugar factory, drawn up by Kahlil Osman, the Sudanese chairman of the Kuwaiti company, Gulf International, and "Tiny" Rowland of Lonrho.

The guidelines for economic development outlined in the Five Year Plan became impossible to follow. In November 1972, recognising this difficulty, the Sudanese authorities drew up a supplementary "five year interim programme of action". This was to incorporate projects in the fields of transportation and industry as dictated by the types of loan received from western sources, as well as to make room for projects financed by direct private foreign investment. The result, a collection of disparate projects, hardly formed an integrated development programme.

During 1973, the inflow of foreign capital peaked at around £S123 million. By the end of 1975, Sudan's total outstanding debt was £S371.7 million. But, despite this large capital inflow, the average rate of plan implementation in the public sector was only 52.4%, while actual expenditure was more than planned expenditure. The big jump in expenditure is explained by the marked escalation of project costs. Table 4.1 illustrates this for three major projects.

Table 4.1: Cost escalation in some development projects during the Sudan's five–year plan, 1970-5

Project	Estimated cost (in £S millions)		
	1973	1974	1975
Kenana Sugar Factory	55	129	200
Khartoum-Port Sudan Pipeline	8	40	97
El Rahad Scheme	33	95	125

Source: Internal files, Ministry of Planning, Khartoum.

The five year plan did not achieve its targets. The overall rate of growth was estimated as 4% as against a target of 7.6%. The majority of projects were not completed, while others were completed but remained inoperative owing to technical problems. Table 4.2 illustrates the poor performance of the plan by comparing the planned balance of payments against that which was actually achieved.

Instead of a surplus of £S20 million, the trade balance showed a deficit of £S122.2 million. This deficit was the result of imports exceeding and exports falling short of expectations. If it had not been for a sharp rise in export prices (averaging 23.2%) the shortfall would have been more pronounced. There was also a sharp increase in the value of imports resulting from a 7.2% increase in volume and a 27% rise in prices. Additionally, in contrast to an expected contraction of the invisible account deficit, it grew rapidly. This was mainly due to the growth of invisible payments, in particular interest on foreign loans and payments for transportation and travel.

Over the plan period, the Sudan became more dependent on foreign official borrowing to finance its external deficit. This was mainly from the Arab countries. Nearly two thirds of this capital came from Saudi Arabia and Kuwait. The result was that the country's outstanding foreign debts increased from £S110.6 million in 1970 to £S372 million in 1975.

Table 4.2: The performance of the balance of payments during the five year plan (in £S millions)

year	trade balance		invisible balance		capital account		balance of payments	
	planned	actual	planned	actual	planned	actual	planned	actual
1970/1	4.0	-12.5	-11.5	-10.6	-10.9	-0.4	3.4	-21.6
1971/2	9.0	-16.9	-11.3	-13.3	8.9	5.8	6.6	-22.2
1972/3	14.0	17.7	-11.0	-17.2	6.8	0.4	9.8	0.4
1973/4	18.0	-3.9	-10.2	-26.6	8.9	15.3	16.7	-15.6
1974/5	20.0	-122.2	-9.3	-38.1	9.2	108.6	19.9	-51.9

Source: The Five Year Plan of Economics and Social Development, 1970/71-1974/75. Bank of Sudan, Annual Reports, 1970-76.

High hopes and expectations dashed by the failure of the plan were once again raised by a new idea — the Sudan as the breadbasket of the Middle East. This idea was promoted by the Arab oil producers with a view to reducing their dependence on western food imports.

In order to pursue this policy, Sudan began to borrow heavily from Kuwait and Saudi Arabia. Foreign borrowing in this period has been described as an "hysterical process". A former minister reported that "Any minister could go to the President with a project, tell him it was a good idea, and get his go-ahead for it (Financial Times 1980). New loans contracted during the period 1975-6 alone amounted to $US1.8 billion.

STRUCTURAL IMBALANCE AND THE FOREIGN EXCHANGE CRISIS

The majority of foreign loans contracted in order to finance the five year plan were tied either to specific projects or to the purchase of certain commodities. This had profound effects on the intersectoral distribution of expenditure and can be seen as having contributed to a structural imbalance. The original FYP allocated 38% of total expenditure to agricultural expenditure and 14% to transport and communications. The amended plan altered this distribution — 32% to transport and 27% to agriculture. Moreover, the amended plan made no allowance for investment in electricity or power. This shift in emphasis was to a large extent responsible for the structural imbalance which underlay the foreign exchange crisis in the post-1977 period.

In particular, the investment in the transport sector, desirable in itself given the poor state of transport infrastructure, involved massive drawings. In the period 1970-7 external loans allocated to this sector amounted to some 42.3% of total foreign loans. The proportions for agriculture and industry were 20.4% and 10.3% respectively. An already alarming picture was made more so by the terms and maturity structure of the loans. Of the total external public debt which stood at £S502 million in 1978, £S328 million were short term loans with five to ten years to maturity. The rate of interest charged on 41% of these loans was higher than 6%. This meant that within a fairly short period export earnings needed to be substantially increased to meet the country's import and debt repayment bills. In the absence of such an increase, Sudan would become increasingly dependent on additional loans to finance the balance of payments deficit. Under such circumstances, a foreign exchange crisis would arise when capital flows dried up.

Over the planning period 1970-5, the projects which were meant to increase export earnings capacity were limited to the Rahad agricultural scheme together with three sugar factories. The Rahad Scheme, which was initiated in accordance with the World Bank's Rural Development Strategy for the Sudan, was meant to produce cotton and groundnuts for export. The scheme was meant to be operative by 1976. However, the first phase was only completed in 1977/8. It made a small contribution — 5 per cent— to total cotton production. The three sugar factories, Kenana, Sennar and Asalaya, were part of the government's plan to promote the Sudan as a major sugar exporter by 1979. The sharp increase in import prices as a result of accelerated international inflation, the growing disputes between the foreign financiers of these projects, together with administrative and manpower constraints, made timely completion of these projects impossible. In 1980, the Sudan still imported 64% of its sugar.

In addition, the existing export-oriented production units, and in particular the Gezira Scheme, were neglected over the plan period. As a consequence, these projects not only failed to increase their contribution to the country's export earnings, but also failed to maintain their past contribution. The situation was further vitiated by the government's decision to promote self-sufficiency in wheat and rice, following increases in the import prices of cereals in 1975. Cotton acreages were reduced and those of wheat and rice increased. This policy was not expected to reduce cotton production since average cotton yields were expected to increase. In the event, average yields declined, and hence cotton output.

During the period 1970-7, the volume of cotton exports deteriorated by an average of 1.3% per year. This was just offset by an increase in the production of other traditional exports, and the average rate of growth of total export volume remained virtually stagnant. Yet export proceeds increased, as a result of the increase of export prices, by an average of 13.3%. At the same time, import prices increased by 26.5%, and the barter terms of trade moved against the Sudan by an average of 13.2%.

The combined effects of sluggish export growth and increased import prices had a marked influence on the country's external account. This is particularly true for the years following the 1973 oil price rise and its inflationary consequences. The current account balance, which had recorded a surplus of £S6.4 million in 1973, turned into a deficit of £S103 million in 1974 and £S166.3 million in 1975. At the same time a large proportion of the country's foreign debts began to fall due. In 1976, the ratio of debt repayment to export earnings reached a peak of 22%. Confronted by this situation, Sudan relied heavily on borrowings from Saudi Arabia, not only to finance the growing current account deficit, but also to repay past debts.

Under these circumstances, in April 1977, the government launched its second development plan. The Six Year Plan (1977/8-1983/4) was a clear reflection of change in the government's development philosophy. The idea of building an economically independent Sudan was abandoned. Instead, the SYP contained:

a well designed policy to attract foreign private investment in strategic fields of the economy

and

a portfolio of well prepared bankable development projects was made ready to attract foreign capital (Ministry of National Planning1977: 63).

The dream of making the Sudan the "breadbasket of the Middle East" was incorporated in the plan in the form of projects to be jointly funded by Saudi Arabia, Kuwait and the Sudanese private and public sectors. The plan projected that sufficient foreign capital would be available to finance public development expenditure. These projections were based on "informed judgements taking into consideration past experience, the current situation and future possibilities" (Ministry of National Planning 1977: 63).

Contrary to the confidence implied by this statement, the developments which took place during the first year of the plan brought the inflow of capital to a complete halt. Early in 1977, the IMF acquired new powers through the creation of the Witteveen Facility (also known as the Supplementary Financing Facility).

The Witteveen Facility meant that surplus countries could lend their surpluses to the IMF (instead of lending directly), which would then re-lend, and impose its own conditions on each borrower. Having consented to be the major contributor, the Saudis were promised by the IMF that it would ensure the safety of their money by enforcing the strongest disciplinary measures. The situation became even tighter when President Numeiry declared his support for the Egyptian-Israeli peace initiative proposed by President Sadat in November 1977. As a result, the Arab oil countries curtailed their financial assistance to Sudan. Early in 1978, in the middle of severe shortages of basic food imports and fuel, the Saudis and other creditors made it clear that the flow of their financial assistance would be conditional upon the country's acceptance of an IMF arrangement. In June 1978 the Sudan signed a one-year stand-by arrangement with the IMF.

THE STAND-BY ARRANGEMENT AND THE DEVALUATION DEBATE

The report prepared by the IMF and the World Bank mission to the Sudan identified the country's foreign exchange crisis with an over-valued exchange rate, and argued for devaluation. The immediate reaction of some Sudanese economic advisors was a complete rejection of the IMF proposal. This reaction was summed up by El Hassan:

> although the Sudanese economy is currently characterised by rather serious internal and external imbalances, it is indeed doubtful whether the conventional text-book prescription of devaluation is appropriate or relevant (El Hassan 1978).

In the event, the Sudanese Minister of Finance formed a consulting panel to examine the IMF's proposal. In his submission, El Hassan argued that irrespective of the economic theory backing the proposal, the elasticities of demand for exports and imports play an important role in the success of any devaluation. He added:

> It is indeed surprising that despite the crucial importance of checking the elasticity magnitudes prior to the advocacy of adjusting the

exchange rate, the recent IMF and IBRD proposals did not make any attempt to ascertain the values of the elasticities in question (El Hassan 1978).

He provided evidence that the demand for the country's exports and imports were extremely insensitive to price changes. On the other hand, the IMF officials admitted in an internal memorandum that:

the demand for imports is likely to be inelastic in the short-run as imports have already been reduced to essentials by quantitative restrictions (IMF).

Yet they argued that by providing price incentives to producers, and hence increasing the supply of exports, devaluation would improve the balance of payments.

This argument was also attacked by Sudanese officials who stated that the numerous structural rigidities which characterise the Sudanese economy, together with the highly inelastic nature of the supply of agricultural production, would militate against any immediate or even long-term increase in the supply of exports. The IMF officials responded to this criticism by amending their original note, which endorsed devaluation, stating that the improvement in the trade balance resulting from the proposed devaluation would:

probably be moderate in the short term, but would become greater over time as the cropping pattern is adjusted, new land is brought under cultivation, and the Sudan moves into the production of the commodities which have a higher elasticity of demand (IMF).

The economic logic underlying the IMF statement was weak. The adjustment of the cropping pattern, the bringing of new land under cultivation and the shift to new commodities, are all long-term measures, which if judged desirable can be achieved by administrative or planning measures. This is particularly true because the bulk of the country's exports are produced by the public sector. It is only when these measures are introduced and the country shifts to the production of goods with higher price responsiveness, that the IMF logic makes sense. As a Sudanese official commented, "the IMF logic is like putting the cart before the horse".

Considering the inflationary effects of devaluation, the Sudanese officials argued that devaluation would increase the budgetary cost of development expenditure substantially because of the large import content. According to the IMF's own estimates the proposed 25% devaluation of the Sudanese pound would result in a 24.3% increase in prices of imported consumer goods. No estimates were given for the increased prices of capital goods, fuel, parts and materials.

On the question of the hardships which the inflationary consequences of devaluation might bring to the Sudanese people, the IMF officials argued that:

in the countryside and for the lower income groups the import content of expenditure amounts to little so that the price effect would be less than 6-7%,

and that,

the increase in the cost of living from devaluation would affect mainly the urban population particularly the higher income group (IMF).

This statement is hardly convincing. To start with, the IMF's own estimates of price increases in the different imported consumer goods were much higher than the 6-7% mentioned, and in addition most of these items loom large in the consumption basket of the low income groups. Examples can be taken from the IMF's own estimates: tea, coffee and medicine with IMF estimated price rises of 17.6%, 22.2%, and 25% respectively. Secondly, it is well-known that inflation cannot be geographically confined — thus the economic burden of inflation, measured by the loss of real income, cannot be confined to an "urban" population.

Given the country's poor foreign exchange situation, with its creditors pressing for the IMF measures, the devaluation debate was an academic exercise. On 15 February, 1978, Mr. Osman Hashim, the Minister of Finance, surprised the Sudanese public not only by accepting the IMF conditions, but by supporting them too. In the government controlled newspaper, El Sahafa, he wrote on 15 February 1978:

the devaluation of the Sudanese pound will help to increase production in the agricultural sector and hence the income of farmers who represent the majority of our people. Devaluation will offer them more incentive to increase their production and their supply. This will restore domestic price stability and will increase the country's exportable surplus...Devaluation will stimulate the flow of foreign capital and strengthen our economic relation with the world. All of which will result in improving our balance of payments (El Sahafa 1978).

In June 1978, the Sudanese pound was devalued by 25%. In return, a stand-by arrangement of £S10.4 million (equivalent to Special Drawing Rights (SDR) of 30.2 million) was agreed, as well as drawings on the Trust Fund of £S15.1 million (SDR 30.2 million), and on the Compensatory Financing Facility of £S12.9 million.

One year after the devaluation, the trade balance deteriorated drastically from a deficit of £S23.7 million to £S83.7 million. This resulted from a 25% increase in the value of imports and a 2% decrease in the value of exports. The rise in the value of imports was caused entirely by the rise in import prices, the volume of imports remaining virtually unchanged. The fall in export proceeds was entirely due to a fall in cotton output, from 3.6 million to 2.5 million kantars. Export proceeds other than those of cotton, increased by 14%.

As a direct consequence of the stand-by arrangement with the IMF, the Sudan received the sum of £S26 million from Saudi Arabia. This included £S10 million representing drawings on the US$200 million loan from Saudi to meet the repayment of Euro-dollar loans, and £S16 million from the same donor for balance of payments support. In addition, three EEC members — West Germany, UK, Netherlands — decided to write off some £S109 million outstanding loan repayments due to them.

THE EXTENDED ARRANGEMENTS

In May 1979, one month before the expiry date of the stand-by arrangement, a three-year Extended Fund Facility totalling £S200 million was agreed. According to the accompanying letter of intent, the objectives of the Extended Facility programme were to raise the sustainable rate of growth, to reduce the rate of inflation, and strengthen the balance of payments. The programme objectives were to be achieved by the following measures:

i) liberalisation of trade. This measure included the termination of the bilateral trade agreement with Egypt, and the abolition of all quantitative and qualitative restrictions on currency payments;
ii) exchange reform. This included the replacement of the multiple exchange rate system with a dual market comprising an official and

65

parallel rate. This was to be the first step towards a gradual unification of the exchange rate regime. The exchange reform measures also included the abolition of all exchange taxes and subsidies, as well as the "nil-value" licensing system;

iii) a reduction in the overall government deficit, including tax increases on selected sales, stamp duties, and many other fees and charges, reductions in subsidies on petrol and sugar, the curtailment of development expenditure, and concentration on on-going development projects;

iv) reductions in bank credit to the government and private sector; and

v) the removal of all controls on profit repatriation to encourage private foreign investment.

Fifty per cent of the SDR 200 million drawing was to be supplied through the Witteveen Facility.

Of the total amount, SDR 37.8 million would be made available immediately, while the rest would be disbursed in six monthly instalments, subject to satisfaction of certain performance criteria. The Fund also promised to convene a rescheduling conference for Sudan's outstanding debt.

The new Minister of Finance, Mr. Bader Eldien Sulaiman, who was appointed specially to carry out the IMF recommendations, stated that the aim of the policies was to stimulate production by allowing the free flow of imports. He described the government's control over imports and foreign exchange as "fetters which bind the potential of everybody" (Financial Times 1979).

To ensure the free flow of trade, the IMF advocated termination of the country's bilateral trade agreement with Egypt and some other developing countries. The history of these trade agreements goes back to the early 1960s. Their essence was to provide the country with guaranteed export markets at contracted prices, avoiding fluctuations in export proceeds and consequent effects on domestic income and employment. These fluctuations were particularly large in the case of Sudan because of its dependence on cotton. The bilateral agreements also provided the country with imported goods at contracted prices.

The IMF objection to bilateral trade agreements springs from its "free trade" outlook which calls for the widest possible movement of goods and capital. Yet this free trade philosophy is enforced only on poor countries, while various forms of trade agreements are practised by developed countries which are leading members of the IMF. An example of this is the European Economic Community which encourages trade among its members and discourages trade from outside the community.

The IMF did not, however, object to the semi-formal bilateral trade agreement between the Sudan and the US, which took the form of the "Sudan-United States Business Council". Formed in 1978, after the IMF stand-by arrangement, the council's objective was to promote trade and investment between the two countries. In 1977, US exports to Sudan amounted to US$14 million while those of the Sudan to the US were US$17.1 million. In 1980 the respective figures were US$235 million and US$14 million, a trade ratio of about 14:1 between the two countries.

The extended programme included explicit conditions relating to the encouragement of direct foreign private investment through the relaxation of controls on profit repatriation. In March 1980, the Sudan-United States Business Council supported this policy by lobbying the passage of the new investment Act which offered foreign investors guarantees against nationalisation and sequestration (Sudanow 1981). This Business Council included, from the one side, representatives of 40 US firms which were aiming to increase their investment in the Sudan. From the other side, it included Sudanese businessmen (some of whom were able to influence government policies) who were running investment partnerships with US firms. This is one illustration of how IMF programmes, which poor consumers find hard to accept, often find support from a small but influential minority of people who benefit from them.

In the first year of the programme, the Sudanese authorities carried out every aspect of the extended arrangement. The dual exchange rate was established with an official rate of US$ = £S1 and a parallel rate of US$1.25 = £S1. The official rate was to be used in 92% of export transactions (including cotton) and in 70% of import transactions. The parallel rate was to be used in all other transactions. This implied a 20% devaluation for cotton and a 38% devaluation for 30% of imports.

On the fiscal side, subsidies on petrol and sugar were reduced. New taxes yielding £S100 million were introduced and development expenditure was curtailed. In agriculture, farmers were made to grow more cotton, pay more for water charges, and restrict the expansion of the wheat crop. On the monetary side, the net domestic assets of the Bank of Sudan were kept well within their IMF ceiling.

Despite these measures, the performance of the economy was worse than in the previous year. Even with the large increase in tax revenue, and the reduction in services, the overall government deficit continued to increase. In 1978/9 the fiscal deficit had been £S174.1 million; it widened to £S340 million in 1979/80 and £S480 million in 1980/1. This was attributed to the devaluation-induced increase in the government import bill, domestic inflation and the valuing of foreign components of development expenditure at the parallel exchange rate. With ceilings imposed on net domestic assets, the government deficit was increasingly financed by external loans.

Increased taxes, reduced government services and domestic inflation brought immediate hardship to the majority of the population. These were reflected in street riots and a five-day strike by railway workers demanding wage increases and reductions in the cost of living. The seriousness of these actions can be understood if viewed against a background where strikes had become illegal and were punishable by imprisonment. The tenants of the Gezira also went on strike and refused to sow the 1979/80 crop. The immediate cause of the strike was their disapproval of the IMF endorsed policies which advocated the reallocation of crop areas in favour of cotton and against wheat. This meant a loss of income to the farmers since the Gezira share-cropping formula entitled the government to share cotton proceeds, while wheat proceeds went in their entirety to the tenants.

The strike caused a delay in sowing and inadequate irrigation. As a result, cotton output dropped by 32%. However, this was more than compensated for by the increase in export prices in domestic currency, and cotton proceeds increased by £S24.2 million between June 1979 and June 1980. At the same time export supply of other commodities dropped by 21% while the proceeds of these exports rose from £S139.9 million to £S207.4 million.

Despite this large increase in export proceeds, the trade balance widened sharply from a deficit of £S83.7 million in 1978/79, to a deficit of £S199.3 million in 1979/80. This adverse out-turn resulted mainly from the dramatic increase in the money value of imports from £S307.2 million in 1978/9 to £S488.2 million in 1979/80. Within this increase, government imports rose by £S95.4 million, while private imports increased by £S85.6 million.

According to the Bank of Sudan, the marked rise in government imports was due to the increase in the prices of petroleum, raw materials and other essential consumer goods. The increase in private imports was said to be due to the expansion of private sector business enhanced by the newly launched policy of trade liberalisation (Bank of Sudan 1979: 1980). As a result of the abolition of the nil-value system of imports (thereby leading to the channelling of savings by Sudanese nationals working abroad through commercial banks) invisible receipts increased from £S120.2 million in June 1979 to £S237.3 million in June 1980. Accordingly, the invisible account recorded a surplus of £S72.1 million. This was insufficient to bridge the trade gap, and the current account recorded a deficit of £S127.2 million in June 1980, compared with a deficit of £S77.9 million twelve months earlier.

During the first year of the programme the IMF made available an amount of £S55 million from Saudi Arabia. Capital inflows from other sources were not attracted by the IMF agreement.

Under the auspices of the IMF, and within the framework of the consortium to support the Sudan, meetings to reschedule Sudan's official debt of US$850 million (£S425 million) were held with the country's principal creditor nations and the international agencies. In March 1980 an agreement was reached to reschedule the country's official debt. Such creditors are not altruistic; their aim is to ensure that countries which provide markets for their products do not completely collapse, renege on their existing debts or withdraw from the western trade system. By 1980 about 90% of Sudan's imports were from Western countries.

With regard to the country's commercial debt, a rescheduling agreement with commercial bank creditors (known as the "Club Banks") proved difficult to achieve. In the initial negotiations, the "Club Banks" proposed rescheduling terms which included: a three-year grace period, seven-year maturity and a possible US$100 million new money facility. In return, the country was to resume repayments of interest arrears as well as make regular payments on current and refinanced interest.

The Sudanese negotiators described these terms as impossible to fulfil and negotiations broke down. By October 1980 it became apparent that what rescheduling terms the Sudan would be able to meet would depend crucially on additional IMF assistance. Consequently, the original Extended Arrangement of SDR200 million was augmented by SDR227 million subject to the same performance criteria as the original agreement. The augmented agreement helped to restore dialogue between the Sudan and the "Club Banks". However, it took Morgan Grenfell (a British bank appointed to advise the Sudan government on rescheduling its debts), and a team of foreign experts, a complete year to draw up a rescheduling offer acceptable to the commercial banks. By the time the offer was made, in November 1981, the Sudan had already used about 90% of the total amount made available by the IMF under the original and augmented Extended Arrangement.

In December 1981, five months before the expiry date of the 1979 agreement, the Sudan concluded an additional one-year stand-by arrangement of £S126.3 million, containing further disciplinary measures. This time the IMF conditions involved the abolition of the dual exchange rate and the establishment of a single exchange rate at US$1.25. This implied a 37% devaluation in the official rate which was then applied to approximately 90% of exports and 70% of imports. In addition, the IMF pressurised the Sudanese government to abolish the share-cropping formula in the Gezira Scheme, and to establish the individual account system.

Thus at a time when inflation was running at a rate of 63%, the country had to devalue for the third time in four years. The second IMF measure, the establishment of the individual account system in the Gezira, was justified on the grounds that it would increase production by promoting the optimal allocation of resources. The idea of the individual account system had been around since 1966 (IBRD 1966), but had been strenuously resisted by the Sudanese authorities because of its political and social implications. In 1981, because of their weak bargaining position vis-a-vis the IMF, they gave way to the IMF-IBRD pressures and the new system was introduced in the 1981/2 season.

In itself this provides an excellent example of how the IBRD and the IMF work together to impose their policy conditions on developing countries. The 1966 agreement between the two institutions clarifies the nature of the Fund-Bank teamwork. The essence of this agreement is that the Fund has the primary responsibility in matters related to exchange rates, balance of payments and modes of adjustment. A World Bank Mission visiting a troubled country must adopt the Fund's established views regarding these matters. On the other hand, the Bank has primary responsibility with regard to project evaluation, development programmes and priorities. In such matters the Fund adopts the Bank's views and enforces them, as was seen in the case of the Sudan.

CONCLUSION

The preceding analysis shows how the Sudan's dream of socialist economic development turned into a nightmare of foreign exchange crisis, economic collapse and IMF intervention. The point of departure came when the Sudan turned to Western countries seeking their assistance to finance the five year plan which had been drawn up by the Russian experts. The practice of aid-tying led to remarkable changes in the project specifications contained within the original five year plan. Investment was diverted from agriculture and power to the transport and communications sector. For the same reason a large proportion of the investment expenditure contained in the plan financed prestige projects with no appreciable impact on output. The outcome was the failure of the plan to achieve its desired economic and social objectives. The nationalisation of private domestic and foreign businesses, and the transfer of their ownership to the government, which marked the first move towards socialism, was replaced by denationalisation and an open door policy to foreign investment. The country's debt repayment capacity deteriorated and outstanding debts accumulated. Being dependent on foreign aid to finance its payments deficits, the consequent drying up of capital inflows caused the country its first major foreign exchange crisis, and hence the IMF intervention.

REFERENCES

Bank of Sudan (1970) *Annual report 1970,* Khartoum.
Bank of Sudan (1979) *Annual report,* Khartoum.
Bank of Sudan (1980) *Annual report,* Khartoum.
El Hassan, M. (1978) "An evaluation of the adjustment in the exchange rate of the Sudanese pound", unpublished paper submitted to the Consulting Panel constituted by the Minister of Finance, March 1978.
El Sahafa (1978) 15 February, Khartoum.
Financial Times (1979) September 6, London.
Financial Times (1980) August19, London.
IBRD (1966) *Gezira Study Mission* (also known as the Rist Report), Washington.
IMF Memorandum and IBRD Report, Ministry of Finance, Internal files, n.d.
Ministry of National Planning (1977) *The Five Year Plan of Economic and Social Development, 1977,* April, Khartoum.
Sudanow (1981) March p.22 Khartoum.

5

A Background Note on the Final Round of Economic Austerity Measures Imposed by the Numeiry Regime: June 1984-March 1985

Richard Brown

INTRODUCTION

The last package of austerity measures introduced by the Numeiry regime during February and March 1985, which culminated in the food riots, strikes and popular overthrow of the regime, should be understood in the context of the seven-year long rescue operation that Sudan's "international community" of main donor governments and multilateral agencies had until then successfully pieced together.

The main purpose of this note is to attempt to put some of these pieces together, with a view to shedding further light on the circumstances in which this particular policy package was formulated and implemented. In doing this, we also try to illustrate the lengths to which the donor community, led by the government of the United States, was prepared to go in its efforts to avert, or at least forestall, the social and political manifestations of the deepening economic crisis which Sudan had been enduring for ten years or more. It is also argued that this last rescue operation differed from those of previous years in one important respect, perhaps signalling what was to have been the start of a new phase in the International Monetary Fund's relations with the authorities of Sudan, and which also brought out into the open the direct involvement of the US government in persuading the international donor community to commit the extraordinary levels of foreign aid that had been necessary to maintain some semblance of stability in an otherwise explosive environment.

THE IMF'S ROLE IN PREVIOUS RESCUE OPERATIONS: 1978 TO MAY 1984

As argued elsewhere (Brown 1984a) the IMF's Stabilisation Programme in the Sudan since 1978 had differed from other Third World country programmes in a number of important respects which need to be taken into account when assessing its effects. The main function of the Extended Fund Facility and Standby Loan Arrangements (see Hussein in this volume for details of these) negotiated on an almost annual basis since 1978 had been to provide the country's main donors, the USA in particular, with the legitimisation which their governments required to obtain the ever increasing amounts of economic aid needed to fill the unfinanced gap in Sudan's balance of payments. In this sense, the most important "effect" of the programme had been to allow the country's authorities to avoid introducing the the sorts of economic policy changes that would have been necessary in the absence of the external resource flows from the donor community at large.

Until the middle of 1984, this "bailing out" procedure worked rather smoothly. As Sudan's balance of payments problems approached crisis proportions and it began defaulting on its foreign debt service payments, the country's authorities would appeal to the US, Saudi Arabia and other donors for more aid in the form of debt relief, balance of payments support, commodity aid etc. These donors would then informally agree among themselves to provide the necessary support, but would stipulate that the authorities should first come to some agreement with the IMF on the "corrective" economic policy measures to be implemented in the course of the following year. Negotiations for a new arrangement with the IMF would then begin, in which a number of policies, targets, performance criteria and conditionality clauses would be included. An agreement in principle with the IMF would be reached, subject to the condition that the projected unfinanced gap in the balance of payments in the forthcoming year would be filled by increased aid disbursements, over and above those already promised. With the US being the most powerful member of the IMF Executive Board, Sudan never encountered much difficulty in obtaining the required votes, given that the US and other donors were already committed to the bailing out operation of which the Arrangement was an integral part.

With the formal approval of each new Standby Loan Arrangement, Sudan's aid donors would then meet and agree collectively on the details of the rescheduling of its existing and anticipated arrears on bilateral foreign debt (this group became known as the Club of Paris), and their individual contributions to the increased aid monies required for the coming year. With these commitments made, the IMF's Standby Loan Arrangement would come into operation and Sudan would immediately receive the first purchase (drawing), usually amounting to 25 to 40 per cent of the total loan. However, after the Stabilisation Programme which began in 1978, most of Sudan's annually negotiated Standby Loan Arrangements became inoperative midway. Usually this happened because the authorities failed to comply with the performance criteria and/or conditionality clauses contained in the Standby Loan Arrangement. In immediate financial terms, this was not usually very important because the total amount of the loan was extremely small in relation to the total of the other aid monies already obtained or committed from donors at the time of signing the Standby Loan Arrangement with the IMF. In more recent years, the total value of the loan barely covered the amount due to the IMF from Sudan during the period in question.

Normally, however, the suspension of a Standby Loan Arrangement would make it very difficult for the country in question to enter into a further agreement with the IMF without a protracted period of tough negotiation, and without meeting a number of policy preconditions even before the Standby Loan Arrangement became operative. Similarly, the suspension by the IMF of an existing Standby Loan Arrangement is usually interpreted by the country's main donors and creditors as meaning that it has lost the IMF's "seal of approval" and should therefore be treated less favourably in future aid and commercial loan negotiations. In Sudan's case, this would have implied that the country's authorities would have faced increased difficulties in entering into new rescheduling and aid agreements with donors because donor governments could no longer use the IMF "seal of approval" to elicit approval of further aid to Sudan from their own parliaments. In the case of Sudan, however, this scenario does not seem to have operated as one might have expected. Suspension of an existing Standby Loan Arrangement did not deter the IMF (which was no doubt under considerable pressure from the US administration) from almost immediately re-entering negotiations with Sudan for another Standby Loan Arrangement for the following year. With a new round of negotiations successfully concluded, yet more arrears on foreign debt service payments would be rescheduled, new increases in balance of payments support and other aid monies would be committed, and so on. It is in this sense, I maintain, that the IMF's treatment of Sudan under Numeiry can be considered "lenient" in comparison with the experience of, for example, Tanzania or Jamaica under Manley; not because the IMF itself has a "soft spot" for the regime, but because of the power of the US administration (and other allies including Saudi Arabia) within the IMF's decision-making process. In other words, the determination of the US-led donor consortium to prevent the collapse of the Numeiry Regime led it to force the IMF into negotiating a series of functional paper agreements which neither it nor the IMF really believed would be successfully implemented.

Until early 1984, all parties concerned appeared willing and able to play ball, by which time the IMF had entered into five "upper tranche" agreements with the Sudan in the space of six years. Four of these had been rendered inoperative midway. Sudan's foreign debt amounted to US$8 billion, and debt service payments due represented more than 100 per cent of export earnings. The Paris Club had already met four times and all debt arrears which could technically be rescheduled, both past and anticipated for the next year, had been rescheduled. Necessary aid disbursements to fill the 1984 balance of payments gap were estimated to be more than US$1 billion (or about 150 per cent of total export revenues) and were not expected to become any less in the foreseeable future.

However, in the summer of 1984, which also coincided with the introduction of martial law, a number of Islamic reforms, as well as with the heightening of the conflict in the South, Sudan entered a new phase in its relations with the IMF, the US, and the international community at large.

By early 1984, negotiations were already underway with the IMF for a new Standby Loan Arrangement, to be effective from May 31. By February, however, Sudan had run into arrears on payments due to the IMF totalling US$18 millions. Under the terms of its constitution, the IMF is not allowed to enter into any formal negotiations with a member state that is in arrears. Almost immediately, however, the US government stepped in and diverted US$18 million of USAID monies already committed for Sudan, to pay these arrears. Negotiations with the IMF resumed, and a new Standby Loan Arrangement was agreed in principle. For this to operate, the unfinanced gap in the Sudan's balance of payments had to be filled by May 31. This was estimated at some US$60 million after allowing for already agreed debt rescheduling and aid disbursements for the same period.

By May 31, however, the additional funds needed had not been found. Normally, this would have rendered the Standby Loan Arrangement inoperative, but the IMF agreed to an extension of the deadline to June 7. Again, efforts to raise the necessary aid increases among the international donor community failed and, under much pressure from the US, the IMF consented to a further extension of the deadline to June 14. During this week, the US$60 million aid commitment was found, but, unfortunately, from the Sudan government's point of view, it was already too late. Although the projected unfinanced gap could be filled, Sudan had in the meantime run into arrears once again on its payments due to the IMF. Until these could be paid, the Standby Loan Arrangement could not come into operation. The US Congress, having learned of the February US$18 million "misuse" of USAID aid monies blocked any effort for this to be paid on Sudan's behalf by the US government. Saudi Arabia also refused to pay the US$25 million necessary to square Sudan's account with the IMF. Finally, having failed to raise the funds through the official international donor community, the US government arranged the payment indirectly, by concluding the negotiation of a bridging loan on Sudan's behalf on June 25. This was paid directly to the IMF. On receipt of this payment, the IMF released the first SDR20 million purchase on the 1984/5 Standby Loan Arrangement to the government of Sudan. This was then immediately used to repay the commercial bridging loan. Through this masterpiece of financial juggling, the US government had managed, in spite of the apparent refusal by all other bilateral donors to co-operate, to bail out the Numeiry regime yet again, and temporarily at least, forestall a direct confrontation with the IMF and the rest of the international donor community. However, this period of grace was short-lived. Before the Paris Club or Consultative Group members could meet to organise yet another salvage operation for the coming year, as had been planned for later in 1984, the Sudan yet again went into arrears on its payments due to the IMF. The newly activated Standby Loan Arrangement was immediately frozen. If the Paris Club and Consultative Group members had met, there was very little they could have orchestrated to avoid the debt-servicing problems that followed. For, at this time, almost all debt service payments falling due were with respect to multilateral loans which, constitutionally, were not subject to rescheduling. As each month passed, Sudan's arrears on payments due to the IMF, World Bank, AFSED, ADF and others, compounded rapidly. This led to the suspension of all aid disbursements due by these organisations for the financing of a number of critical development projects, including the all-important Gezira rehabilitation scheme. As these were jointly financed with a number of bilateral lenders and donors, some of the West European governments and the US were also forced to freeze part of their already committed aid allocation for 1984. By the end of the year, Sudan's accumulated arrears to the IMF alone amounted to about US$82 million. In addition it owed over $30 million to AFSED. To quote an African Economic Digest report:

> a simple bail-out to keep the economy ticking over was no longer on the cards by December — even if the essential prerequisite of a functional IMF standby could be achieved. "None of the donors can afford to bail Sudan out; the amounts are simply too large", a US State Department source said, "It is going to require a joint effort by all donors and that's only going to occur under the umbrella of some kind of IMF/World Bank programme" (African Economic Digest 1984: 30).

Unfortunately, it seems, at about this moment a so-called rift developed between the IMF on the one hand, and the World Bank, US government, and other donors on the other.

The precise details of this "rift" were not public at the time of writing, but what seems to have happened is that during discussions on the scenario of a possible bailing-out operation for Sudan, the IMF was openly criticised by the USAID mission in Khartoum and other donors, for failing to recognise the underlying structural nature of the Sudan's economic crisis, and the need for a policy package that took into account the "longer term structural adjustments" necessary for economic recovery, as opposed to the shorter term "shock tactic" measures usually advocated by the IMF. USAID then contracted a group of Princeton University (USA) academics to advise on an "alternative economic strategy" for the Sudan. The details of their recommendations were not officially announced. In a public lecture at the Development Studies Research Centre, University of Khartoum, Professor Branson was openly critical of the IMF's insistence on an "active" exchange rate policy which sought a real devaluation and argued for a "passive" policy, amounting to a "managed float" in terms of which the real value of the pound against a basket of other currencies was to be preserved.

By late January 1985, there was increasing speculation that the IMF was about to declare Sudan ineligible for further borrowing. Food and fuel shortages in Sudan, as well as the open market exchange rate, reached unprecedented levels. By the end of January, Sudan's arrears to the IMF had reached US$110 million. In early February the newly appointed Minister of Finance and Governor of the Bank of Sudan visited the US, in what was seen as a last desperate effort to persuade the IMF not to formally cancel the still operative 1984/5 Standby Loan Arrangement. In spite of this effort, which also involved a token payment of US$10 million by Sudan to the IMF, on February 8, the Standby Loan Arrangement was formally suspended by the IMF Board. In its place, however, the Sudan's authorities negotiated a special deal directly with the US administration which we shall label the "USAID-Princeton package", it being, presumably, the outcome of the USAID's attempt to find an alternative to the IMF's policy package which could be sold directly to the Reagan administration and the US Congress as a last ditch effort to bail out the Sudanese government.

THE USAID-PRINCETON PACKAGE AND ITS IMPLEMENTATION

What this policy actually consisted of was not clear, its contents were not publicly announced. Even some of the individual components were not announced by the authorities, such as the fuel price increase which was simply implemented in March without any prior explanation. However, from the scant information available, the package included the following elements:

i) a virtual unification of the exchange rate on a "managed float" basis through the commercial banks;
ii) an increase in fuel prices ranging from 60 to 66 per cent;
iii) an increase of flour and bread prices of about 75 per cent;
iv) the establishment of a special oil facility (funded mainly by donors) in order to permit the purchase of the country's oil imports at the much lower spot market prices;
v) the revision of the recently introduced Islamic taxes, and other recently introduced commercial laws;
vi) the reduction of central government expenditure by an unspecified amount.

As well as these economic policy changes, a number of political measures were introduced. These included the imprisonment of leading members of the Muslim Brotherhood. What seems clear is that the US administration and other donors agreed collectively on the need for these policy changes to be implemented by April 1 1985, as a precondition for the release of previously frozen aid monies, and the resumption of negotiations on a programme of economic support for the future. It is therefore not coincidental that when Presidents Numeiry and Reagan met in Washington on April 1, the US government was able to announce the release of US$67 million which had been previously allocated under the 1983/4 budget.

What still remained to be seen after the April 1 meeting was how the Sudan was to settle its arrears with the IMF (by now in the region of US$ 130-150 million) and the other multilateral donor agencies with whom debts could not be rescheduled, and how, if at all, the US and the Sudan's other main bilateral donors were going to manage future salvage operations. In this connection, it is worth raising a few question concerning the future of Sudan's relations with the IMF.

The analysis would suggest that since the summer of 1984 there had been a definite hardening of the IMF's attitude. It seemed that the days were over when it was prepared to agree to a purely functional Standby Loan Arrangement on paper, the terms and conditions of which it knew were not going to be met, but which would serve to legitimise a US-led bailing out operation. At the same time, however, one should not conclude that the IMF had washed its hands of the Sudanese authorities. The so-called "rift" between the IMF and USAID *et. al.* should not be seen to imply that from then on the role of broker between the Numeiry regime and the international donor community would be played directly by the US administration through USAID. For, even if the IMF had been inclined to avoid suspension of the 1984/5 Standby Loan Arrangement, technically it could not formally have negotiated the more recent economic policy package on behalf of the international community, in view of the Sudan's arrears.

It would appear that by appearing to criticise the IMF's Stabilisation Programme, and contracting the Princeton Group to formulate an alternative, USAID was simply seeking an immediate and politically expedient solution to the problem of persuading the US Congress, and the rest of the donor community, to release the aid monies frozen in late 1984, with a view to paving the way for a 1985 IMF- approved salvage operation. Throughout this period, the IMF was consulted and its blessing for the final package was obtained. The implementation of the package can therefore be seen as a sign of movement on the part of Sudan's authorities towards an accommodation with the IMF, rather than a rejection of its Stabilisation Programme in favour of USAID's so-called "alternative".

With respect to the USAID-Princeton Package, it is interesting to note that almost every component announced was identical to measures contained in the previous IMF Standby Loan Arrangements that were never implemented. It is also interesting that the full implementation of the package was stipulated as a precondition for the release of frozen aid monies — a degree of conditionality never previously imposed by the IMF in any previous agreement with Sudan. From this perspective, it could be concluded that the apparent hardening of the IMF's relations with the Sudan are but a reflection of a more general hardening in attitude on the part of the international donor community at large, in which case the austerity measures were perhaps simply a first, small sample of what was to come thereafter.

CONCLUDING REMARKS

The details of these transactions in the twelve months prior to the downfall of Numeiry raise a number of important questions. These concern both an understanding of the role of the international donor community in ousting the Numeiry government as well as the difficult task of formulating and financing a programme of economic reconstruction.

As far as the former is concerned, there can be little doubt in anybody's mind that it was the economic austerity measures announced in March 1985 that provided the final straw. One crucial question this raises is why the US administration, which until then had pressurised the IMF into softening its terms, imposed such harsh terms as a precondition for releasing US$67 million of aid monies frozen under its 1983/4 programme? One must conclude either that this was a big mistake, or that it was a deliberate move to topple the regime. By June 1984, it had become clear that the West in general was losing patience with the regime, as evidenced by the reluctance of the donor community to finance the $60 million projected balance of payments deficit, thereby stalling the final agreement on the crucial 1984/5 Standby Loan Arrangement, soon thereafter freezing parts of their 1984 aid monies, and postponing indefinitely the all-important Paris Club and Consultative Group meetings. Either way, the West will be eager to come to new aid agreements with the post-Numeiry regime, hoping to avoid mass-starvation in the countryside devastated both by droughts and the failed policies of the previous regime, as well as a less friendly administration backed by other less friendly powers.

While it is also true that Sudan will remain dependent on substantial external funding for some time to come, it can bargain on the terms of this dependence from a position of relative strength in view of the West's fears of the alternatives to agreement with it. It is in this context, and from this perspective, that the formulation of a programme of economic reconstruction must surely be the immediate task of the Sudanese people themselves.

NOTE

This chapter was written in 1985 at the time of the popular uprising precipitating the fall of President Numeiry in April of that year. It was written hurriedly in the present brief form for two reasons. First, time was of the essence, and I thought it more important to offer my humble contribution to the immediate discussion and debate on economic policy and other matters that followed Numeiry's downfall, rather than to concern myself with more formal academic presentation. Since then, two articles have appeared (Brown 1986a; Brown 1986b). Secondly, I am aware that the present note contains some errors, both of fact and of judgement which should be corrected as more information becomes available. The inevitability of such errors stems from the secrecy with which the IMF, World Bank and other international donors, concluded their business with the Numeiry regime. Only when the precise contents of the numerous negotiations and agreements of that regime are made public, will we be in a position to undertake more rigorous assessment of past economic policies, and be better equipped to formulate alternative proposals. This note is a first step toward this end and an invitation to those better-informed to point out errors.

REFERENCES

This list contains material additional to that referred to in the paper, providing a source for other researchers in this important area.

African Economic Digest (1984).

Bank of Sudan (1978-83) *Annual report*, Khartoum.

Bank of Sudan (1978-84) *Economic and financial statistics review*, Khartoum.

Bank of Sudan/Ministry of Finance and Economic Planning (1983), *External foreign currency obligations*, Khartoum (also referred to as "Peat Marwick Mitchell Report").

Brown, R. (1984a) "Sudan's Balance of Payments Crisis and the role of the IMF since 1978" Sudan Research Workshop, Final Seminar, Institute of Social Studies, Den Haag and Development Studies and Research Centre, Khartoum, July.

Brown, R. (1984b) "On Assessing the Effects and Rationale of the IMF

Stabilisation Programme in the Sudan since 1978", Finance in the Periphery, Policy Workshop, Institute of Social Studies, Den Haag.

Brown. R. (1986a) "International Responses to Sudan's Economic Crisis: 1978 to the 1985 Coup d'Etat", *Development and Change*, Vol. 17, No 3.

Brown, R. (1986b) *"On assessing the effects and rationale of the IMF stabilisation programme in Sudan under Nimeiry: 1978 to the April 1985 popular uprising"*, McGill University Monograph, McGill University Press, forthcoming.

Consultative Group (1983) unpublished Proceedings of the Consultative Group for the Sudan.

Joint Monitoring Committee (1983) Consolidated Report to the Consultative Group Meeting, December 1983, on Implementation of the Economic Recovery Programme in the Sudan, Khartoum.

Killick, T. (ed.) (1984a) *The quest for economic stabilisation*, Heinemann, London.

Killick, T. (1984b) *The IMF and stabilisation*, Heinemann, London.

Ministry of Finance and Economic Planning (1982a) *Bulletin of development statistics 1980-81*, Khartoum.

Ministry of Finance and Economic Planning (1982b) *Financial planning and development budgeting in the Sudan*, Khartoum.

Ministry of Finance and Economic Planning (1982c) *Prospects, programmes and policies for economic development 1982/3-1984/5*, Khartoum.

Ministry of Finance and Economic Planning (1983a) *Joint venture investments in the Sudan*, Khartoum.

Ministry of Finance and Economic Planning (1983b) *Prospects, programmes and policies for economic development 11*, 1983/4-1985/6 Khartoum.

Ministry of Finance and Economic Planning (1983c) *Sudan foreign trade analysis 1970-1981*, Khartoum.

Ministry of National Planning (1980) *Second Three Year Investment Programme 1980/81-1982/83*, Khartoum.

Mustafa, A.M. (1982) "Current Affairs", *Sudanow*, Vol. 7, No. 4, Ministry of Culture and Information, Khartoum.

Newsweek (1984) "Strange Days in Sudan", 25 June.

Sudan News Agency (1984) "Fitzgibbon Speaks to the Press", *Daily Bulletin*, No. 4895, 17 June 1984, Khartoum.

Sudanow (1984a) "Debts Rescheduled", Vol. 9, No. 6, June.

Sudanow (1984b), "Benefits For All", Vol. 9, No. 6, June.

World Bank (1980) *The main difficulties, policy issues, government action, reform and balance of payments in the Sudan*, Washington.

World Bank (1982) *Sudan: Investing for economic stabilization and structural change*, Washington.

World Bank (1983) *Sudan: pricing policies and structural balances* (three volumes), Washington.

6

The Jonglei Scheme: The Contrast Between Government and Dinka Views on Development

George Tombe Lako

INTRODUCTION

The Jonglei Scheme is Sudan's most ambitious development project. Its aim is to recover water lost in the *sudd* through evaporation and to make it available for irrigation in the North and in Egypt. To achieve this, construction of a 360km long canal was started in 1984 and was under construction until work was stopped in 1985 due to insecurity in the area as a result of activities by SPLF/SPLA forces. Excavation was done by the world's largest single mechanical digger and thus little labour was required. Finance for the scheme was shared equally by Sudan and Egypt.

The implementation of the project was to be divided into two phases (Executive Organ 1976). Briefly, Phase 1 was to include the digging of the canal and concurrently the implementation of various development programmes (Executive Organ 1976: document 11). These were to include improvements in agriculture, livestock production, education, health and social services. Phase 2 was to involve the digging of an irrigation canal west of the main one together with canalisation and irrigation of reclaimed land. The body entrusted with the implementation of the scheme is the National Council for the Development Projects in the Jonglei Canal Area (National Council) through its executive organ based in Khartoum, but with branches in Bor and Malakal. There is also a joint Sudanese and Egyptian Technical Committee (JPTC) which supervises the work of the contracting company, the Compagnie Constructions Internationale (CCI).

The aim of this paper is to present the views of the Government as well as those of the Dinka people in the light of the implementation of the Jonglei Scheme. To do this, an analysis of Government thinking about the Dinka subsistence semi-nomadic economy is presented, based on Government information releases, reports and speeches. A contrasting section on the attitudes of the Dinka towards the scheme then follows. This is based on a survey of a sample of Dinka carried out in 1981. Finally, some comments are made on the debate between Government and Dinka in the light of recent developments.

GOVERNMENT ATTITUDES TOWARDS THE SUBSISTENCE ECONOMY

The present Jonglei Canal Project is viewed by the Sudan Government as capable of transforming the traditional subsistence economy. In a major policy statement on the scheme, the then President of the Southern Regional Government (now defunct) in Juba stated:

> We have elected to enter into the modern economy in preference to the subsistence tribal economy...(Alier n.d.: 20).

The Government hoped that people like the Dinka would join the modern economy, since modern irrigation would be introduced, particularly in Phase 2 of the project. They would retain their livestock, but in modern ranches using improved animal husbandry techniques. Clearly, government policy towards the people of the canal area entails a radical transformation of the economic and social basis of these societies. Within the bounds of this paper, we cannot describe the Dinka or any other of the local societies. In any case, adequate information is available from other research (Lienhardt 1961; Deng 1972).

In following such a policy, the Government assumed that the response of the people to such a radical change would be positive, because they are also assumed to be dissatisfied with the existing hazards such as floods, drought, soil erosion, birds, predators and plant diseases (Executive Organ 1982). All these are assumed to disappear the moment Phases 1 and 2 of the canal project are completed. In the event of people rejecting such radical changes in their semi-nomadic way of life, it could only be taken to mean from the Government's perspective that "people do not necessarily know what is best for them" — to quote the words of an official of the Executive Organ. And so, the Government has to impose "development", although in some way also taking into account the need to minimise the physical and social costs of the project.

To convince the local inhabitants of the benefits of the canal, a massive "enlightenment" campaign was undertaken in the villages of the canal zone. These campaigns were carried out by the "Basic Units" of the Sudanese Socialist Union (SSU), the country's only political party at that time. The basic "attractions" being presented to the people were apparently clear solutions to the hardships and deprivations that they were assumed to face. People were told that the canal would put an end to the present shortage of water for themselves and their animals during the dry season. More pasture would become available, and so the quality and number of livestock would be improved. Veterinary services would be readily available. Obviously, nothing touches a Dinka's heart more than the care or prevention of the diseases that beset his cattle.

In the sphere of agriculture, the government has been persuading the people by encouraging the belief that the canal would bring them prosperity akin to that enjoyed in the Gezira Scheme in the North. Their land would become "a second Gezira" through the introduction of modern irrigation and new commercial crops such as cotton, sugar cane and rice. It was further argued that hunger, not an uncommon phenomenon, would cease to exist since adequate food would be produced. This argument was further instilled into people by statements made by returned labour migrants who had witnessed the outcome of developments in the Gezira.

Additional attractions were those regarding health and education which were included in the development programmes associated with the canal. Some efforts were made to construct schools and dispensaries in Kongor, Ayod and the two Duks.

In addition, the canal project purported to lead to the development of easier and better roads linking the various villages. This was said to be possible since a major road was to be constructed on the eastern side of the canal and all other roads would be linked to it.

The declared intentions of the government were based on certain assumptions concerning subsistence economies. These were regarded as incapable of, or at least "too slow" in, joining the modern sector. Alier's statement quoted above that "we have elected to enter into the modern economy", demonstrates the general attitude of government towards the subsistence economy. The dissatisfaction with, and outright dismissal of, the subsistence economy is coupled with a determination to impose the canal on the people as the only way that can and will lead to development and modernisation. Thus:

If we have to drive our people to paradise with sticks, we will do so for their good and the good of those who will come after us (Alier n.d.: 21).

The Government contended that not only was the subsistence economy incapable of entering the modern sector through its own internal dynamic, but also that this may take place too slowly or never at all. This is believed to be so because of the alleged inherent weaknesses and impotence of subsistence economies to extricate themselves from the environmental and physical constraints to both agriculture and animal husbandry (these points are discussed in Lako 1983). In addition, the present social and political organisation of the people are considered too "primitive" or "rudimentary" to suit the needs of a "modern" society. For example, people are said to be unwilling to increase commercial off-take from livestock because of their "cattle complex", at a time when they are apparently willing to part with their animals for social, ritual and cultural purposes.

In order to strengthen the basis of the above contentions, and hence the "appropriateness" of the decision to implement the canal project, a number of policy-oriented studies were sponsored by the Government. One such study by Payne (Payne 1977) on the livestock industry, concluded that the present livestock practices among the Dinka and the Nuer can be improved on only through the introduction of programmes of modern cattle ranching and management. The recommendations to the Government included: a) the import of water buffalo from Egypt and the establishment of a breeding herd; b) the mechanised production of hay on intermediate grazing areas — the *khor* bottoms. The import of the water buffalo as an alternative to the Nilotic herds was an idea based on the contention that "though Dinka cattle are hardy and tolerant to some extent to diseases and parasites, their growth is stunted and milk production is low" (Payne and El Amin 1976). This proposal for the import of water buffalo was in part the cause of the riots in Juba in opposition to the canal in 1974. Most Dinka expressed their disbelief and amusement at the news of the coming of the buffalo. Fortunately the buffalo is not coming, for the idea has been discarded.

A study on health and nutrition among the Dinka, concluded that though the general impression was that many young men and girls appeared well nourished,

many of the children were hungry and suffering from diarrhoea and sickness ... many of the people had eye troubles caused by dung smoke and flies ... many of the children may have been anaemic, as indicated by the paleness of the red of their eyes (Ogilvy 1977: 14).

The existence of disease in the area is not disputed. But it is doubtful whether this is any more prevalent or widespread than in other parts of rural Sudan. Despite the seasonal occurrence of hunger, caused mainly by shortage of dura supplies, the Dinka diet is generally rich and varied, consisting of various food crops, meat, milk, milk fats, fish and game. The fact that "there is never a surplus of food" (Ogilvy 1977: 15), does not seem sufficient to justify the conclusion that "the Dinka receive only 75 per cent of their minimum food requirements" (Ogilvy 1977: 15).

The preceding is but a small sample of the many studies often cited by the government to substantiate its contentions regarding what is best for the development of the Dinka. To say the least, the conclusions reached are not by themselves conclusive or sufficient to warrant the complete rejection and destruction of the present traditional subsistence economies. Despite this, the planners are convinced that their project is the optimal one for developing the Dinka and other tribes living in the area. This optimism is further extended to include the belief that not only is the choice right, but that the Dinka themselves think so too and are willingly awaiting its implementation and completion.

Far from an insular fear of the Jonglei Canal Project, there is every indication that the people await it with anticipation. It has become, in fact, a manifestation of their desire for change; which is why development must be implemented at an early stage in the wake of the canal (Executive Organ 1980: 18).

The above contentions and attitudes of the government contrast sharply with those of the Dinka we talked to in Kongor.

THE ATTITUDES OF THE DINKA TOWARDS THE JONGLEI SCHEME

It is by no means an easy task to gauge people's attitudes, but it is important to attempt to do so. We held guided interviews and lengthy discussions with fifty Dinka of both sexes in Kongor and other settlements, as well as with some of those working in the government or private sector.

Over three quarters of the people interviewed first heard of the project from lorry drivers and passengers who travel up and down the road between Juba and Khartoum. Some had heard from educated Dinka who made home visits to the villages, as well as from other returning migrants. Most important, the canal is now almost two-thirds complete and so many have seen the physical evidence of the cut with their own eyes.

But though most people now know the reality of the Canal, their views on and responses to it often differ from those declared by government. The idea that the canal will provide more water for people and their animals had captured the imaginations of most of the Dinka to whom we spoke. While the government regards the Canal as an alternative that would end annual dry season migration to the *toiches* (the portions of the swamps used during the dry season), most of the people considered it an addition to the already existing wells and bore-holes. Most people think that they would like to continue travelling to the *toich*, since it is there that they can catch fish. Moreover, it is in the cattle camps in the *toich* that traditional leaders like the "masters of the fishing spear" and the "leaders of the cattle camps" have their influence. Since so much of their socio-political organisation centres around these figures, it is not surprising that most of the people interviewed do not contemplate an end to or even a disruption of the working of these institutions.

In addition, people do not consider that the reorganisation of animal husbandry along the lines of modern ranches is commensurate with their present practice. Indeed, they fear that such a reorganisation may lead to their having to abandon their traditional system of animal husbandry as well as their social and political organisations. Insofar as the proposals seem to promise an easing of their hardships and an easier subsistence, they are quite willing in principle, to accept any suggestions. Their ready acceptance of veterinary drugs and new crops, such as okra, maize and groundnuts, demonstrates their receptiveness to innovations and changes. But because they cannot know what will be required of them through irrigation as planned by the government, they have generally adopted an attitude of wait and see.

Most people are not aware that the changes required by the canal would entail a radical transformation of their present traditional economy. The paramount chief of Kongor summed up the feelings of his people as follows:

We do not know how the government wants us to change our way of looking after cattle and digging the land, and so we shall wait and see. If it turns out to be bad for us, then we shall refuse it, although I do not know how we can fight the government. You know the government is very powerful. I was told by the people in Bor [by which he meant the Provincial Commissioner and his officials] that things will be alright and better for us.

In our discussions with them, many Dinka expressed the view that the canal should be dug more to the east of their permanent settlements so as to create a permanent barrier between them and the Murle who frequently raid for cattle and children. Indeed, many see the main benefit of the canal as putting an end to the "Murle Menace", rather than appreciating the benefits publicised by the government. An old man in the village of Payom, which suffered a Murle raid in November 1980, described his feelings as follows:

My son in Bor came home and told me all about the canal. But in my seventy years in the area, I have learnt to rely on myself and not the government, and so I did not believe what he said about the benefits of the canal. But somewhere in my heart I still worried if I was not wrong and he was right. The last raid by the Murle convinced me that we need the canal to keep out the Murle and they can have all the land to the east of the canal.

The Dinka also fear the settlement of other tribes who might come to work on the scheme. Most people questioned the need for such settlement and some proposed that if these were necessary at all, then they should take place to the east of the canal line and the number of such settlers should be kept small so as not to disturb their way of life. A few recognised the authority and ability of the government to settle people in their land, even against their will and tribal interests, though they were uneasy. A thirty five year old man in Panyagoor village told us that:

if other tribes come and they don't cause troubles, than we can stay with them in peace; but if they don't maintain peace, then we can easily clash.

One of the oft-cited aims of the Jonglei Scheme is the improvement of land and river transport in the area. Thirty of the fifty people interviewed expressed indifference towards these proposed improvements. Again the paramount chief of Kongor summed up:

> We do not wish to leave our land and so we do not need roads or
> steamers. We want schools for our children and more medicines for
> us and our animals. That dispensary over there has remained as a
> mere foundation for five years. You see that ruin over there? We
> used to receive drugs for our cattle from there before the war with the
> Arabs. Why has it not been rebuilt?

One of the ways in which the canal may affect the lives and the
economy of the Dinka is through the expansion of trade and commerce.
We felt it necessary therefore to ask people about their general attitudes
towards this possibility and particularly towards the *jellaba* traders.
Most of the people we talked to welcomed the fact that the traders have
brought them goods which are not available locally or which are not
produced locally in sufficient quantities. For example, clothes, beads,
cooking pots, shoes, batteries for torches, empty sacks and barrels are
not produced locally. People also appreciate that the traders supply
such foodstuffs as cooking oil, salt, rice, lentils, etc., which are
imported from the North or from towns in the South. Dura is the most
important commodity produced locally but not in sufficient quantities.
Most of the people interviewed agreed that they bought dura from the
traders when their granaries were low, usually at the start of the
cultivation season.

Not surprisingly, therefore, most Dinka regard any expansion in
trade as beneficial. A young man in Paliau village described the
feelings of his people as follows:

> We already buy goods from the *jellaba* and if more will be
> available, because the canal will enable steamers and lorries to
> bring goods here quicker, then we welcome it. But the *jellaba* are
> not good people. They sell their goods at too high prices. We do
> not have enough money. The government should control prices.
> I think that if these traders were Dinka they would not cheat their
> brothers in this way.

An old man standing by nodded his head and proposed that:

> the government should close all the shops, giving them to the local
> Dinka and then fix lower acceptable prices that a Dinka could
> afford to pay.

Apart from accepting the goods provided by traders and at the same time expressing dissatisfaction with the level of prices charged for them, the Dinka (especially the older people) complained that the expansion in trade hampers efforts to produce some items locally. For example, one person commented "Some people do not make more effort to produce enough grain because they think they can buy it from the *jellaba*". The same sixty year old man continued that some of the goods in the shops were unnecessary in any case. Pointing to his friend, he said "Look at Majak over there. He bought a radio, but it talks in Arabic and sings strange songs which he does not know".

Most of the interviews and discussions with the Dinka in their villages were very cordial and frank. This was not the case with educated Dinka, who form a substantial proportion of the civil service in the South and work in towns like Juba, Bor and Malakal. Those in top positions of authority in government preferred to recount the familiar "benefits" of the project as stated by the government. However, in private, most of the Dinka elite expressed doubts about these benefits. Because they craved confidentiality, we can only present a general outline of their attitudes. They feared that the scheme could lead to the destruction of their tribal system of social and political organisation, at a time when such institutions in other tribes remained undisturbed. They feared that the Dinka would lose their identity, which is a source of pride to them. Moreover, in their opinion, the resources earmarked for the construction of the canal could have better been used for the provision of more health and educational facilities as well as the improvement of agriculture and livestock production. In this they were close to the position of the elder quoted above. In addition, they refer to the likely adverse environmental effects of the project such as the drying up of the lakes and swamps, the reduction in fish supplies and the desertification of the area through the reduction in convectional rainfall caused by the vast swamps.

A third group of Dinka, comprising big and also small businessmen, cattle traders and top civil servants, whose eyes were set on owning large farms in the forthcoming Jonglei Scheme, expressed total and unqualified support for the project. Their model of development for the Dinka is the Gezira Scheme. We were often told by this group that the Gezira Scheme is the backbone of the Sudanese economy and that it has brought prosperity to the people living within it. Thus, they proudly refer to the Jonglei Scheme as "the second Gezira", meaning that it will not only become the backbone of the economy of the Southern Sudan, but also that it will bring prosperity to such people as the Dinka. They do not share the fears about adverse social, political and environmental effects of the canal. A Dinka merchant who owns four shops and a fleet of lorries and trucks in Bor and Juba, said:

> Our people are too lazy and will never develop. The canal will enable us to invest in irrigated agriculture, commerce and agro-industry. We shall make them work and pay them well so that their standard of living will improve. Why worry about adverse environmental, social and political effects when we shall all be richer?

Clearly then, different groups have different views of the canal project depending on their economic and educational positions. Whereas the government intends to transform the social and economic basis of their society, the Dinka in the villages either do not believe this to be the case or simply can hardly envisage such a change. Furthermore, the vast majority of educated Dinka who form a substantial proportion of the civil service in the South, reject the canal project because they think that it may lead to the destruction of the present social and political system and also that the environment may be adversely affected. Despite contrary views by the few who form the third group of Dinka whom we discussed above, the views and attitudes of the Dinka in villages and most of those in the civil service or schools do not, on balance, indicate any great enthusiasm for or anticipation of the completion of the canal. They have not been persuaded of the need for it.

IMPLICATIONS OF THE SCHEME FOR SOCIAL DIFFERENTIATION

The process of social differentiation in Dinka society has been dealt with elsewhere (Lako 1981). There, it was suggested that certain forces making for social and economic differentiation in Dinka society do exist. These forces are based on the kinship-marriage relationship, herd size, the development of trade and the effects of migration. Thus, some groups of Dinka, such as the cattle traders, retailers, tailors, *merissa* (beer) brewers and tobacco sellers are richer than others. The emergence and continued growth of these groups is a fairly recent development, though it is likely that they will continue to grow.

Since the views of the Dinka which were discussed in the preceding section are also expressive of social and economic positions in society, we deem it appropriate to identify winners and/or losers in the context of the impact of the scheme on social differentiation. And also, since the scheme is still not complete (as was earlier noted, work has now come to a halt), our discussion of its impact must necessarily be rather speculative. However, we contend that the development envisaged under Phase 1 of the project may intensify the existing types of differentiation without producing any profound changes. The situation could be different under Phase 2.

The programme under Phase 1 will open up opportunities for the presently better-off groups to enhance their economic and social standing. If the canal and an all-weather road are completed so that the transport of goods by water and land is made easier and perhaps cheaper, then local retail and cattle traders may profit. At present, during the rainy season, the *jellaba* and Dinka traders are unable to continue retailing because transport by land is impossible and so they cannot replenish their supplies. Increased trade should mean more profit.

By being able to trek cattle, the cattle traders may also benefit from the canal road or from river barges. At present, it is not possible to trek cattle over long distances such as to the market at Juba during the long wet season. Similarly, supplies of cloth and thread should be available all the year round and so tailors will benefit too. The *merissa* brewers may also benefit indirectly as more people are able to travel and to purchase beer. Dura supplies may be increased either through the improvement of local production, as planned in Phase 1, or through supplies from outside. As for those Dinka who produce and sell tobacco, if the improvements in local agriculture take effect, then they might be able to increase production and sale of the crop.

The livestock improvement programmes may increase the quantity and quality of livestock. This, however, does not mean that the distribution of livestock among households will be any more equitable than at present. Households with large stocks may increase their herd, and the increase of the herd of those with less may not offset the existing disparities. Therefore, it is reasonable to assume that the motivation to migrate, based on the need to obtain money to buy cattle for marriage (as is the case at present), will remain strong, since some households will still have significantly more cattle than others. The process of out-migration is likely to continue and the impact of returned migrants (who form the majority of tailors, retailers and cattle traders) on differentiation will remain. Generally, Phase 1 programmes are not likely to lead to a dramatic change in the present

95

social and economic base of Dinka society.

Phase 2 could have a more profound impact on the traditional economy and so on the processes of social differentiation. In general, the changes envisaged are radical in that they include programmes designed to move the Dinka traditional economy away from rainfed cultivation and the traditional system of husbandry towards modern irrigation and cattle ranching. The tribal subsistence economy may be transformed so much that the present privileged strata are reduced in status.

Phase 2 may affect the institutions of the "masters of the fishing spear" and "the leaders of the cattle camps". The annual seasonal movement of people and their animals from the elevated villages to the *toiches*, across the intermediate grazing lands, is based on these two institutional offices. Since the aim of phase 2 is to put an end to, or greatly reduce, the process of seasonal migration, the functions of these "leaders" and "masters" will be greatly reduced and may completely disappear.

The ending of seasonal migration and the reorganisation of animal husbandry may spell the end of the traditional system of husbandry and so vastly alter the role of cattle. At present, cattle are central to the entire Dinka social, political, ideological and economic world. The introduction of "modern" cattle ranching would mean that the purpose of the exploitation of animal wealth would no longer be mainly to meet household food requirements, but for commercial exploitation and increased off-take. The profit-motive whether in the case of individual, cooperative or state-run cattle ranches, does not exist under the present methods of husbandry, except insofar as a few individuals do now trade in cattle.

At present, the social use value of cattle is dominant. If the emphasis is shifted towards commercial exploitation, then the kinship-marriage element of social differentiation may gradually decrease in importance. For example, people may prefer not to use cattle in bridewealth transactions, and may choose to pay partly in cattle, partly in money or entirely in money. Since some members of poor households, notably those with inadequate numbers of cattle, migrate primarily because of a desire to earn some money to buy cattle for marriage, then the process of out-migration might itself be reduced. Of course there may be other reasons for out-migration.

Furthermore, it is planned that new, commercial crops will be introduced. This may directly affect one group of presently privileged Dinka, the tobacco sellers. At present, tobacco is the only cash crop, but the introduction of new ones may make it more likely that some other crop or crops may become more profitable. In fact, cotton has been emphasised as the main cash crop to be grown in the new irrigated farms, and the government intends to encourage it. Thus, the position of tobacco sellers may be reduced in status or they might shift towards the production or sale of new, more profitable crops.

Thus, if we consider the groups of rich Dinka that we identified earlier, it is only the cattle traders, retailers, tailors and beer brewers who are likely to maintain a measure of their present economic and social dominance. However, because the changes in phase two are so radical, it is possible that a new Dinka, or non-Dinka, elite may emerge. If this occurs, then the basis for the analysis of social differentiation in the "new" society may be different. It is this "new" society that the Dinka in the villages and the vast majority of the middle or lower rank officials or students fear, and so generally oppose the scheme. Present instability in the area, although influenced by other considerations, could yet be said to be in part a result of such resentment and opposition to the canal, contributing to the work being brought to a halt.

Certain groups of Dinka, such as the top civil servants and merchants (earlier identified as the third group), support the project wholeheartedly because they see it as an opportunity for profitable investment. These groups may be attracted by the possibilities for commercial cash cropping that phase two will offer, so they may invest in irrigated agriculture, cattle ranching and dairy farming. In fact, since the Jonglei Scheme is viewed as an engine of growth by the government, any Southerner or Northerner with the necessary capital may see it as profitable to participate in agriculture, cattle ranching and trading, and trade in general.

Finally, government views, attitudes and intentions have completely ignored the question of the distribution of wealth in Dinka society. We have suggested that not only is Dinka society non-egalitarian, but also that with the Jonglei Scheme, social and economic inequalities will persist and the vast majority of Dinka may have little to gain. We contend that the question of the impact of the scheme on income distribution and social differentiation should be subjected to further intensive and critical appraisal.

REFERENCES

Alier, A. (n.d) *Statement to the People's Regional Assembly on the proposed Jonglei Canal,* Executive Organ Publication, No.1, El Tamadlon Press, Khartoum.

Deng, F.M. (1972) *The Dinka of the Sudan,* Holt, Rinehart and Winston, New York and London.

Executive Organ (1976) *The Jonglei Canal: Phase I,* Khartoum.

Executive Organ (1979). *Proposals for a mid-term programme and a crash programme for the development of agriculture, livestock and socio-economic services in the Jonglei Canal Area,* document no. 11, Khartoum.

Executive Organ (1980) *Jonglei Canal — a development project in the Sudan,* Printing and Packaging Corporation Ltd, Nairobi.

Executive Organ (1982) *Jonglei Canal — a development project in the Sudan,* Khartoum.

Lako, G.T. (1981) *Social differentiation and the market: the case of Kongor in the Jonglei Canal area,* School of Development Studies, University of East Anglia.

Lako, G.T. (1983) "The Impact of the Jonglei Canal Project on the Development of the Southern Sudan and the lives of the Dinka People", unpublished Ph.D. thesis, University of Manchester.

Lienhardt, G. (1961) *Divinity and experience: the religion of the Dinka,* Clarendon Press, Oxford.

Ogilvy, S. (1977) *A preliminary study of the food and nutritional status of the Dinka in the Jonglei area,* Executive Organ, Khartoum.

Payne, W.J.A. (1977) *A preliminary report on the livestock industry in the Jonglei area,* UNDP/Economic and Social Research Council/Executive Organ, Khartoum.

Payne, W.J.A. and El Amin, F.M. (1976) *Interim report on the Dinka livestock industry in the Jonglei Area,* UNDP/Economic and Social Research Council/Executive Organ, Khartoum.

7

On Becoming Sudanese

Paul Doornbos

INTRODUCTION

The introduction of Shari'a law in the Sudan and its application to everyone present on Sudanese soil regardless of region or religion, cast doubt on the country's claim to act as a bridge between the Arab and the Black African worlds and to seek unity in diversity. Trends towards furthering a more Islamic lifestyle and national identity have been going on for some time, both formally and informally. Formal measures have included prohibition in many provinces, banning of forms of gambling, and government support for Islamic banking, insurance and missionary activities.

This paper deals with the informal spread of a more Arab-Islamic lifestyle in Western Darfur. It focuses on the definition of "Sudanisation" and describes the role of the wandering preachers in spreading orthodox Islam.

Over a period of five years, the author has witnessed the virtual disappearance of tribal dancing and a growing polarisation within communities. This polarisation is concerned with opinions as to the proper way to live as a Muslim. The different ethnic groups of the area have lost a great deal of their original cultural identity over recent decades. This change represents the conversion from what is considered an increasingly irrelevant, narrow ethnic ethos and worldview to a new, prestigious and powerful ideology and praxis. While splitting some local communities, "Sudanisation" simultaneously strengthens certain class and national identifications.

SUDANISATION

The use of the term "Sudanisation" is problematic. It is usually employed to describe the taking over by Sudanese nationals of jobs held by expatriates. In the present context, the term is used to define provisionally the process of conversion of ethnically diverse population groups living in the Sudanese periphery to the dominant and prestigious lifestyle of the central Nile valley region.

It might be argued that "Arabisation" would be a more suitable term (James 1971: 20; Bender & Malik 1980: 5), the latter authors also use the term "Arab-Islamic imperialism" (Bender & Malik 1980: 4). However, there are a number of reasons why "Arabisation" and similar terms should not be used. Firstly, the term is often employed in relation to the spread of Arabic among non-Arabic speakers. What is here termed "Sudanisation" is far more comprehensive than mere linguistic change. Secondly, "Arabisation" suggests that all Arabs in Sudan are similar and that the conversion process occurs among non-Arabs only. In reality, the majority of Sudanese who can claim to have Arab origins are engaged in animal husbandry or in farming, and they are as far removed (especially socio-economically) as the non-Arab populations from the "Sudanised" lifestyle. Thus, Arab and non-Arab aspirants to this lifestyle are engaged in "Sudanisation" rather than "Arabisation". Thirdly, the term "Arabisation" suggests an assault on traditional African cultures. This is indeed what is happening today, but those who are engaged in "Sudanisation" aim to become fully "Sudanised", not to catch up with the mainstream of Arab culture. To be "Sudanised" means to be able to participate spiritually and materially as a member of the top stratum of traders and officials and to be taken seriously, be considered trust- and credit-worthy throughout the Sudan and its trade periphery beyond international frontiers. It should be noted that with regard to pan-Arabism, personal and collective experiences of Sudanese with nationals of other Arab nations through study, labour migration or business travel has often led to ambivalence in this respect.

Notwithstanding these brief remarks, the spread of Islam and Islamically-sanctioned notions about personal appearance, eating and drinking, the place of women, conceptions of time, are tightly linked with the spread of the Arabic language. The fact that Islam was revealed to an Arab and was subsequently spread by Arabs, has made Arab ethnic origin the most prestigious among Sudanese Muslims. A large number of non-Arab populations nowadays claim — with the aid of myths of origin and elaborate genealogies — that their ancestors were

Arabs too. On an individual basis, "Sudanisation" could easily be called imitation of a more "Arab" way of life. In remote villages, "Sudanisation" represents the first wave of linguistic and cultural Arabisation under the aegis of a second or third wave of Islamisation.

What is "Sudanisation"? Sudanisation is conversion by Arab peasants and pastoral nomads, and by non-Arabs, sometimes recently Islamised ethnic groups in Sudan and parts of Ethiopia, Zaire, Central African Republic and Chad, to a lifestyle which has historically emerged along the Nile, and which has been spread outward by itinerant traders-cum-*fuqura* (lay priests). In remote areas these men were considered "wise strangers", who were well-versed in the Koran and the Arabic language, and often introduced new techniques and products (tools, crops, etc.), and who exemplified in their day-to-day contacts with indigenous people a way of life "superior", both materially and spiritually.

Today there are still parts of the Northern Sudan which have not been Islamised, notably the Nuba mountains in Kordofan region and the part of Central region which borders on Ethiopia. In the late 1960s, Wendy James studied the Uduk people of that area. In the past they had lived on hilltops in order to defend themselves against Arab slave raiders. In this century, the Uduk came down and settled at the bottom of the hills, and today,

> in the areas where money has become an essential (along the main roads and around important trading centres), the local people have assimilated themselves so thoroughly to the culture and values of the dominant group, the immigrant merchants, that they have accepted the social categories of that group and maximised their own status in terms of those categories (James 1971: 202).

Today in Western Darfur, as in many other parts of the region, Sudanisation no longer depends on immigrant traders and religious men from the Nile Valley. Having been Islamised long ago, and having benefited from a proliferation of government services in the wake of a rapid development of trade, indoctrination and conversion in Western Darfur take place in village primary schools and local market centres, where Sudanised and aspirants of indigenous ethnic groups teach and learn, buy and sell, and where the Sudanised increase numerically at the expense of other cultural identifications.

In many respects, Sudanisation is a revolutionary ideology and praxis, most of all because it constitutes a comprehensive assault on traditional social organisation and culture. For individual aspirants, conversion means complete surrender to the reference group and desertion of one's peer and kin group. Traditionally-minded people are subsistence farmers, pastoral nomads, day labourers and craftsmen, while the aspirants and the fully Sudanised try to engage in non-manual occupations. The traditional people differ among themselves with regard to whether they share an economic household with their wife, drink alcohol, engage in traditional dances, practise female circumcision, or say their prayers aloud. On the other hand, the Sudanised and the aspirants attempt to abstain from alcohol and tobacco, seclude their women, avoid manual labour, and as a rule, pursue religious knowledge of a formal, orthodox nature, as well as working as traders or salaried officials.

With respect to proficiency in Arabic and Islam, eating, drinking and clothing habits, conceptions of time, division of labour within the household as well as many other criteria, there exists a clear-cut dichotomy between the ideal lifestyle in either direction. Also, as argued above, Sudanisation cannot be studied in isolation from "Arabisation", together with wider trends in the Muslim world towards fundamentalism — its heralds and preachers in Darfur being graduates from religious establishments such as Omdurman Islamic University. Other vehicles of a more tolerant Islamisation are the religious brotherhoods, of which the Tijaniyya is the most influential.

THE PATH OF THE PROPHET IS THE ROAD TO SALVATION

The most important agents of religious purification and orthodoxy in Darfur are the wandering preachers (Ar. *wa'iz*, pl. *wu''az*) some of whom belong to one of the religious brotherhoods, but most of whom are without any formal affiliation. They are generally fundamentalist in inclination and uncompromising with regard to the precedence of Islam over other, worldly, concerns. The message they preach is highly discriminatory, practical and directed towards the teaching of an alternative, superior and divinely sanctioned way of life which guarantees its practitioners a place in heaven. It leaves little or no room for mysticism or religious introspection, and by its continuous stress on the individual's responsibility for himself and his kith in the face of God, it expressly negates the idea of intercession or mediation on behalf of the individual by live or dead agencies. In this respect, both Darfurian and Chadian Islam differ from Islamic beliefs in the Nile Valley, where *tariqa* sheikhs or the tombs of deceased holy men play a central role in popular Islam.

In this section an attempt will be made to elucidate some of the main tenets of Islam as preached by wandering preachers in contemporary Darfur. Particular attention will be paid to their sermons, in which the proper way to live is invariably contrasted with the improper way common to the majority of people who form the audience. In such sermons three topics are always treated in an exhaustive fashion:

i) the importance of prayer and the ritual cleanliness it requires; its timely performance; the appropriate verses and genuflections for each of the five prayers; the conditions which can make its performance null and void;
ii) the position of women, particularly in the family context;
iii) the perils of alcohol and tobacco;

It is with regard to these three often related fields that the religious message of Sudanisation formulates its frontal assault on traditional lifestyles. The right and wrong conduct in each field is exemplified in sermons with the aid of relevant quotations from the Koran and the Traditions, funny and sad anecdotes drawn from real life, and moralistic stories attributed to the life and works of Islamic celebrities like 'Abd al-Qadir al-Jilani, all the threads woven into a tight ideological fabric.

Most preachers begin their sermon with a series of axioms concerning the nature of Islam, the Koran, worldly life, Good and Evil, and the individual believer's personal status and responsibilities within this realm.

To begin with the nature of the Koran. Every Muslim in Darfur has learned about the existence of four revealed religions, Judaism, Mazdaism, Christianity and Islam. Islam as the Seal, the final and last of the revealed religions, incorporates the good aspects of the preceding religions, has added new revelations, and has been shaped into a more consistent and authoritative creed than any of its predecessors. Naturally, therefore, Islam is considered superior to the others by Muslims. Other religious systems in Africa are considered paganism. To win converts from any of the non-Muslim creeds is highly meritorious for the individual Muslim as well as for the Muslim community as a whole.

As for the nature of the Koran, God revealed it to the Prophet Mohammed in order to command and restrain mankind with its message. He gave the Koran to mankind as an *amana* (lit. goods given in trust), and each individual Muslim has to safeguard and protect its message, because when Man, who is God's own creature, returns to Him, he will be asked whether God's *amana* has been safeguarded and whether His message has been obeyed.

Regarding the nature of worldly life, the world by itself has no sense. One's own worldly conduct has, and "what one sows on earth, one will reap in the hereafter". What does one sow as a Muslim? First of all, one adheres to the five pillars of Islam, that is basic. Secondly, in worldly life the true Muslim must abstain from the *haram*, the evil or forbidden. Preachers admit that the tendency to commit evil is present in every man's heart, and that man is led to commit forbidden things because of four different forces: Satan, who scatters people; worldly life, which cheats people; the wind, which diverts people; and the self, which leads people into utter darkness.

Haram, as a general umbrella category for forbidden worldly acts, encompasses a great many injunctions of a social nature which are universal, and which pertain to murder, theft, adultery, lying, rancour, slander, eavesdropping etc. Other forbidden acts include the consumption of certain kinds of food and drink, smoking and chewing tobacco or hashish, matters of ritual and personal cleanliness. In addition, there are those to do with women and matrimony. Another, mainly orally evoked category of *haram*, is concerned with aspects of worldly amusement and "hypocrisy". These are vague and arbitrary categories, in which a plethora of transgressions against the proper way of life is incorporated on an ad hoc basis by the wandering preachers. Thus, whether a particularly sharp business practice is condemned as *haram* by a preacher varies with time and place.

Halal (tr. lawful, good) is the opposite of *haram*, while *makruh* (tr. hateful), constitutes a threshold category with regard to *haram*.

A preacher was asked by a member of his audience whether one could accept a gift from someone who had no steady occupation. The preacher answered:

The man who is neither a cultivator nor a butcher, and whose only occupation is to brew beer, is rare. If he gives you a present and you know that he only sells liquor, don't accept it. But when someone else comes to you and says "Hey, you, this is a present from me for the sake of God", take it and keep silent. Don't examine, don't ask, for what is concerned is the outer, not the inner thing. Don't examine people's hearts, don't examine.

The same man from the audience:

But if you don't know how the present was earned?

The preacher:

We don't say: "Did you get this from growing tobacco or from growing tomatoes?" No, we don't examine. If we examined like that, people, would there be anyone who would eat anything pure (*halal*)?

There is no clear-cut dividing line between *makruh* and *haram*, at most it is a matter of degree:

Al-Makruh leads you to *al-Haram*, and the *haram*, if you commit the *haram*, God will leave you, and you will be led to places of which God disapproves. If God told you "Don't drink alcohol", and you drink it. If God said: "Don't commit adultery", and you did it, you did the *haram*. *Al-Haram* gives birth to disobedience and that in turn results in damnation!

Later on in his sermon, the preacher employed the term *nijis*, impure, and *rijis*, filthy, atrocious, as parallels for *makruh* and *haram*. The following excerpt exemplifies his use of the terms and is also representative of the vehemence with which the wandering preachers attack the practices of drinking *merissa* (fermented beer):

The prophet has said: "Whoever drinks liquor, whether man or woman, is forty times damned. Damned as the enemy of God and enemy of Islam!." God forbade it and made it *haram*, as a final decision. He did not say that it was *nijis*. He said it was *rijis*. *Rijis* is seventy times worse than nijis. When he says it is *nijis*, we will find a way to purify and eat it. When he says it is *rijis*, then that settles the matter once and for all.

There is no such calamity as the *sitt al-andaya*, the lady who sells beer. She is damned, there is no good in her in this world or in the next. She strangles the sons of the believers. Even if she wants to repent, he does not find a way to repent [the preacher mimics the beer seller].

"Say, customer, I put the *merissa* ready for you. Why don't you come?"

"I have repented".

"Hey brother, what is wrong with you? What would you eat in this world if you abandoned *merissa*? Come and drink and repent tomorrow!"

The Prophet has said ten kinds of people are doomed, and those are the sellers of *merissa*, the buyer, the person who prepares it, the one who sieves it, the one who carries the water, all of them are damned; and the one who allows people to drink it in his compound, and the one who ate the *saman* [residue left after brewing], and the one who collected the *mushuk* [dregs] and fed them to his donkey, and the one who shows a stranger the way to where it is drunk, and the one who gives his guest money to go to the *hilla* [village] to drink ... all are damned. May God help you, what a calamity...

To bring this discussion of the preliminary remarks of a sermon to an end, a brief word will be said about the nature of the believer's individual responsibility. In worldly life, "every one is a shepherd looking after his flock". In other words, every individual is to a large extent responsible for his fellows, especially his family, and when they commit evil they must be corrected. Correction can be accomplished in three ways: with the hand, the tongue and the heart.

Wives, sons, and daughters must be corrected with the hand if they fail to pray, drink alcohol, and in the case of women, if they resist seclusion. The worldly ruler must also punish by hand, for example, thieves, adulterers, and beer sellers. Only the ruler has the authority to do this, and he should use it. If correction with the hand fails, the husband must divorce his wife, the father send away his recalcitrant son, the ruler exile the beer seller. Correction with the tongue is the domain of the *ulama* — the Islamic teachers. When they see evil and corruption, they are obliged to speak out loudly in public and elucidate Islam, explain what is *haram* and what is *makruh*, and where they lead the believers. The purpose of Islamic teaching and preaching is to show the people that they have left God's side, but that there are ways to repent. Finally, correction with the heart is done in circumstances when the believer sees something which is disapproved of in Islam, and is in no position to alter it, so he has to pass by. He cannot do anything except to murmur wholeheartedly an appropriate quotation from the Koran.

A number of themes which have already been alluded to will reappear in the following verbatim extract from a sermon delivered in Foro Boranga in March 1981. It was attended by hundreds of men and several dozen women, who unanimously considered it "first rate" — by which they meant it was impressive in its elocution and build up, choice of examples, quotations and consistency. Even the most objective outsider will grant that the sermon and its delivery were impressive, the preacher leaving no trick or technique unused to woo, threaten and frighten his audience into changing their views. The excerpt, which was translated by Dr. Lidwien Kapteijns, covers fifteen minutes from the ninety minute sermon and deals principally with the Day of Judgement.

The first thing that God will ask you on the Day of Judgement is: "Did I not send you the Prophet, who told you everyone is a shepherd looking after his own flock? Good! Why then did you let your flock stray into other people's fields? Why?"

If you answer "No, they did not", well, God knows the truth. — Atit and Rakib [angels] will be present. They wrote down that Fulan ibn Fulan's daughter on that and that day went to the market; that Fulan ibn Fulan's wife sold things on the market. Such a man's case is already decided.

Your file will be brought along with you in this way. Be careful that Malik Ruman does not come to you. Be careful on that day to write down what you used to do in the world. Remember that Ruman visits you after they have buried you. Remember that the world is not simply sweetness, not beautiful clothes and nice food. No! The important thing is how the human being goes to God who created you from Adam and Eve [repeated twice].

It is not the human being who is important, it is God who is. God is stronger than the strong. You must settle between yourselves and God. Your fate is not linked up with the *'alim,* the *wa'iz* or the *murshid* [respectively the Islamic scholar, preacher and spiritual guide]. No, settle for yourselves between you and God.

Look what God will do to you when you have died. When they have buried you and the people have gone home, Ruman will come. Ruman makes you get up from your place, saying "Get up, O Fulan!".

If you belonged to the people of the prayer, you will find perfect blessing there, but if you belonged to the people of *barjala* (tr. dividers), if you let your herd stray in other people's fields, you will find Ruman a different kind of person. He will say:

"This place of yours is not the world anymore, it is the Hereafter. Get up and write!"

"What should I write?"

"Write what you did before you came to the grave, while you were in the world!"

"What should I write with? I have no pen."

"Write with your thumb!"

"But I have no ink."

He will tell you to use your spittle.

"But I have no paper."

He will tell you to use your shroud, and will tear off a piece.

"Go ahead, write!"

"But in the world I could not write. I was illiterate."

Ruman says:

Write with God's help. Put your thumb in your mouth. Make it wet, and after you have written the *bismillah*, you begin. If you have ever deceived God and the Prophet, write it down. If you went against what God ordered and against the Koran, write it down. If you stretched a verse and did not act according to it, you write: "On such and such a day, I went to the house of Fulan and drank liquor." And as for your wife, God has said, "Give her long dresses and do not let her go out", while you gave her a very short dress and she went to the market. All that you must write down.

On that day you cannot play around. You have died. Ruman sits on your neck until you have completed your writing. Then, when you have finished your writing, Ruman leaves and who is next to visit you? Munkar and Nakir, the two angels who had been awaiting you at the grave from the beginning.

"Get up, O 'Abdalla!"

If you were one of the people of prayer, and diligent in religious classes, and your friends were your brothers in Islam, then there is no need to fear. You will get up happily like rising from sleep. The story will have a happy ending, and will continue even better. You will be allowed inside [Paradise]. On both sides, left and right, as far as the eye can see, you will see people. You will be like the bride brought in procession, especially arranged for you. That day you will be overjoyed. That is the blessing conferred upon you by God! But if you had been told by your teachers to memorise sixty or seventy lines and you said to yourself "If I made myself free for that reading, what would my children eat?" But God told you in the Koran that he would not leave you without guidance and that he who depends on God belongs to His party. Those very words you locked inside a suitcase and then abandoned it. But God did not leave you alone and was kind to you. He told you:

"Order your wife to pray and order your daughter and son to pray, and be patient until the grave."

But you refused! Today I find you in Geneina, tomorrow in Nyala, the day after in Foro Boranga, then in Am Dukhn. You leave no market unattended in any of the seven days. And meanwhile, your flock scattered. Some at the lady's fingers [okra], some the tomatoes, some the millet and sorghum. All these things are divisive and every single thing constitutes a single case against you. All these cases will be added up for you, you with that beard over there! They will be put on the scales on the Day of Judgement... Our women, our children, our wealth, God gave them to us. If you

ordered your wife to do what is approved of by God and the Prophet, you will be saved. If not, you will not be saved!
Imagine you get up early to go the mosque to your morning prayers. You leave your wife and children asleep and when you return they are still asleep. You do not say anything and go inside to your papers. The next day the same thing. The day after, if you accept it again, they will have become hypocrites. If you divorce your wife it is a disaster, but if you leave her in peace it is a double disaster. And if you throw out those sons it is a disaster, but if you let them stay it is a double disaster. You may argue that they got out of hand, send their mother too, and your daughters too, but that you yourself remained faithful to God. In that case there will be no one who will listen to you. If you ask them to do their duties, they will call you a dervish. If you scold your son, he will ask to be transferred to Nyala because his old man will not leave him in peace, and they will transfer him. Alright, what has the whole thing become? It has become a divisive thing and it has been your own fault! I pray to the Prophet." [The audience answers.]

Preachers continually impress upon their audiences the obligation to repent and to dissociate themselves from the enemies of God as in the following:

Whoever acts counter to God's precepts should be rejected, even if they are close relatives. Abandon him. Keep your distance. Why is this done to the wrongdoer? So that he will return to the straight path and repent.

It is quite common for Darfurian men in their middle age to foreswear alcohol and to devote themselves to religious study. This is a repentance pure and simple, with a view to the approaching Day of Judgement. Another reason for repentance is that the routine consumption of alcohol by men whose age and wisdom entitles them to respect, meets with social disapproval. Failure to foreswear alcohol in time may result in a poorly attended burial. Usually a standing prayer is said before and after burial. It is believed that if at least forty men participate in it, God will consider this a recommendation to grant the newly deceased a place in Heaven. However, the Koran expressly states that the prayer over the grave of an unbeliever is forbidden (Koran 9, 84). The new orthodoxy in Islam, of which our preacher is an outstanding and enthusiastic representative, considers a Muslim who drinks as equivalent to an unbeliever, as evidenced by the following exchange:

> Questioner:
> If your brother dies while being drunk, do you go to his burial?
> The Preacher:
> Don't go. Go and tell his companions who drink with him. Tell them "Brothers, Fulan has died. Come and take away your friend." So they take him and bury him. But if that does not happen, we bury him, but we will not make a nice grave. We make his grave in a rough way because we are angry with him.
> The questioner:
> Then while praying we should not greet him?
> The Preacher:
> What does the ritual ablution mean? Isn't it meant to purify and to make us brothers in God? Or what? He has no power with God, so why would you come and do the ritual ablutions? Abandon him!

Another subject which is treated in graphic detail in sermons is the position of women. The message of orthodox Islam is that wives and daughters must live a secluded life and may not go out without valid reason. Leaving the house to shop is frowned upon; selling produce in the market is absolutely wrong. In public, women are enjoined to wear long sleeved garments which reach to the ground, and to cover their heads and bodily features with a *tawb* [a robe]. A feature derived more from the Koran and traditional practice in Darfur, than from the Nile Valley, is that it is undesirable for women to remain single, and that it is the duty of their relatives and the community at large to find them a spouse as soon as possible. Thus daughters should be married off at maturity to the first available suitor, without regard to hopes of receiving a higher brideprice. Preachers fulminate against the practice of delaying marriage in hope of a higher payment, which is gaining ground in Darfur, and which, in their own words "force the young men to migrate to Libya to earn the high brideprice, while the girl and her family's honour may be compromised every day for years on end." This marriage ethic exists also with regard to widows and divorcees, and in Darfur — in stark contrast to the Nile Valley — these categories usually remarry again, often several times during their lifetime. Of course, women should perform their prayers as regularly as men. The following excerpt illustrates the necessity for strict control of women by men:

You go to the shop. Fatuma has stayed at home. These days, may

God have mercy upon our women, our mothers, wives, grandmothers, but they do wrong as only God knows. After you have left, she puts a *tawb* over her head and goes out aimlessly, like a spreading disease. Twenty houses of the neighbourhood she visits without your permission. And the Prophet said that if she goes out without your permission, she will be damned. But she goes out and meets wrongdoers who cheat her and say: "Listen, ya Fatuma, you are with child, and it drinks all your blood. You have no blood left", and they persuade her to drink a calabash of *merissa* with which she is not acquainted. [The preacher mimics how she begins to feel drowsy and belches and comes home only to fall down on her bed.] Fatuma's husband comes home, finds her eyes are all red, asks what is wrong. She says she has a headache, "Give me Cafenol". He gives her a blow instead. [Laughter.]
First thing, they made your wife's heart impure. Secondly, the son whom she nurses becomes impure himself. The community of Muslims should live according to Shari'a!

Another subject which is often tackled by orthodox preachers is the widespread custom in the region of considering virginity at marriage as worthy of special honour and material reward, instead of it being the norm from which digressions should be sanctioned.

People, does this happen or not? Yes, it happens! Good, any woman who married off her daughter and who goes to her in-laws and says "Give me the sheet with the blood to attach it to the top of my house" is damned! ... Dishonour! You have dishonoured your daughter! Don't go and say "give me the *bishara*". No! That sort of thing is not in the Shari'a. *Bishara* [tr. glad-tidings, rejoicing, and by extension the sheet which gives rise to such] does not exist, only *Sadaqa* [almsgiving].
All this is heresy and innovation, and is abominable, not good. Look! Listen! There is another thing that the women do. They grab the girl and say they will examine her. If that is written in the Koran, say it is in the Koran. Say our fathers and ancestors told us to examine our future daughters-in-law. This is abominable, it is not Islam, it is shameful. Don't bring shame upon Muslims because whoever brings shame upon a Muslim, shame will be brought upon him on the Day of Judgement. Don't bring shame upon your daughters, that is not acceptable. Keep this kind of talk at a great distance.

As for the bridegroom, if without this abominable thing on the day of consummation, you too beware of saying that you found the girl not a virgin. God willing, if the Shari'a were applied, we would take your eye out, or you'd be given eighty lashes, or you'd be forced to bring forward the man who took the girl's virginity!

Female circumcision has long been a difficult topic for preachers among the sedentary peoples of Darfur, where the practice has gained some acceptance — slowly and grudgingly — in the wake of the spread of Sudanisation among the native-born aspirants to Sudanised status. Whereas the harsh and extreme "Pharaonic" circumcision has been practised for several centuries in the Nile Valley, in Darfur the Fur, Masalit and others have hesitantly begun to practise the milder Sunna form, which moreover, has been given a degree of legitimacy by prominent orthodox functionaries in the Nile Valley, mainly in order to act as a counterweight to the colonial, and later, the national government's ill-fated efforts to outlaw the practice altogether. Wandering preachers rarely discuss the practice, and will only do so when challenged. However, it is spreading rapidly among wives of aspirants to Sudanised status who are eager to emulate their immigrant or already converted representatives, and circumcisions of mothers of three children are by no means uncommon.

A final topic worth mentioning with regard to the content of sermons by orthodox preachers is that of the "hypocrites". Thus far, the excerpts from sermons have depicted the social and religious universe in terms of binary oppositions, good and evil practices. Confronted with this manichaean universe, a common strategy employed to combine religious duty with earthly pleasures is to abstain from alcohol until the fifth and final prayer of the day, performed at about 2015. In the orthodox view, this is "hypocrisy". Moreover, from this perspective, the peasants, craftsmen and casual labourers who are both numerous and poor, whose *merissa* often constitutes their best source of calories and vitamins, and who pray and adhere to the fast as scrupulously as their better-off Sudanised patrons, are judged higher than "hypocrites" — they are sinners, but not beyond redemption.

A true "hypocrite" differs from the poor peasant and working man in that he has the means (financially, educationally, by descent) to know which path he ought to choose, and fails to do this, either by not giving up the *haram* in its many forms, and/or by adopting alien, often Western habits. The "hypocrite" either goes only a little way in the direction of leading a life according to Islam, or has been brought up in this vein and has relented and begun to indulge in the lesser, coarser and evil pleasures of worldly life. In either case, the "hypocrite" tries to combine the virtuous with the vile.

A man from the audience:
Ya mawlana, teacher, every drinker smells!
The preacher:
Indeed, I take refuge in God, he really smells. By God, brothers, it is a big calamity, particularly the drinker who reads God's book and drinks *merissa*. I take refuge in God, there is no power except Him. That is an ugly calamity of his, brothers. Praying and drinking out of his cup at the same time!

It is the conviction of the (newly-) orthodox Muslims and their heralds in remote regions, the wandering preachers, that "hypocrites" are growing in numbers almost daily, mostly as a result of the sudden material advancement due to trade, job security in an official capacity, and westernisation via the media and exposure to the way of life in the national capital. In sermons, but also in private conversations, the "hypocrites" exist in all walks of life. They range from whisky-drinking business tycoons to hard-drinking officials and teachers in what are for them outposts. They include such vague categories as people who go to the cinema, have their pictures taken in a photo studio, play cards, wear western clothes and shoes with lifts when they do no need to, or have "Afro" hairstyles, read books other than religious ones, listen to cassette tapes other than religious ones — even, as one preacher proclaimed, those who use a plastic toothbrush and toothpaste rather than the seven kinds of twig which he claimed to be sanctioned by Islam.

What has been depicted thus far in this section is the third wave of Islamisation in Western Darfur, with other socio-economic changes temporarily left out of account. Its target is properly to Islamise the already Muslim population. This population has for several decades served as a labour reservoir, primary production area, and target for scorn and discrimination, for the core area of "true" Islam in the country, the Nile Valley and its outliers. The preachers, however, often drawing upon ethnic backgrounds and traditions differing from "mainstream" Islam in the Nile Valley, offer a number of differences in their religious message with regard to modernity and the role of the modern state.

It seems that despite their formal and non-formal education, ranging from learning from *fuqura* in three or four different countries in an unquenchable thirst for religious learning, to graduation from al-

Azhar University in Cairo or Omdurman Islamic University, followed by travels abroad and early pilgrimage to Mecca, these wandering preachers have a rooted objection to social change. It seems they have never thought about world affairs or even the causes of the present economic problems which beset the Sudan, in part caused by fellow Muslim countries. Indeed, it appears as if they have refused to contemplate modern developments in the Muslim world, and instead have willed themselves into an historical dream from which they draw new energy for themselves and a new message for their fellow Muslims, the era of the Prophet Mohammed and his first four Caliphs, the unspoilt Golden Age of orthodox Islam.

Thus, modern primary education is attacked by some preachers as being "the school of the Turks", drawing on the widespread belief in the region that the Turco-Egyptian regime was a dreadful era in the Western region (although it lasted less than ten years as compared to sixty years in the Nile Valley). Alternatively, the practice of teachers of sending a pupil to buy a packet of cigarettes, is exploited by some preachers to show how pupils are taught smoking by their teachers. The moral of their attack on modern education is that the institution as a whole is corrupt.

Orthodox preachers may also disagree about such minor matters as the appropriate dress and personal appearance of a true Muslim. Short garments and no beards are prescribed by some. Long garments and beards advocated by others. The smaller fry among the preachers try to make a living and become known in the region by delivering fiery diatribes against modern affectations such as village schools and smoking, in an environment which is already thoroughly anti-school, anti-teacher and everything they represent. The bigger preachers are more knowledgeable, better schooled in Islam and in Arabic, and they dare concentrate on real, fundamental issues.

To be a preacher is to pursue a career like everyone else. This applies to local *fuqura* today, it is a spiritual, economic, and at times, political, profession. As in the past, it pays to be a renowned *faqih*, considering the gifts and fees received for officiating at rites of passage and during crises, when they are asked to read the Koran, write amulets, or intervene in other ways. A wandering preacher is rewarded materially by his audience by means of gifts of money and hospitality.

The final question to be answered in this section on orthodox preaching is who are the audience? The overwhelming majority are men and women who aspire to become good Muslims, and have already made a few steps in the right direction and want to know more.

The minority is split between those who have already reached the desired state of purity and virtue (a few merchants and officials) and who are curious to hear what infamies the preacher will use this time to force his audience to repent. They attend these sermons largely out of curiousity. They pretend to stand above it all, consider themselves sometimes better versed in Islam than the preacher, who talks in colloquial Sudanese Arabic with heavy Darfurian idiomatic overtones and who uses "silly" examples to make his religious points. On the other hand, there are the habitual drinkers and husbands who allow their wives and daughters to brew *merissa*, distil gin, and to leave the house. Many of them are impressed and convinced of the truth of the message of the preachers, but they quite convincingly argue that they are financially unable to enforce what the preacher enjoins them to do.

SPLIT COMMUNITIES?

Can communities be split into two mutually exclusive and excluding parts as is done by the wandering preacher? The answer is, of course, that this is impossible. The extreme forms of the two ideal typical ways of life can certainly be found in actual practice. For example, in the person of a subsistence farmer or a butcher, and a wealthy merchant or headmaster. But as R.S. O'Fahey (1980: 122) has noted:

> From nominal conversion, via the insinuation of Islamic practices or interpretations into traditional beliefs, to an acceptance of Islamic/Arabic culture represents an almost infinite gradation, conceptually, but not in practice susceptible to analysis.

The range of actual accommodations to the ideal is very wide indeed. In social reality, the type of dichotomy as espoused by orthodox preachers can only exist because of a third, ambiguous and ambivalent category situated in between. This third category gives the extremes the right to exist without causing the complete disruption of the community or society of which they form part. After all, the ultimate consequence of the preachers' message is that social life would become impossible.

The religious component of the ideology of Sudanisation is extremely divisive, because it creates and encourages tensions and conflicts within families and communities, and between neighbours, friends and relatives. Taken literally, its stress on repentance and on the responsibility of each individual "to look after his own flock" is socially disruptive in its consequences, which are divorce, dismissal, exile and social isolation of those who do not, and more importantly, those who cannot conform. The preachers' orthodox message is discriminatory in that it forms the basis of the ideology used by the ruling stratum to justify its divinely sanctioned right to judge its own productive basis morally, socially, economically, politically and judicially, as members of local courts of law.

The attraction of Sudanisation is its consistency and comprehensiveness. In worldly life, the Sudanised thrive materially and will find even greater blessings in the hereafter. Conversion to this way of life by people who were brought up within a narrow ethnic context and outlook, is the most dramatic form of social change taking place in remote parts of the Sudan and beyond. An attendant feature of the conversion process, to be treated in more detail elsewhere is detribalisation. Instead of crossing ethnic boundaries in the traditional sense, implying that one discards the ways of one's own group and adopts that of another ethnic group, aspirants to Sudanised status gradually, in stages, attempt to shed their traditional ways in order to adopt the manners and customs, ethos and worldview, and the jargon of an entity which transcends the ethnic group. Their aim is to become Sudanised, a member of the family, stratum, new tribe which, regardless of one's own ethnic origin, is taken seriously, considered trust- and creditworthy by fellow-Sudanised in the largest towns and remotest hamlets, where they are the people who matter. As far as the most vigorous and purely Sudanised, the traders and merchants are concerned, their diaspora in search of profit has led them to countries like Burundi, Zaire, Cameroon and Nigeria, and there they play the same role as their counterparts who live and work in the remote regions of Sudan. The trading network and map of the Sudanised in these parts of Africa deserves further study.

It is noteworthy that this form of conversion is a one-way process. Although in the Sudan full conversion is becoming increasingly more difficult to accomplish (in many regions the saturation point has been reached with regard to shopkeepers, merchants and salaried officials), rapid conversions still take place, in the marginal areas and beyond, in regions which are only partly Muslim. Everywhere, aspirants fail to qualify completely and remain suspended in a marginal position in relation to both extremes, with the result that both extremes consider them as not serious and only half trustworthy. Once individuals have begun to discard their old ways and to adopt the new ones, they may succeed or fail to qualify, but complete reversion to the old ways is unheard of.

In the preceding sections, an outline was given of what is required to move from the traditional to the Sudanised pole. Those who have responded to the preachers' call and have not completed their conversion, constitute the buffer category between the two extremes. The numerical strength of the two categories is subject to constant change. In the unit of study for this research, the small towns of Beida and Foro Boranga, they may be estimated at 10, 30 and 60 percent, for Sudanised, aspirants and non-Sudanised respectively, whereas the population of the towns' respective trade networks would show a ratio of 5, 15 and 80 percent. Even more extreme differences can be expected in regions in which Islam has only recently begun to spread. On the other hand, in regions nearer to the Nile Valley, the three categories are spread more evenly in terms of percentages, the non-Sudanised percentage constituted to a large extent of labour migrants, while in the Northern Region, the Sudanised form the majority of the population, albeit without everyone being a merchant, trader or official.

The process of full conversion can be compared to a hurdle race, whereby each hurdle represents one aspect of exemplary social conduct. From hindsight, the dialectic between the ideological and socio-economic aspects of Sudanisation can explain to some extent why so few men have succeeded and so many failed. Those who succeeded were ruthlessly ambitious at a time when enterprising aspirants — under the patronage of immigrant wholesale merchants — could rapidly develop new trade networks and set themselves up independently. Those who have failed thus far, generally lacked this singular ambition and failed to clear one more of the hurdles. Alternatively, to be over-ambitious, boastful while under scrutiny, by attempting a further hurdle which others have yet to clear, can cause irreparable damage, as for example in the case of an imaginary aspirant who prances in full Sudanese dress in the market while his wife is hoeing her field. This person would be ridiculed by his reference group and "levelled" by his former companions.

The easiest hurdles to clear are those pertaining to the consumption of alcohol and the regular performance of prayers and attendance at study groups. The ability to say one's prayers aloud is a clear sign that progress is being made. These are "cheap" hurdles, in that they represent a sacrifice which costs nothing except a certain amount of restraint and discipline. The next hurdles are more costly: seclusion, new food and dress habits, offering proper hospitality, all these cost money. To afford this one needs a minor salaried occupation or a reasonably profitable trade, independently or on a commission basis. At this stage the hurdle of linguistic competence becomes crucial, along with a healthy dose of enterprise. The ability to create and exploit networks of real people and names of people one does not know personally, depends initially upon one's personal charm and linguistic skills, coupled with the image that one is trust- and therefore creditworthy. The failure rate is very high among aspirants who are native to the town in which they try to qualify, because besides social pressures from friends and relatives exerted to frustrate their attempts at social climbing, they are also linguistically distracted insofar as they are not speaking Arabic all day. Thus, aspirants, whether indigenous or immigrant, have to be extremely ambitious and to have a degree of luck on their side with regard to the economic situation of the moment. To succeed completely and become an independent trader is easier for second generation Sudanised and immigrant aspirants. More or less the same applies to completing one's education and qualifying via the path of salaried employment.

The attitude of the non-Sudanised towards aspirants and fully Sudanised varies considerably. They resent the aspirations of their fellows to become Sudanised, and will exert every conceivable social pressure to frustrate their efforts. Their attitude towards the Sudanised varies between grudging admiration and blind rage. Quite a few non-Sudanised fulminate at being taken advantage of by traders and agents who make considerable profits, first by speculating in the crops they have grown, secondly, by the sizeable profit margin the traders add to the cost price of their daily necessities. They fulminate against corrupt officials whom they have to bribe in order to obtain identity papers, or a licence, while those who are Sudanised are left in peace. They fulminate against medical assistants whose drugs and medicines remain in the Sudanised circuit, and against the Sudanised judges who punish them severely, but have never tried a corruption case against one of their fellows. Some even fulminate against the wandering preachers.

The sermon which was partially quoted above was tape-recorded by a friendly teacher, while I remained — out of sight and within hearing distance — in the compound where I spent most of my evenings with a *shulla*, a drinking party of ten to twenty men. That evening only one of the "regulars" was there, all the others attending the sermon. The man, who had three wives and seven children scattered in several villages further to the north, was engaged in preparing the evening meal for the others. I joined him in the cooking hut and asked him why he had not joined the others. He replied that he hated *fuqura* [holy men], that they made people soft, that they were people who earned their money with their tongues, especially the travelling ones. He then winked appreciatively in the direction of the neighbouring compound, whose owner had turned up the volume of his huge portable radio to obliterate the voice of the preacher.

Throughout the sermon my host supplied a running commentary on what the preacher said. When he turned to the subject of *zinna*, adultery, he burst out:

> Listen to that, who is talking about committing *zinna* to wives and daughters? Their husbands? Their parents? Do they learn about it from them? No! It is from them they learn it [pointing to where the preacher was holding forth]. They are always talking about it, every day, they are almost teaching it. If it were not for them, we would have no *zinna* here at all.

Later, during an injunction to parents to engage in sexual intercourse in a discrete manner, the man exploded:

> Suppose you have a wife and three children and only one hut, and it has been raining for two days? Do you send the children away into the rain?

Finally, when the preacher broached the subject of appropriate women's dress, he snarled with flashing eyes:

> Listen to that! The traders are going to be happy with the preacher's talk tonight. They will give him fifty piastres or even a pound afterwards. And tomorrow they will raise the price of sugar by five piastres to recoup their money.

When the sermon was over, the other members of the *shulla* returned, quite impressed. While a few men who rarely prayed, performed their prayers, the four–gallon pot of *merissa* was carried to its usual spot between the two long mats. The preacher was praised for his elocution and for the purity of his sermon, in which apparently everything was derived from the Koran and the Traditions, in which nothing was "made up", as other preachers did. During the sermon, a notorious drunkard had publicly sworn off *merissa*. A member of the hard core of the *shulla*, a man with two wives, five children and a tiny salary as a guard, said:

Still, only rich people can tell their wives to stay at home and do nothing all day.

And his remark passed without comment. His two wives brewed *merissa* for subsistence.

The next morning the sugar price went up by five piastres. The notorious drunkard soon began to miss the company of his friends and resumed his routine three days later.

Older non-Sudanised probably foster most resentment against the representatives of the new religious, economic and political order which has relegated them and their traditional values to the background. They are suspicious and defensive when dealing with outsiders who, they feel — sometimes unjustly — ridicule their religious devotions, laughing at their traditional skills, scoff at personal valour as a criterion for judging other people, and who have, in the eyes of such elders, enticed the younger generation out of the villages and into the towns, where their heads have been turned so that they have become corrupt and soft.

REFERENCES

Bender and Malik (1980) *Gaam Dictionary*, SIU, Carbondale.

Fadl Hassan, Y. (ed.) (1971) *Sudan in Africa*, Khartoum University Press, Khartoum.

James, W. (1971) "Social Assimilation and Changing Identity in the Southern Funj", in Yusuf Fadl Hassan.

Kapteijns, L. (1985) *Mahdist faith and Sudanic tradition: the history of the Masalit Sultanate, 1870-1930*, Routledge and Kegan Paul, London.

8

Towards an Understanding of Islamic Banking in Sudan: The Case of the Faisal Islamic Bank

Elfatih Shaaeldin & Richard Brown

INTRODUCTION

Since the formation of OPEC and the first oil price hike of 1973/74, Middle East based finance capital, particularly the banks, has come to play an increasingly important economic and political role, not only in the Middle East, but also within the international financial system (The Economist 1981b). Associated with this development there has been a revival, and indeed a considerable upsurge, of Islamic –style, interest–free banking practices. Islamic banks are now spreading to other parts of the Muslim world and, in some instances, branches have been opened in the Christian West (Hamdi 1981; Cooper 1981).

In the Sudan, the first bank of this sort, the Faisal Islamic Bank (FIB), began operations in May 1978. The authorised share capital of £S6 million was immediately oversubscribed, and subsequently increased to over £S40 million, the shares being divided between Saudis, Sudanese and other Muslims in a ratio of 4:4:2 respectively. As of 1982, the FIB's performance has exceeded most expectations, clearly outstripping all other commercial banks both private and nationalised, in terms of both growth and profitability.

The appearance and immediate success of Sudan's first Islamic bank sparked off a lively debate in academic, business and other circles on a number of issues. This mainly concerned the principle of interest-free banking, concepts such as usury, exploitation, interest and profit, and the actual practices of the FIB in relation to its stated principles and objectives.

121

The purpose of this paper is twofold. In the first part, we trace the origins and examine the principles and practices of interest-free banking and then go on to analyse and interpret the practices and the significance of the bank in the broader context of the role of banking capital in relation to its two counterparts — merchant and agro-industrial capital. Our main point of departure is that the past and future activities and performance of the bank cannot be analysed, and should not be assessed purely in terms of the Islamic principles and ideology which it claims to represent. It is also fundamentally necessary to analyse it in relation to the particular and class fractional interests with which its operations can be identified.

THE PRINCIPLES OF ISLAMIC BANKING: A THEORETICAL SETTING AND A FRAMEWORK FOR ANALYSIS

Although the first Islamic bank was established, in Egypt, as recently as 1963, the principles on which 'interest–free' banking are based can be traced to early Islamic writings. The spread of commodity production and the monetisation of exchange that Arabia was witnessing at the time are reflected in the long-distance trade. Cities such as Mecca and Medina had become major centres of commercial activity in which the rich merchants were powerful both economically and politically. However, moneylending and usury were also becoming prevalent at this time, and with it there arose a concentration of wealth in the hands of a relatively small group. We do not have much information on the extent of moneylending practices, nor of the relative power wielded by the moneylenders. It seems, however, that moneylending was mainly for consumption purposes and not for production. In addition, there is some evidence that the increasing activities of moneylenders caused people to draw a comparison between usury and profit. Thus, in the Koran, one reads:

> Those who live on usury shall rise up before Allah like men whom Satan has demented by his touch, for they claim that usury is like trading. But Allah has permitted trading and forbidden usury (Koran, The Cow:2:275).

Also:
> Believers, have fear of Allah and waive what is still due to you from usury, if your faith be true; or war shall be declared against you by

Allah and his apostle. If you repent, you may retain your principal, suffering no loss and causing no loss to anyone (Koran, The Cow: 2: 276).

Although some Islamic writers argued that low interest charges were legitimate, others argued strongly that the charging of interest in any financial transaction should be abolished on the grounds that it will reduce the debtor to poverty, and also because it is believed to retard economic development by encouraging those with access to finance to make a livelihood from moneylending rather than other productive forms of economic activity. On the other hand, there are some who believe that low interest charges are legitimate, and yet others who extend the definition of *riba* (interest) to include all other forms of surplus appropriation such as monopoly profits in trade.

INTEREST, PROFIT AND SURPLUS: A CONCEPTUAL DISCUSSION

By failing to analyse and theoretically conceptualise relations of production and exchange specific to capitalist vis-a-vis earlier precapitalist society, the participants in the profit versus interest debate have erred in their treatment of the process of surplus extraction and their conceptualisation of its appropriation and realisation as profit or interest in both precapitalist and contemporary social formations.

Under precapitalist conditions, in which independent commodity producers sell their final commodities to the merchant, and/or borrow money from the moneylender, the capitalist has no direct control over production, and therefore, the generation of surplus. He derives his profit or interest through unequal exchange with the independent producer. The merchant's profit depends upon his ability to buy cheap from one producer, and sell dear to another. The moneylender's interest likewise depends on his ability to sell to the independent producer a sum of money now in return for a greater future sum. In both cases, these capitalists rely entirely on their ability to deprive the independent producer of a part of his own surplus through an unequal exchange relationship when buying his finished commodity or lending him money. The capitalist has no direct control over the total amount of surplus actually generated by the producer. However, under these production and exchange relations, one can envisage a situation in which production is destroyed and the independent producer impoverished by the greed and usury of the merchant or moneylender.

Under capitalist production and exchange relations, on the other hand, the actual producer of the commodity — wage labour — does not sell a finished commodity to the capitalist, rather he sells his capacity to produce, his labour power, to the capitalist for a given wage. In this situation, the capitalist does not appropriate surplus from the worker by depriving him of part of what he has already produced. For the worker has already relinquished his labour power to the capitalist in exchange for a wage which, like the price of any commodity, represents its exchange value in accordance with its reproduction cost. In so doing, the producer has relinquished his control over production to the capitalist, who now owns and controls the surplus which he gets the worker to produce for him. As it is the industrial capitalist who controls the generation of surplus, the merchant and moneylender are no longer dependent on exchange relations with the producer of surplus for appropriating their share of the surplus. Indeed, it is with the industrial capitalist that they must now engage in exchange in order to appropriate a share of the surplus that he has extracted from the worker. It is in this sense that the appropriation of profits, rent and interest is essentially a question of the allocation of surplus in the sphere of exchange relations. The surplus already exists in the commodity or money form, it originates in the sphere of production, and its magnitude is determined by the intensity of the exploitation of labour, i.e. the ratio of surplus value produced to the value of labour power. Thus, while the industrial capitalist, merchant and moneylender are forever in potential conflict over the distribution of the given surplus between them, they share a common class interest in maximising the total amount of surplus available through an increased rate of exploitation of labour. However, insofar as the activities of the merchant and moneylender are confined to the sphere of exchange, they are dependent on the industrial capitalist for extracting the surplus in the first instance. They can, of course, have an indirect influence on this process by facilitating production through the trade and moneylending services they render to the industrial capitalist.

The implications of the foregoing discussion should by now be obvious. It implies that all forms of surplus appropriation, whether it be capitalists' profit, merchants' profit, moneylenders' interest or landowners' rent, have a common source in the extraction of surplus from wage labour in the production process. Thus, moneylenders' interest is no more the villain of the piece than other forms of surplus appropriation. Nor can we attribute the impoverishment of the working class and the increasing polarisation of wealth in capitalist society to any one fraction of the capitalist class in particular.

Although it is in the sphere of production that exploitation and impoverishment is, in the first instance, located, all fractions of the capitalist class share an objective interest in the maintenance and intensification of this process without which there would be insufficient or no surplus appropriation. In other words, "interest", and its substitution by another form of appropriation, "profit", would have little or no direct implication for the overall share of income between the exploited and the capitalist classes. It would only affect the distribution of surplus between the different categories, profit, rent and interest. Finally, as exchange and financial relations are restricted to the sphere of circulation, and as circulation is only one part of the overall process of capital accumulation, it is difficult to conceive how any reforms confined to the sphere of circulation, such as the abolition of interest, could achieve a fundamental change in the socio-economic organisation of production.

However, it is conceivable that the prolonged economic and political dominance of either merchant or moneylending capital could frustrate and retard the development of capitalist production. In such a case, it is therefore conceivable that changes of this sort undermine the hegemony of the merchants and/or moneylenders, paving the way for the consolidation of a national, industrial bourgeoisie, being, as it were, the midwife of transition.

MODERN BANKS, MERCHANTS AND MONEYLENDERS: A FRAMEWORK FOR ANALYSING BANKING IN THE SUDAN

Historically, commercial capital — merchant and interest-bearing — long preceded the emergence and ultimate dominance of industrial capital. With the transition to capitalism in the now advanced capitalist economies in the West and its extension to the colonial periphery, interest-bearing capital underwent a fundamental transformation of its function and form in the overall process of capital accumulation. From relying on usury to appropriate surplus from independent producers, self-employed artisans and wealthier spendthrifts, as well as the powerful merchants on whose trade they ultimately depended for their existence, interest-bearing capital became, in effect, subservient to the requirements of industrial capital. Their activities, and in particular the credit system, were thereby adapted in accordance with the laws of motion governing the process of capital accumulation with both its cyclical up and downswings, and its secular tendency towards increasing internationalisation of production and centralisation of ownership and control.

However, in view of the historically uneven nature of development and spread of capitalism throughout the world economy, it does not necessarily follow that the role and functions of interest-bearing capital comply, in each and every concrete situation with this abstract conceptualisation specific to capitalism in its pure form. In some parts of the contemporary capitalist world, merchant capital has succeeded in retaining its economic and political hegemony over other fractions of capital at the level of the national economy, although perhaps being subservient to industrial capital at the international level, and even in spite of the existence of a nascent, national industrial bourgeoisie within the same social formation. By the same token, this transformation of the function and form of interest-bearing capital under capitalism does not imply that precapitalist forms of moneylending (including usury) altogether cease to exist in either the advanced or the underdeveloped parts of the world economy. Nor do they necessarily cease to play an important role in the accumulation process. Indeed, throughout the capitalist world, a not too insignificant part of moneylending activities exist outside the organised financial system, and is carried out between independent moneylenders (who may themselves also be traders or landowners) and self-employed small farmers or artisans (who may be independent producers possessing their own means of production). Here, moneylending often retains the form of medieval usurer's capital in relation to such borrowers, despite its taking the form specific to capitalism in relation to other borrowers. The coexistence of the usurious *shail* (forward selling) system of moneylending and a modern banking and financial sector extending to most parts of Sudan, is a clear example of this (Wilmington 1955; Adam and Apaya 1973).

Thus, while any analysis of interest-bearing capital in a country such as Sudan cannot ignore the particular forms and characteristics of moneylending which are specific to capitalism, one also needs to incorporate into the analysis due consideration of those features which are specific to the particular concrete situation with which one is concerned. Indeed, in order to understand the role of banks and other financial institutions in the process of accumulation in the Sudan, it is necessary to understand two phenomena:

i) the continued hegemony of merchant capital, and in particular its relation to international capital on the one hand, and domestic banks on the other, and,

ii) the continued existence of certain medieval moneylending practices in relation to small-scale farmers, self-employed artisans and other petty commodity producers.

We maintain that the recent emergence of the FIB and other banks as an alternative to the existing banking system should not be seen simply as an ideologically inspired aberration from existing, commercial banking practices, but instead needs to be explained in relation to the rising aspirations of the hitherto nascent national/ domestic bourgeoisie, in their struggle to control the process of capital accumulation. Indeed, to the extent that these banks have played a role in extending finance to productive investment in Sudan's main surplus-generating sphere, agriculture, this has been restricted to the activities of the relatively small, specialised, Agricultural Bank, or it has occurred only indirectly through their lending to large merchants who in turn are involved in the extension of credit to farmers through the *shail* system.

On the other hand, one cannot necessarily attribute the continued dominance of the *shail* system in providing finance for much of Sudan's traditional agricultural activities to the neglect of agriculture by the modern banking system. The main clients of that system — the merchants — are to a large extent the main agents and beneficiaries of the *shail* system. They have an interest in its continuation. But it is also clear that in those parts of the country where large-scale capitalist agricultural and agro-industrial undertakings have been recently developed, the modern banking sector has been very quick to respond, and has had very little difficulty in extending its services to agrarian capitalists in those regions. Thus, we are hypothesising that a precondition for the extension of the service of the traditional banking and other financial institutions to agriculture is the transformation of production relations in these spheres. Without capitalist production, it is difficult to conceive how a transformation of the financial system could occur. At the same time, however, without access to the loans and advances of the traditional commercial banks, development banks and other financial institutions, it is difficult to see how Sudan's aspiring small agro-industrial bourgeoisie could succeed in effecting a transformation of production, unless a new source of borrowing and financial support were to appear.

Therefore while it is perhaps correct to argue that as Sudanese agriculture is in the process of transformation to capitalist relations of production, the continued existence of the *shail* system can be interpreted simply as as transitory phase, doomed to extinction with the development of capitalist production. There is no telling how long this phase might last.

During the transformation, it is inevitable however that certain conflicts will emerge between the various fractions of capital. In particular these will be between those who have a vested interest in maintaining the status quo (the merchants cum rural moneylenders), and those whose interests are in the development of capitalist production — the emerging indigenous industrial and agro-bourgeoisie and the foreign investors and lenders. This also suggests a potential source of conflict between different branches of financial capital. On the one hand, there will be the traditional banks which are closely connected to some of the powerful merchant class, a class whose interests we have suggested are in maintaining the *shail* system and traditional agriculture. On the other, there will be the "progressive" banks which either establish a direct interest in financing the international trade side of the "modernisation" of production (the foreign banks) or new banks which materially and/or ideologically become associated with the aspiring indigenous agro- and industrial bourgeoisie.

We believe that it is from this perspective and in this context that the past and future policies and practices as well as the ideological and political associations of the FIB have to be analysed. This is the task of the next section.

THE ORIGINS AND PRACTICES OF THE FAISAL ISLAMIC BANK IN THE SUDAN

The emergence of the Faisal Islamic Bank was a result of both regional and domestic developments. Domestically, Sudanese capital was eager to penetrate the banking sector after it was denationalised. In fact there have been attempts by indigenous capital to enter the financial sector since the late 1950s. By then foreign capital was in full control of the banking and insurance sectors. Afterwards, inter-imperialist competition led to the establishment of new foreign banks. The sixties witnessed a gradual Sudanisation of banking. In 1960, the

Sudan Commercial Bank was established mainly with Sudanese capital. In 1963, Credit Lyonnais liquidated its Sudanese branch and was replaced by Bank El Nilein with 60 per cent Sudanese ownership. Similarly, the foreign-dominated insurance sub-sector experienced a gradual process of indigenisation at about the same time. In the early 1970s, the then radical government nationalised the entire commercial banking sector, thereby severely restricting the direct influence of foreign capital over Sudan's banking, insurance and export-import business. Total state control was, however, short-lived. By the mid-seventies private banks, though entirely foreign at first, were allowed to begin operating in Sudan again, side-by-side with the nationalised banks.

It is interesting to note though, that it has been mainly US and regional capital that has moved in, replacing the earlier European influence. As yet, these banks are restricted in their dealings with Sudanese citizens, although they can open accounts for import-export agents and for Sudanese nationals working abroad.

Meanwhile, pressure from the Sudanese business community to relax state control over Sudanese–owned banks was mounting. At the first national conference of the Sudanese Businessmen's Association in February 1979, a motion was passed requesting that the Sudan Commercial Bank be restored to private ownership. Fath El Rahman El Beshir denied that businessmen were aiming at the total denationalisation of banks — "It just seems inappropriate that foreign commercial banks such as Citibank should be able to operate here while there is no Sudanese equivalent" (Sudanow April 1979).

Regionally, the huge increase in oil revenues since 1973 has been accompanied by the emergence in the Gulf of a wealthy class consisting in the main of merchants with close links to US and other foreign capital. Since the base of accumulation in these countries is small in relation to the available investible surpluses, this class looked for alternatives in the immediate region. This was perhaps accelerated by the worsening of relations between the Arab states and the West immediately after the 1973/4 oil price rise, with the Saudis eager to establish alternative sources of food and raw materials.

At the ideological level, the revival of Islam was closely associated with the drive for the extension of capital accumulation in the region. The revived interest in Islamic banks followed the oil boom and massive accumulation of petro-dollar surpluses in the Middle East after 1973. The first to appear was a development bank based in Saudi Arabia, while in Abu Dhabi the first Islamic commercial bank was established. This was soon followed by the establishment of a whole group of Faisal Islamic Banks in several Middle Eastern countries. It was in 1976 that an agreement was reached with the Sudanese government to establish the Faisal Islamic Bank (Sudan) as a public, joint venture company. Sudanese merchant capital warmly welcomed this partnership. The weakness of Sudan's indigenous agricultural and agro-industrial capital is reflected by the ease with which this sector became dominated by large, joint venture agricultural schemes, as in the case of the partnership between the Aboulela Company and Mohammed El Faisal.

Thus, a basic feature of the FIB (and this is also the case with most other recently established Islamic business enterprises) is that its ownership is multinational with its shareholders belonging to a particular geo-political region, sharing a common religious and ideological background. The claim, therefore, that the FIB is first and foremost a Muslim institution has been effective in stilling certain sensitivities in the Sudan to the penetration of foreign capital, and in particular, to foreign banks. The recent emergence of Islamic enterprises should be seen essentially as an attempt to assert and promote "regional" capital vis-a-vis other branches of international capital in the Middle East. This was succinctly expressed by Mohammed Faisal, the Saudi prince behind the FIB, when he outlined the main motivations underlying his promotion of the bank as (i) the desire to check the foreign cultural domination of Muslim countries, and (ii) the intention of eradicating any feelings of Muslim inferiority in relation to the West.

While these general economic and ideological motivations might be common underlying features of emerging Islamic enterprises, the way they are manifested in each individual national situation will depend on and vary according to the particular political-economic conditions and configurations of class forces in each case.

THE PRACTICES OF THE FAISAL BANK

The FIB has claimed that it operates according to the economic principles of the Islamic Shar'ia code. These principles are stated as follows:

i) prohibition of interest in all forms of transaction;
ii) undertaking business and trade activities on the basis of fair and legitimate (*halal*) profits;
iii) giving of *zakat* (alms);

iv) prohibition of monopoly;

v) co-operation for the benefit of society and development of all *halal* aspects of business that are not specifically prohibited by Islam.

(FIB 1979: 1)

The Bank provides for three types of account. Current accounts, as in most other commercial banks, offer chequebook facilities and carry a service charge, but depositors receive no interest or other income on their balances. However, the bank obtains the explicit permission of the account holder to use his/her funds for other business activities. Saving accounts only differ from current accounts insofar as they do not carry a service charge. There are no restrictions, and they can be drawn on without notice, but the saver is entitled to special borrowing facilities. Investment deposit accounts, on the other hand, earn the holder a share of the bank's profits, provided that the deposit has been held in the account for a period of at least six months. The minimum deposit is £S100 which is invested by the bank in a twelve-month joint venture by a borrower. The bank then claims 25 percent of the net profit on the client's investment account.

As can be seen from Table 8.1, over the four financial years 1979-82, FIB's equity, including both paid up shares and reinvested profits, increased by more than 350 percent, while total commercial banks' equity grew by only 70 percent. By 1982, its share capital represented 30 percent of total commercial bank share capital.

Table 8.1. FIB's capital in relation to total commercial capital, 1979-82 (£S '000)

	1979	1980	1981	1982
FIB share capital	3579	4466	10212	19216
FIB share capital	17%	16%	30%	
equity	2%	2%	4%	

Source: Annual Report of Board of Directors, FIB, 1980, 1981, 1982, 1983. Bank of Sudan Annual Report, 1980, 1981, 1982. Bank of Sudan Economic and Financial Statistics Review, Vol. 21, No. 3.

Table 8.2 shows that during the same four–year period, total deposits with the FIB increased almost 14 times, while total commercial bank deposits increased by less than a half. FIB's share of total commercial bank deposits thereby increasing from 4 percent in 1979 to 15 percent in 1982.

Table 8.2. FIB's deposits in relation to total commercial bank deposits, 1979-82

Year	1979	1980	1981	1982
FIB's deposits (£S '000)	21774	49512	102319	302373
as % of total bank deposits	4%	7%	12%	15%

Sources as for Table 8.1.

Although its activities are still concentrated very much in Khartoum, new branches have opened in many parts of the country, including not only Port Sudan, but also some more rural towns such as El Obeid and Kosti.

Table 8.3 shows the composition of FIB's deposits over the last few years. It is interesting to note that while deposits in all accounts increased dramatically between 1979 and 1982, investment accounts have grown proportionately faster than other accounts, increasing their share of total deposits from 12.5 percent in 1979 to 39 percent in 1981. In contrast, the share of deposit accounts has declined from 84 percent in 1979 to 63.4 percent in 1982.

Table 8.3:
Composition of FIB's deposits, 1979-82 (£S '000)

	1979	%	1980	%	1981	%	1982	%
current account	18285	84	40152	81	59527	58	128196	63
savings account	770	4	1295	3	2710	2.6	7797	3.8
investment deposits	2718	12.5	8065	16.5	40082	39.2	66379	32.8
Total	21774	100	49512	100	102319	100	202372	100

Source: Annual Report of Board of Directors, FIB, 1980, 1981, 1982, 1983.
Note: Current accounts include both local and foreign currency deposits.

These figures would seem to suggest that the bank is being more successful in attracting relatively wealthier investors in search of a good return on their savings than small savers attracted by the bank's policy of not paying interest on credit balances.

As charging of interest is prohibited, the FIB offers four alternatives to interest-bearing loans (Sadik 1981: 1). *Musharaka* is a joint venture between the banks and an investor in which each partner provides part of the capital, and shares the profit (or loss) in a ratio agreed in advance. This could also take the form of a lease or "self-liquidating" partnership (*ijara*) whereby the full ownership of the investment passes to the investor, who is the bank's customer, after an agreed period. *Mudharaba* is again a joint venture, but in this case, the bank provides the full finance for the operation and the client contributes his/her entrepreneurial skills—a form of agency. The client receives a share of the profits and the bank bears the full burden of any losses. *Mudharaba* is essentially a form of trade credit, in terms of which the bank actually purchases and becomes legal owner of whatever the client has ordered, and then resells it to the client on delivery, at a previously agreed, higher, price. However, the client has no legal obligation to buy what the bank has purchased on his/her behalf. Finally, there is *Kard Hassan*, which is in effect a free loan on which the bank earns no interest at all.

In return for its promotion of so-called *halal* business activities, the FIB enjoys certain privileges which are not normally afforded to other commercial banks. For example, all assets and profits of the bank, and all salaries, wages, gratuities and pensions of its employees enjoy full tax exemption. The FIB also enjoyed guaranteed government protection from confiscation or nationalisation of its assets. It enjoyed complete freedom in the transferability and use of its foreign currency deposits. It could be argued, however, that these rather generous concessions have more to do with Sudan's eagerness to attract foreign capital, Saudi in particular, than the government's commitment to Islamic banking and bankers.

Although we do not have a breakdown of the bank's advances in terms of the different types of funding arrangement discussed above, we have figures for the total advances extended over the same 1979-82 period. Table 8.4 shows that new "investments" increased more than tenfold between 1979 and 1982.

FIB's share of overall commercial bank outstanding advances, although still relatively small, increased from 3 to 8 percent between 1979 and 1982. At the same time, there was a clear shift in the FIB's lending policy over the latter part of this period. In the first Annual

Table 8.4: FIB's advances 1979-82 (£Sm)

	1979	1980	1981	1982
new advances	27.6	56.5	73.7	277.9
outstanding advances	12.5	30.4	52.3	91.6
advances	460.9	592.9	719.1	1142.5
FIB's share of outstanding advances	3%	5%	7%	8%

Sources: As for Table 8.1.

Report of the Board of Directors, 1980, it was stated that the bank's main strategy was to minimise risks and realise "reasonable profits in the shortest possible time". No particular sector or stratum of the business community was singled out as the bank's main target for funding although there was specific mention of financing trade and working capital for industry. In the following year, 1981, however it is stated in the report that:

> a distinct — though small — departure was made during 1980 to go into medium-term financing of industries in the small business and artisan sectors.

The main features of this policy are:

> i) the average financing period is three years;

> ii) the bank charges reasonable profits ranging from 10 percent to 15 percent [sic.] on the tools or machines or raw materials provided by the banks to the client...

> (FIB Report May 1981: 6).

It is this shift of strategy that we consider central to any appreciation of the bank's activities and which is the subject of some comments in a later section of this paper.

As demonstrated in Table 8.5, the bank's profits have not been insignificant. Net profit (before *zakat*) increased from just over £S1 insignificant. Net profit (before *zakat*) increased from just over £S1 million in 1979 to over £S21 million in 1982. The latter figure represents more than 100 percent of paid-up share capital and 40 percent of total equity funds. More than 30 percent of 1981 profits and 36 percent of 1982 profits have been ploughed back into the bank's equity. Dividends to shareholders in the first three years of the bank's existence have already repaid them 90 per cent of their original investment (20 percent in 1979 and 1980, and 25 percent in 1981 and 1982).

Table 8.5. FIB's profits 1979-82 (£S '000)

Year	1979	1980	1981	1982
net profit (before *zakat*)	1052	2588	10288	21202
zakat	125	170	473	734
dividends	499	893	2553	4804
reinvested profits	208	723	3157	7800
net profit/share capital (%)	29	58	101	110
net profit/ total equity (%)	21	23	44	41

Source: Annual Report of the Board of Directors, FIB, 1980, 1981, 1982, 1983.

The experience of the FIB as Sudan's first Islamic bank, in spite of its immediate commercial success, has been met either with a sceptical suspicion and, in some instances, scorn, or with little or no interest at all on the part of academics, planners, policy-makers and others presumably concerned with current developments in Sudan's political economy. The debate among social scientists has focused almost exclusively on conceptual, definitional and ethical questions concerning the FIB's principles with respect to "interest" vis-a-vis "profit" on the one hand, and its actual banking practices in relation to its principles on the other. While we agree that these are important issues that need to be considered in any analysis of Islamic banking, we also believe that concern with these questions should not be allowed to dominate the debate to such an extent that we lose sight of the potentially far-reaching implications that the current commercial success and expansion of the FIB (and others which will doubtless follow in its tracks) could have for economic and political developments in Sudan's medium and longer term future. For this reason, we concerning the various forms of surplus appropriation and the relationship between different fractions of capital in the process of surplus extraction and distribution. We feel that it is even more important that some attempt is made to analyse, explain and assess the wider role that the FIB is playing at this particular stage of the Sudan's economic and political development.

THE ECONOMIC AND POLITICAL SIGNIFICANCE OF THE FIB

It is our view that the emergence of these new, jointly owned private commercial banks and the immediate success of the first, the FIB, is perhaps the most significant of all policies and developments in Sudanese banking which we have witnessed over the last two or three decades. It reflects the gradual emergence of a new finance capital. A cursory glance at the data on commercial bank advances, presented in Table 8.6, shows that until the late 1970s, despite nationalisation, there was very little change in the overall pattern of commercial bank lending. By far the largest proportion — 80 to 90 percent — of total commercial bank credit was made up of short term loans. More than 40 per cent of all advances were extended to import-export merchants, but an increasing proportion was for industrial (trade) credit. Loans to agricultural and industrial producers for investment purposes were, until the late seventies, negligible, and even in the latest year for which data is available, accounted for less than 20 percent of total advances. Furthermore, when one explores the details of these loans, it is apparent that it is only a handful of monopoly, industrial, capitalists who have benefited, as in the case, for example, of the Sharaf and Gulf Corporations. Similarly, if one looks into the operations of the specialised agricultural and industrial banks, one finds firstly that the total amount of their lending is insignificant in relation to total bank advances, and secondly, by far the largest part of it is lent on short term and not for capital investment purposes.

It is perhaps also significant that when the foreign-owned banks were allowed back, it was a condition that the only Sudanese nationals with whom they could do business, apart from those outside the country, were import-export merchants. Also significant is the statement, quoted above, by Fath El-Rahman El Beshir that it was not a total denationalisation of Sudanese commercial banks that the businessmen wanted. It is perhaps more likely that he was appealing, on behalf of the growing number of Sudanese businessmen, in both

Table 8.6: Breakdown of Commercial Bank Advances: 1965-82

composition of total by type

year end	total (£S '000)	short term (%)	trade (%)	indust. (%)	agric. invest. (%)	industrial invest. (%)	other (%)
1965	45748	85.2	55.5	16.6	2.0	5.3	20.6
1968	70817	86.3	60.9	17.3	0.5	4.8	16.5
1971	69830	85.8	50.0	25.4	0.5	3.7	20.4
1974	123215	90.8	40.3	32.5	0.4	2.9	23.9
1975	186071	94.0	44.2	32.0	0.2	2.0	21.6
1976	228394	92.0	42.8	32.4	0.2	2.7	21.9
1977	264587	84.3	40.8	28.4	0.2	9.9	20.7
1978	343228	84.8	38.5	31.2	0.2	11.9	18.2
1979	460903	79.2	34.5	29.4	0.6	17.7	17.8
1980	592861	78.0	35.5	28.7	0.8	19.3	15.7
1981	777526	78.6	37.0	29.2	0.2	17.8	15.8
1982	1142523	78.7	44.0	23.5	0.3	16.2	16.0

Source: Bank of Sudan: Economic an Financial Bulletin, Vol.XVI, No.4, Vol.XXI, No.3, Vol.XXIII, No.4.

commerce and industry, for at least some access to commercial bank credits, access that had never been, and was in the future unlikely to be, forthcoming from either the nationalised or foreign-controlled banks. By contrast, the experience of the FIB, though short, so far indicates a lending policy which seemed at the beginning to explicitly favour smaller new businesses with a particular ideological orientation. The FIB started by giving explicit anti-monopoly policy statements. Table 8.7 shows the average size of its advances.

Table 8.7: Average size of FIB's advances 1979-82

	1979	1980	1981	1982
total advances (£Sm)	27.6	56.5	73.7	183.4
total no. of advances	208	779	1471	1831
Average advance (£S '000)	13.3	72.5	50.1	100.2

Source: Report of the Board of Directors, FIB, 1980, 1981, 1982, 1983.

However, it is also worth noting that the size of its average loan increased from £S13.3 thousand in 1979 to over £S100,000 by 1982. Furthermore, the explicit policy statements on the bank's commitment to the small artisans and producers disappeared from the 1983 Annual Report.

On the bank's lending side, although FIB has been mainly concentrating on the traditional banking sphere, it has also penetrated some areas in which no other banks are currently engaged. Examples of this are the purchase of trucks worth US$12 million, insecticides and herbicides worth US$7.5 million, as well as the purchase of oil. Table 8.8 shows that foreign trade still constitutes its major sphere of activity. Internal trade makes up 12 per cent of all the bank's activities. In particular, internal and external trading in sorghum created a very negative public image of the bank in a period of drought and famine.

Table 8.8: Breakdown of FIB's advances up to 1983

sphere	value in US$m	no. of clients	%
export	168	96	48
import	119	528	40
domestic trade	-	298	-

Source: Faisal Islamic Bank, Annual Reports.

On the borrowing side, FIB's Islamic principles open up to it a potential clientele who would otherwise be unwilling to deposit their savings with the commercial banks. However, in the 1980s, several other banks have started operating on the same Islamic basis. These include El Tadamon Islamic Bank (1983), the Sudanese Islamic Bank (1983), Western Sudan Islamic Bank (1984) and others. Thus, the FIB is now facing some competition. In addition, the government is in the process of persuading all other banks to adopt the same principles. Also, with the recently imposed tight credit ceiling, based on a quota system, it is inevitable that competition between banks, including the FIB, will be much greater. This phenomenon does not stem directly from the FIB's own borrowing and lending practices, but is one which might well bring it into more direct competition with other banks in the future.

On the other hand, since the FIB is promoting those groups with whom it is identified ideologically — namely the Muslim Brotherhood — it faces open hostility and objections to its privileged status. In fact, the well-known ideological and political leanings of the FIB have led to the establishment of rival banks representing the interests of competing political and merchant factions, for example the Sudanese Islamic Bank.

CONCLUSIONS

On the basis of our analysis, it could be concluded that the past success of the FIB can be attributed more to the existence of objective economic forces with which it has identified ideologically, than to subjective support for the Islamic ideology it has employed in advancing its financial interests.

As for its future, we contend that this will depend more on the type of borrower, and hence class fraction, with which it finally aligns itself than with the success it has in promoting the cause of Islamic banking principles and Islamic ideology in Sudan's political and economic life. At this stage, it is still unclear where the FIB actually stands with respect to Sudan's economically and politically dominant merchant class.

REFERENCES

Adams, F.H. and Apaya, W. (1973) "Agricultural credit in the Gezira", *Sudan Notes and Records*, Vol. LIV, Khartoum.

Ali, Abdalla Ali (1973) "Sudanese financial institutions and their functioning", in Ali Mohammed El Hassan (ed.), *Growth Employment and Equity*, ILO/ESR, Khartoum University Press, Khartoum.

Ali, A.A. (1982), *The political economy of banking in Sudan 1970-1977*, DSRC Seminar Series, Khartoum.

Bank of Sudan (1970), (1974), (1980), (1981), (1982) Annual Reports, Khartoum.

Bank of Sudan (1982) *Economic and Financial Statistics Review*, Vol. 21, No. 3, Khartoum.

de Brunhoff, S. (1973) *Marx on money*, Urizen Books, New York.

Cooper, R. (1981) "A calculator in one hand and the Koran in the other", *Euromoney*, pp. 44-64, November.

The Economist (1981a) "Banking or prophet", London, November 14.

The Economist (1981b) "A foot in the door: a survey of banking in the Middle East", London, November 21.

Faisal Islamic Bank (n.d approximately 1979) *Faisal Islamic Bank: Its objectives and operational methods,* Faisal Islamic Bank, Khartoum.

Faisal Islamic Bank, (1979), (1980), (1981), (1982), (1983) *Report of the board of directors,* Faisal Islamic Bank, Khartoum (in Arabic).

Fine, B (1980) *Economic theory and ideology,* Edward Arnold, London.

Hamdi, Abdel-Rahim (n.d. approximately 1981) "The operation of Faisal Islamic Bank (Sudan)", unpublished paper, Faisal Islamic Bank, Khartoum.

Hamdi, Abdel-Rahim (1982) *The experience of Islamic banks with special emphasis on Faisal Islamic Bank,* Faisal Islamic Bank, Khartoum, November.

Harris, L. (1979) "The role of money in the economy", in F. Green and P. More (eds.), *Issues in Political Economy,* Macmillan, London.

Kay, G. (1975) *Development and underdevelopment: a Marxist analysis,* Macmillan, London.

Marx, K. (1978) *Capital: a critique of political economy,* Vol. III, Progress Printers, Moscow.

Ministry of Finance and National Economy (n.d), *Economic survey: 1978/79,* Sudan Survey Department, Khartoum.

Ministry of National Planning (1977) *The Six Year Plan of Economic and Social Development: 1977/78, 1982/83,* Vol. I & II, Ministry of National Planning, Khartoum, April.

Ministry of National Planning (1981) *Second Three Year Investment Programme 1980/81-1982/83,* Ministry of National Planning, Khartoum.

Mohammed, A. N. (1981) "Interest-free banks: the case of Islamic Bank" (sic.), unpublished B.Sc. dissertation, Faculty of Economic and Social Studies, University of Khartoum, Khartoum, March.

Naggar, A. (n.d.), *Manhag el-Islamiyya: simol bil fawaid* (The approach of the Islamic Renaissance: interest free banks), no place of publication.

Sadik, M. (n.d. approximately 1981) *Islamic insurance system as practiced by the Islamic Insurance Co. Ltd. (Sudan),* National Printing and Publishing House, Khartoum.

Saeed, O. H. (1971) *The Industrial Bank of Sudan, 1962-68: an experiment in development banking,* Khartoum University Press, Khartoum, February.

Shaaeldin, Elfatih (1981) "The development of peripheral capitalism in Sudan", unpublished Ph.D. thesis, State University of New York at Buffalo, Buffalo.

Sudanow (1979) "Businessmen confer", Vol. 4, No. 4, Ministry of Culture and National Guidance, Khartoum, April.

Sudanow (1982a) "An uncertain business", Vol. 4, No. 4, Ministry of Culture and Information, Khartoum, April.

Sudanow (1982b) "Must what goes down come up?", Vol. 5, No. 4, Ministry of Culture and Information, Khartoum, April.

Wilmington, Martin W. (1955) *The Middle East Journal,* Vol. IX, pp. 138-45, Washington, 1955, republished in *Development Digest,* Vol. XVIII, No. 3, July, 1980, pp. 71-7.

9

Some Aspects of Commoditisation and Transformation in Rural Sudan

Abbas Abdelkarim

COMMODITISATION OF THE MEANS OF PRODUCTION AND CONSUMPTION AND THE ROLE OF CIRCULATION CAPITAL

Trade and the commoditisation of the means of production and consumption

Trading centres and trade routes connecting parts of the Sudan to the outside world via the western, eastern and northern borders, and later via Suakin, existed for many centuries prior to the advent of the British (Amin 1970; Elhassan 1985). Although there was localised exchange of basic goods between settled farmers and pastoralists, the external trade mainly served the elite of these communities. Intensified commoditisation of the means of production and consumption is of recent origin and has affected different communities in different ways. Its spread commenced at the beginning of this century. British rule opened the way for systematic and wider linkages between the Sudan and the world market through the intensification of money-commodity relations.

Following the flag, British and other companies and individuals moved into the country. Powerful multinationals like Gellatley Hankey, Sudan Mercantile and Mitchell Cotts soon dominated the export import market. Exports began to increase (see Table 9.1).

Gum arabic, groundnuts, sesame and livestock were the country's main export items in the first three decades of British rule prior to the establishment of the Gezira Scheme. These were produced by households, and incentives for increased production could only follow from an increase in the need for cash. Within a few decades, the big

Table 9.1: Expansion of Sudan's total exports and imports 1907-25 in £S millions

year	total exports	total imports
1907	0.4	1.6
1910	1.0	1.9
1915	1.6	1.7
1920	4.7	7.0
1925	3.8	5.4

Source: Beshai 1976: 336.

companies, helped by a network of agents, had flooded the market with new consumer goods, creating new tastes and enlarging the circle of needs of the household producers.

Table 9.2: Quantities of selected principal imports into Sudan in the first three decades of British rule (in '000 tons)

year	sugar	coffee	tea	soap
1907	6.7	0.6	0.1	0.4
1910	10.8	1.1	0.4	0.9
1915	10.8	1.7	0.4	0.9
1920	14.8	4.2	1.1	1.1
1925	13.2	6.3	2.2	2.6
1930	31.2	6.3	2.2	2.6

Source: Beshai 1976: 312.

Table 9.1 clearly demonstrates the increase in production for the external market in the first two and a half decades of incorporation. From 1907 (the earliest data available) to 1925, the total exports of the Sudan had multiplied to almost tenfold. An increase in cash-cropping had been accompanied by an increase in consumption. In a few decades, these changes had affected even the most remote and self-contained communities (see for example Lako 1983; Mustafa 1980; Elhassan, chapter 10 in this volume). When local communities resisted this destruction of their own local production (for example textiles, see Abdelrahim 1963: 8), the state came to the aid of merchant capital by effectively banning local production (for example cotton cultivation and manufacture was banned in the Rahad area of Central Sudan, O'Brien 1980: 166). However, in the main, the goods arriving at the market were either new (sugar, tea, flash-lights), or were able to compete with and ultimately replace the local products.

With the expansion of the reproduction "needs" of the household, commoditisation increased, as did the role of exchange in the reproduction cycle. Increased cash cropping was one way to meet the increased subsistence needs. In Elgayla village in the Western Sudan, for example, the villagers started to grow sesame as a cash crop in the 1920s, and having limited labour resources, they replaced the time-consuming *dukhn* (millet) with *dura* (sorghum) as their main staple (O'Brien 1980: 454). In fact, sesame, cotton, gum arabic and ground-nuts, four of the five most important cash crops in the country, are still mainly produced by household producers. For example, 75% of sesame production in 1979/80 came from this source (Statistical Abstract 1981: 92).

In the absence of cash-cropping, seasonal or permanent migration to local or district employment centres may be the only means of enlarging the circle of household need. Hence the commoditisation of labour power proceeds. The relation between cash cropping or local wage income and migration as alternatives to meet the increased subsistence needs is reflected in the fluctuation of the numbers and sources of migrant labourers coming to the large agricultural (and urban) areas. In the Gezira, for example, the fluctuation in the influx of seasonal labourers does not depend only on the quantity of labour needed in the scheme itself, but also on the conditions faced by households in the sending areas. In 1973, a year of poor rainfall, 18,000 workers were recruited through the Gezira labour recruitment office in Nyala. A year later, after good rains, only 4,000 workers went to the Gezira (Haaland 1980a: 11).

Increased dependence on the market to obtain the means of production has also been characteristic of many farming communities in the Sudan in this century. Hand tools still remain the only means of production for most people. Even in the so-called mechanised farming areas, hand tools remain very significant, and they are increasingly purchased in the market. This is so even in those communities where production is predominantly for subsistence and not for exchange.

Two major mechanical advances have been made in agricultural production — the introduction of water pumps and of tractors. This has not only meant that the forces of production have been raised to a higher level. It has also meant a quantitative change in the process of primitive accumulation. This deepening of the process of accumulation is discussed in detail elsewhere (Ali 1983; Abdelkarim 1985), but some of its features are sketched in the next section.

Trade, finance and increasing pressures towards commoditisation

As household producers become more dependent on the market for their subsistence needs, they face disadvantages. These are of two kinds, the deteriorating terms of trade between agriculture and manufacture, and the monopoly position of the village merchant. As a result of government policies, agricultural products exchange on unequal terms with internally produced manufactures. Data for 1971 (Acharya 1979: 66; ILO 1976: 451) show that Sudanese industrial products had an average rate of protection equal to 107% as opposed to 27% for agricultural products. Thus there can be little doubt that household producers are disadvantaged in the market for internally manufactured products.

In most cases, household producers make their purchases from a small number of resident merchants. They also sell their products to these same merchants, who are thus in a monopolistic position. Nomads are apparently not subject to the same unfavourable exchange relations, because they are able, in the course of their migrations, to choose between many merchants and trading centres.

From this it can be seen that with increasingly unfavourable terms of exchange, household producers will have greater dependence on the market for their subsistence needs. They will experience greater pressures towards commoditisation, increasingly selling their cash crops or their labour power in order to maintain their previous level of consumption.

Household producers also face pressures towards commoditisation in the credit market. *Shail* (credit against a future crop) is widespread in the Sudan. Ahmed (1977: 115-6) shows that 60% of the tenants in the Gezira Scheme entered into such arrangements in 1973/4. *Shail* is an important means of surplus appropriation, and the rates of interest are high, ranging from 50% - 300% (Abdelkarim 1985).

Circulation capital feeds the process of commoditisation and differentiation in a number of ways. It enlarges the household's circle of needs; it leads to a deterioration of the conditions of exchange, and hence to a need for further commoditisation. The increased need for cash forces households to borrow from money-lenders. By intensifying money-commodity relations, circulation capital contributes significantly to the disintegration of the household and of other non-capitalist forms of labour organisation.

144

THE DISINTEGRATION OF NON-CAPITALIST SOCIAL FORMS OF LABOUR ORGANISATION

Forced labour

In the absence of systematic studies of the history of socio-economic formations in the Sudan, it is difficult to follow the development and change in the social forms of labour organisation. However, the work of writers such as O'Fahey and Spaulding (1974), Spaulding (1979), O'Fahey (1980), O'Brien (1980) and Elhassan (1985), point in the direction of some tentative conclusions.

In the four centuries prior to British rule, and certainly in the contemporary Sudan, the terms of subjugation of the direct producers by tribal and religious leaders, and later also by Turkish and Mahdist rulers, seems to have been mainly through taxation, tribute and donations. Labour service, especially in the form of military service, was frequent, although in the case of the Fung and Fur kingdoms, a class of feudal serfs akin to that of medieval Europe does not seem to have appeared. In some cases, slaves were captured through organised raids on neighbouring areas, and, especially during the Turco-Egyptian period (1820-81), a market was created (Hill 1959; Shibeika 1965).

Anti-slave trade measures were enacted by Gordon, the last governor of the Turco-Egyptian Sudan. These were resuscitated during the British administration. But, as O'Brien notes (1980: 164-5), slavery as an institution was not seriously challenged before the early 1920s, when a great demand for wage labour was expected consequent upon the establishment of the Gezira Scheme (see also Ibrahim in this volume).

Evidence suggests that slave labour continued in some places (Asad 1970; Omer 1979). Today some people are still known as being of slave descent, and lack full social acceptance. However, overall, the extent of slavery in agriculture labour seems to have been limited. O'Brien (1980: 513-6) argues that in the majority of cases, slaves were used as a supplement to, rather than a substitute for, household labour. Today this form of labour organisation has disappeared.

Voluntary labour

We can identify two forms of voluntary labour. One entails

reciprocity, the other does not. In the first form, voluntary labour is normally organised from within a narrow social circle of relatives, camp and village mates. In the second form, labour is performed for religious leaders of either local or national significance. Here there is no economic compulsion. At present this form does not seem to be very significant. The surplus appropriated by these religious authorities has been (and remains) largely through channels of regular or irregular donations, or even through specific "fees" for "medical" treatment. Such payments are called *mal al-zoowara* (lit. visit money).

In some parts of the Sudan, productive operations are traditionally done using co-operative work parties. These are known as *nafir* in many places, and as *faz' a* in the Northern Region. In *nafir*, participants are expected to carry out certain tasks, and in exchange they expect to be entertained with food and drink. *Nafir* generally entails an expectation of reciprocity, although this has declined in recent decades. Indeed, in some cases, it has been used by merchants in the process of capital accumulation (Barth 1967), and is probably more frequently used by those households having surplus grain which they can use to support the *nafir* (Elhassan in this volume).

In some recent studies, *nafir* has been reported to be on the decline (Omer 1979; O'Brien 1980; Abdelkarim 1985: Elhassan in this volume). It has been suggested that this decline is associated with the expansion of commodity relations. In many areas, wage labour has replaced *nafir*. In a number of cases, the replacement of *nafir* by wage labour has been part of the radical transformation of the production process to a form where the capital-wage labour relation dominates (as in Gedaref). In other cases, wage labour has developed as a form of monetisation of *nafir*, rather than as a distinctive class relation. In the cases of the Western Savannah (Elhassan 1985) and Um Fila (O'Brien 1980), no landless class exists, and most household producers work alternately for wages for each other, instead of organising the same process through *nafir*.

Changes in the gender division of labour

Different forms of household division of labour are present in different communities. These depend on the source of livelihood, the cultural position of women, and in particular the form of Islam and the consequent degree of female seclusion. The gender division of labour will also vary within different households in the same community.

In comparison, household division of labour based on age is similar in different communities. Generally, children below the ages of twelve and elderly people are assigned only a minor role in the production process if at all. Children may give a hand irregularly in some farming activities, provide services for the working adults, and rear home-based animals. At this age, even in communities which practise women's seclusion, young girls will be expected to perform minor tasks and may mix with other people outside the household.

Regarding the gender division of labour, there are some common features among different communities in Sudan. Women, even if undertaking a full production role, are still assigned domestic labour (see for example the case of non-Arab cultivators in Southern Darfur, Haaland 1980b, and the case of Elgayla village in North Kordofan, O'Brien 1980). What may also be common among nomadic and semi-nomadic pastoralists, regardless of whether they are Muslim or not, is that generally both young boys and girls may engage in rearing home-based animals, and both men and women may milk. But other tasks associated with animal rearing, which may include seasonal migration and travelling long distances are generally assigned to men (Cunnison 1966; Asad 1970; Lako 1983).

Among the Kababish pastoralists, the women perform all tasks associated with the household, including spinning wool and weaving tents, as well as making beds and decorations. The finished products are their property. Baggara pastoralist women perform all domestic labour and also erect, dismantle and move the tents to new sites. Once again, the tent is their property. In both cases, women also process milk, selling the surplus, and may help in milking and other "men's work".

In some farming communities women participate fully in the farming activities. Where there is little or no seclusion, they may be able to cultivate their own land. In some cases in Southern Darfur (Haaland 1980b: 72) and Northern Kordofan (O'Brien 1980: 442), it has been observed that women have separate fields over which they exercise full command, both of the land and its products.

In some cases where seclusion of women is the case, it is their public participation in work which is objected to rather than their participation in agricultural work per se (O'Brien 1980: 359). In fact, to some extent, O'Brien's argument may be generalised to some other communities. In Um Fila, women cultivate small plots within their *hosh* (home compound). Mustafa (1980: 112) also observes the same thing in Radom, Southern Darfur. And Shaw (1961?) argues that in the Gezira, women's participation in agricultural work in earlier times was apparently higher than later when migrant wage workers began to make up a large proportion of the labour force. Where women are secluded and where they cannot cultivate in private because of the conditions of production or for other reasons, their work may be confined to the home. However, this does not mean that they will not be engaged in productive work, as they may be engaged in household production. An example is the case of the married women among the poorer section of the community in Maiurno, who produce foodstuffs and craft goods (Duffield 1981: 107).

The cultural norm of women not participating in the "public" sphere or in agricultural work is no longer adhered to in many communities. A few cases will illustrate this point. In three villages studied in the Gedaref region, where women's seclusion is still advocated, they are not supposed to work in the fields, and are denied the right to inherit land. However, it was found that in three classified income groups — "rich", "medium" and "poor" — the percentage of women engaged in income-generating activities in 1982 were 16, 30 and 50 % respectively (ILO/UNHCR 1984: 42). However, household heads in these villages tended to deny that this level of participation existed. In Um Fila, women's participation is also changing. O'Brien (1980: 326) mentions the case of a merchant-farmer whose mother and two wives worked in the fields. Duffield (1981) argues that women's seclusion among West African migrants to Sudan, who have often been cited as one of the strictest groups in this respect, has been relaxed.

We can conclude from the above that the development of capitalist commodity production is causing changes in the household gender division of labour in many rural communities, especially where previously women were excluded from agricultural and other public work. The increasing pressure on the standards of living of agricultural producers has led some poorer households to relax their ideals and has pushed female household members to work in the fields, either alongside male members of the household, or to replace men who are working away. And even among the wealthier households, attempts to maintain or increase their higher level of consumption has led them to the same position. Obviously, such changes have increased the burden on women.

COMMODITISATION OF LABOUR POWER

Commoditisation of labour power has been developing at different rates in different areas of the Sudan. This can be explored by using a wide range of case study material. In some cases, like Gedaref and

Gezira, wage labour exceeds household labour when total labour inputs are considered. In other cases, household labour continues to be the major form of labour organisation. This is so among the Kababish, in Dongola and in the Western Savannah. In other cases, there is hardly anything other than household labour. The Dinka are an example. Our rural case studies also provide a wide range of comparisons in terms of the "release" and "absorption" of labour power. The Gezira is a case of both intensive release and absorption. Other case studies show release without absorption.

Gezira

The Gezira Scheme undoubtedly marked the commencement of a systematic process of commoditisation of labour power in the Sudan. The colonial government spared no effort to encourage "westerners" (people from both West Africa and from Western Sudan) to settle in the Gezira region even before the inception of the Scheme. Duffield (1983: 49) correctly argues that the West African immigrants "were amongst Sudan's first modern wage labourers". However, in Gezira not all these migrants were landless as some of them were offered small plots on which to cultivate *dura*, while others were even offered tenancies. In both cases, this was to encourage them to settle and to provide the bulk of their labour power as wage labourers.

On the other hand, the establishment of the Scheme began a process of commoditisation of labour power within the Gezira region itself. In the allocation of land in the Scheme, priority was given to the landowners and to their nominees (see, among others, Culwick 1955). Apparently many landowners were not offered tenancies, or did not wish to settle in the Scheme as permanent cultivators. These consisted of pastoralists and pastoralist-cultivators who had been using the interior of the Gezira for grazing and rainfed cultivation. These groups were forced to move away from the Scheme area to the east and the west towards the Blue and White Nile areas. Such moves seem to have adversely affected the rate of increase of their herds, and this made them look for resources to supplement their incomes. They were easy to recruit as seasonal wage labourers because of this need and also because they were familiar with the Gezira and its people.

During the establishment of the Scheme, other groups of people were also landless. These were the slaves, the landless and the small independent peasants who did not qualify for a tenancy. Some of these moved to *bildat* (rainfed) land outside the Scheme area. Others became wage labourers in the Scheme.

With the growth of the Gezira tenant population, and the Scheme being either unable to offer new tenancies or those tenancies being financially unattractive, many people abandoned farming in the Scheme, and started exploring alternatives within and outside the area (Abdelkarim 1985). Naturally, for most people this involved selling their labour.

It can be concluded that the Scheme started a process of free labour formation in the region, although a large number of the people who have lost access to land do not work as wage labourers in the Scheme itself. The other side of this process is that for other areas where free labour formation has begun, the Gezira provides wage labour opportunities, and may have been acting as an accelerator in the process.

In Gezira labour camps, the number of settlers has been rising, reaching about 170,000 in 1980, of whom 41% were found to be economically active (Tamin 1980). Seasonal wage labourers have also been coming in greater numbers. In the ten years between 1969/70 and 1978/9, their numbers grew, fluctuating between 261,000 and 365,000 (O'Brien 1980: 208). However, these wage labourers are not all free of access to the means of production.

Those who sell their labour to the settled people of the Gezira can be categorised as follows:

i) Those Gezira tenants (together with the members of their households) who have smaller holdings, and/or comparatively large households, may sell their labour to other tenants, particularly if they also have low asset endowments (Barnett 1977 and 1984). There is no data available regarding the frequency of wage labouring among the members of tenant households.

ii) As we have seen, inhabitants of Gezira labour camps are not all solely wage labourers. Some are tenants, and the majority are sub-tenants. This was the case in 78% of the households interviewed by the author in 1983 (Abdelkarim 1984). Some are also sharecroppers. The phenomenon of sharecropping between tenants and wage labourers is of recent origin. This development indicates an interesting reversal of the usual process, a decommoditisation of labour power. Sixteen percent of the economically active inhabitants of the labour camps did not undertake wage labour in 1982/3. Instead, they were fully engaged in their sub-tenancies. However, the majority of the subtenants (80% of the sample), reported that they sold their labour as well as working on their subtenancies (Abdelkarim 1984: 84). Such landplot-holding wage workers are in fact in a similar position to those tenants who sell their labour. Both categories are obviously not totally free of access to the means of production, and hence not yet "free wage labourers". They exercise control over their tenancies (or subtenancies), their control being limited by the administration and structure of the Scheme (Barnett 1977).

iii) The third group of wage labourers in the Gezira Scheme are those who have no access to the means of production, save a few animals. This group comprised a minority (22%) of the labour camp inhabitants interviewed in 1983. Also in this category must be included those workers who live in the tenant villages. The number of these is not known.

From the foregoing, we can conclude that the majority of the Gezira settled wage workers are not free of access to the means of production. In addition, in a small survey conducted in 1983, it was found that 92.5% of Gezira seasonal labourers have access to land either as cultivators or pastoralists (Abdelkarim 1984: 5). This suggests that the majority of seasonal wage labourers are also not separated from their means of production.

Gedaref

Wage labour has been present in this area since the days of *harig* (lit. burning) cultivation, prior to the development of mechanised farming. Western migrants had been the main source of labour during the earlier period, and continued to be so after the development of mechanised farming. The scale of commercial *harig* cultivation was limited. However, with the expansion of the Mechanised Farming Scheme, the demand has increased. In 1982/3, it was estimated (Abdelkarim 1985: 266-7), that the number of wage workers involved in Gedaref farming was in the order of 350,000, of whom 49% had no access to land (ILO/UNHCR 1984: 61).

Among the Gedaref labourers surveyed in 1982, only 11% reported that they were born in the region (ILO/UNHCR 1984: 59). This suggests that the rapid expansion of capitalist farming in the region has not been accompanied by a proportionally rapid process of separation of producers from their land. This may in part be due to the the fact that prior to the expansion of capitalist production, the Gedaref region was relatively underpopulated. It may also reflect the possibility that some expropriated producers have moved away. This may be the case with some nomads. However, since the 1970s, pressure on land has been growing (Abdelkarim 1985). The result of this would be that small household producers might have more need of wage employment to supplement their incomes.

Gedaref region is ahead of all other agricultural regions in Sudan, both in terms of absolute numbers and proportions of wage labourers who are totally separated from the means of production. The proportion of landless among Gedaref wage labourers, reported as 49% in 1982 (ILO/UNHCR 1984: 61), must have increased considerably with the influx of Ethiopian and Eritrean refugees in the latter half of 1984 and 1985.

Western Savannah

In the Western Savannah region, 54% of Elhassan's 1980/81 sample (Elhassan 1985) depended on wage labour to meet an average of 22% of their total farm labour requirements. While 40% and 3% of households had respectively hired 58% and 95% of their farm labour, there did not seem to be a landless class in the villages surveyed. In fact, wage labour is provided by landplot-holding fellow villagers. Depending on the size of the land cultivated, asset position and amount of household labour available, households stood in different positions with respect to their involvement in the labour market. There are four categories:

  i) 30.4% only buying labour;
  ii) 27.3% only selling;
  iii) 21.8% both buying and selling;
  iv) 21.65% neither buying nor selling.

It is the conditions of production, the need to mobilise relatively large groups of people for a particular task, which necessitates hiring of wage labour by about 52% of households in the villages studied by Elhassan. From Elhassan's study, it can be seen that the internal evolution of the village economy, though showing clear differentiation tendencies among households, has not yet resulted in the creation of a landless class residing in the villages as full–time wage workers. However, we cannot say from this study whether or not there has been any outmigration, with the resulting creation of free wage labourers whose labour power is realised elsewhere.

The Dinka

Among the Dinka there seems to be a very limited amount of wage labour. These people are mainly cattle breeders with some crop production. In the sample surveyed by Lako (1983), it was found that only 5% of households used wage labour in crop production. This was limited to land preparation. Female wage labour is hired for beer making. Apparently, no wage labour is employed in herding. However, these facts should not suggest that Dinka society is closed and self-reliant. Thirty eight per cent of the people interviewed by Lako reported involvement in labour migration. The ratio of such people at the time of the survey is not known. While Dinka pastoralist-farming household production is not able to meet the requirements of realisation of labour power for all its members, the communities have not yet been sufficiently polarised to allow the absorption of the excess labour force as wage labour within the community. This is possible because of the slower rate of development of the forces of production. Apart from the use of some veterinary drugs, there has been no notable change in the production process. This is, of course, true of many areas of the Sudan.

The Kababish

Most of our knowledge of the Kababish is derived from a study done in the 1960s (Asad 1970). Eleven percent of the households used wage labour in herding. According to Asad, paid herders only work for temporary periods and are usually paid in animals. They work until they have accumulated enough animals to become independent household-ers. Wage labour is also used for digging and repairing wells as well as some other casual jobs. Differentiation among the Kababish is clear, not only with regard to access to political power, mainly in the hands of one section of the tribe, the Nurab, and a few individuals from other sections, but also in terms of animal wealth. From Asad's account we are able to conclude that a permanent class of non-owners of animals did not exist in the 1960s: wage labour was only a transitory phenomenon. The difficulty with Asad's work, as with much other, is that it does not adequately consider the links between the community and the wider system. In particular, it does not tell us much about out-migration.

There is evidence of some out-migration from other sources. As early as the 1930s, Purvess (1935: 171) observed that many Kababish worked in the police force in the northern, riverain parts of the country. Omer (1979: 38-44; 78-81) also notes that settlement of members of nomadic tribes coming from the Western Desert, which is largely inhabited by the Kababish, in Dongola, has been going on for a long time, and had intensified in the wake of a series of droughts. These two statements are an indication that for a long time the Kababish have been able to move out of their community. Thus, there are indications that the community cannot cater for the reproduction of all its members.

Dongola

Omer (1979), our main source on Dongola and on the agriculture of the northern region of the Sudan, does not deal separately with wage labour. Therefore, it would seem that the role of wage labour is not significant in that area, although not because differentiation is absent. There is pressure on the land in all the northern parts of the country. This has led to fragmentation. Under such conditions, a surplus of labour and small plots, we could expect a high demand for wage labour. However, this is not the case. The *Sudaniyya* (a local term used to describe those of slave descent), after being forced from their bond relations, seem to have become the main source of wage labour early in the present period. Ex-nomadic Arabs and poor *ahali* (the indigenous people of Dongola) had also belonged to the category of *jiygols* (agricultural and domestic labourers). At present, wage labour is provided by casual labourers who are also cultivator-tenants and sharecroppers.

COMMODITISATION OF LAND

It seems appropriate to begin this section with a survey of the land tenure system in the Sudan before and immediately after British rule.

Land Tenure

The main source for this is Bolton (1948). By the time the colonial administration was established in 1898, three main forms of land tenure were in existence. These were as follows:

i) where settled farming had been practised, members of the community had rights dependent on the consent of the community leaders. Normally, nobody would claim rights over land cultivated by others. Land may or may not have been inherited, but certainly could be changed if it became exhausted. Abandoned land could be offered to other people. Ties to specific plots were loose.

ii) In some cases, in some communities, land was recognised as being privately owned. This could be inherited, sold or rented. This type of ownership had been established over land which had been cultivated continuously over a long period. For example, in the riverain lands of Central and Northern Sudan, in the Tokar and Gash deltas, land irrigated by floodwaters and in the wadis, and also in the Gezira rainlands and Nuba mountains.

iii) In the case of pastoralist communities, land was normally used communally. Organisation of land among different tribal segments had been, and still is, vested by the community in the hands of their leaders (Asad 1970; Lienhardt 1967).

By means of a series of land settlement ordinances (see also Gaitskell 1959: 42-48) from as early as 1899, the British administration had attempted to "regulate" ownership and to establish itself as the major legal landowner. According to these ordinances, three forms of ownership were registered, and still exist. These are:

i) individually owned land. Although the criterion for registration was continuous cultivation, this was not always adhered to. The riverain land of Central and Northern Sudan and the rainlands of the Gezira which satisfied this criterion were registered to individual owners. In other places, like the Tokar and Gash deltas, wadis etc., this right was not recognised. Instead, land was either expropriated (Gash and Tokar), or was registered so as to be potentially expropriated by the state.

ii) government land subject to community rights. All land not recognised as individual title, or not yet expropriated by the government, came into this category. Government thus established itself as the legal owner of such land. Although the right to use this land was, and is, vested in the hands of the customary leaders, government could and can claim the land. The national governments which succeeded British rule used this right to expropriate hundreds of thousands of feddans to be leased to large farmers in the mechanised farming schemes and in the large irrigated developments.

iii) government land subject to no rights. In this category we find land expropriated in the first two decades of British rule such as the

Tokar and Gash deltas, the basin lands of Karu near Shendi, expropriated in 1938, land incorporated into government sponsored schemes such as the Gezira.

The paradox arising from these land settlement ordinances is that the state formally owns the vast majority of the agricultural land in the country, while the people, most of whom are in fact ignorant of the legal situation, think and act according to custom where land is concerned. This sometime leads to conflicts, particularly where land is taken for new projects and the local people object.

Commoditisation of land: major steps and tendencies

The state has been the major force behind the commoditisation of land. Obviously, its role is conditioned by the socio-economic and political factors prevailing at a specific time. The role played in the transition to capitalism by the large landowning class in many other places, is played by the state in the Sudan.

Due to the absence of a landless class during the early period of British rule, and to the unfavourable political consequences of using forced labour in the Sudan, appropriation of surplus was organised through sharecropping arrangements. This began in the small pump schemes in the northern region and was then transferred to the Gezira. To establish the Gezira Scheme on land where private ownership had prevailed for centuries, the colonial government had to buy or force out the owners. This was the most significant step in the history of land commoditisation in Sudan. Several hundred thousand feddans of land which passed into government control by these means were leased to tenants in smallholdings from the mid-1920s onwards.

The second and third major steps in the process of land commoditisation were largely initiated by rising indigenous capital, in the first as circulation capital, and in the second as productive capital.

Private pump schemes developed first in the northern region. From the late 1940s and early 1950s and up to the mid–1960s, these schemes multiplied rapidly, reaching an area of well over 1,000,000 feddans (Shaaeldin 1981). It is the development of this process of primitive capital accumulation that has led to the emergence and expansion of these schemes.

However, rising indigenous and foreign capital also pressed the state to realise its "formal" land ownership and to lease that land to them, which they in turn leased to tenants. Both the colonial and post-colonial governments had an interest in such a course. Besides the obvious economic benefits, there were political interests as well. As Ali (1982: 1983) and Shaaeldin (1981) have argued, the colonial government was interested in establishing an economically powerful class ally. This group came to power in the post-colonial period, and their interests have been fully represented by post-colonial governments.

The development of the third major step in land alienation started in the Gedaref region. The precondition was the commoditisation of labour and the accumulation of money capital in the hands of a rising number of Sudanese nationals who were prepared to enter productive activities. This rising national capitalist class pressured the government in two ways. First, to realise its ownership on land over which it only had reversionary rights, by taking it from those with mere usufructory rights. Secondly, to lease the land to the capitalist producers. This process began in the Gedaref area in the 1950s and has since spread widely.

Further developments in the process of commoditisation followed. The government lets out such land on long leases, and these are in principle extendable. In addition, although illegal, such holdings are freely transferred and sub-let. Many of the "tenants" consider themselves to be "owners". While the government's rent from the schemes is set on a per feddan basis, there is an active land market in the area, and land is differentiated in terms of rainfall, soil type, and proximity to communications. In 1982/3, the market price of schemes of from 1000-1500 feddans ranged between £S40,000 and £S200,000.

In the Gezira, land rental and sale are very limited, if they exist at all. Because of this limit to the further commoditisation of land, a process of decommoditisation of labour power has apparently been taking place. This has been noted above.

In other places, land alienation is less pronounced. In Dongola, a large part of the land is freehold, but there is only a restricted market. Land ownership, however small, brings social prestige (Hakem 1976; Omer 1979). As a result, fragmentation occurs as inheritance follows the Islamic pattern. This leads to migration and the development of sharecropping agreements.

In the case of the Western Savannah (Elhassan 1985 and in this book) some commoditisation of land seems to be developing. In one village affected by the development of mechanised farming nearby, 4.7% of the people acquired their land through purchase and a similar percentage through rental. There is no landless class, but the majority of the producers also engage in wage labour on the nearby mechanised farms and on each other's plots during peak periods.

Lako's work on the Dinka (Lako 1983), reports that 3% of people acquired their land by purchase, and that 5% resorted to wage labour to assist in land preparation. There is no evidence of a landless class.

What can be observed from these cases is a strong relationship between the process of commoditisation of land and of labour power. Where a clearly distinct landless class has developed, and where wage labour is almost the only form of labour used (as in Gedaref and other mechanised farming areas) the commoditisation of land has reached its highest level. Where an initial step towards land alienation has been taken, as in the Gezira, and where the state has hindered the process of commoditisation of land and labour, a process of decommoditisation of labour has begun. The relationship between these two variables can be observed in other cases, and in other forms, as well. However, it is important to note that as in the case of other social relations, a positive relationship between the development of the two processes of commoditisation can only be described as a tendency, it is not inevitable. At any specific place or time, a number of other variables may play a role and influence these processes in different directions.

REFERENCES

Abdelkarim, A. (1984) *Social forms of organisation of labour in Sudan Gezira*, Discussion Paper No. 171, School of Development Studies, University of East Anglia, Norwich.

Abdelkarim, A. (1985) "Primitive capital accumulation in Sudan", unpublished Ph.D. thesis, University of East Anglia, Norwich.

Abdelrahim, A.W. (1963) "An economic history of the Sudan", unpublished Ph.D. thesis, University of Manchester.

Acharya, S.N. (1979) *Incentives for resource allocation: a case study of the Sudan*, World Bank Working Paper No. 367, Washington D.C.

Ahmed, S.A. (1977) "The integration of agricultural credit and marketing in the Gezira Scheme of Sudan", unpublished PhD. thesis, University of London.

Ali, T.M.A. (1982) "The cultivation of hunger: towards the political economy of agricultural development in the Sudan, 1956-64", unpublished Ph.D. thesis, University of Toronto.

Ali, T.M.A. (1983) "The road to Jouda", *Review of African Political Economy*, No. 26, 1983.

Amin, M.A. (1970) "Ancient trade routes between Egypt and Sudan, 4000 B.C. to 7000 B.C.", *Sudan Notes and Records*.

Asad, T. (1970) *The Kababish Arabs: power, authority and consensus in a nomadic tribe*, Hurst, London.

Barnett, T. (1977) *The Gezira Scheme: an illusion of development,* Frank Cass and Co., London.

Barnett, T. (1984) "The labour market in the irrigated areas of Sudan", in ILO/ UNHCR 1984.

Barth, F. (1967) "Economic spheres in Darfur", in Firth, R. (ed.), *Themes in economic anthropology,* A.S.A. Monograph No. 6, Tavistock, London.

Beshai, A. (1976) *Export performance and development in Sudan* 1900-1966, Ithaca Press, London.

Bolton, A.R.C. (1948) "Land tenure in agricultural land in Sudan", in Tothill, J.D. (ed.), *Agriculture in the Sudan,* Oxford University Press, London.

Culwick, G.M. (1955) "A study of the human factor in the Gezira Scheme 1951-55", manuscript, Sudan Gezira Board Archive Centre, bib. No. 460/18.

Cunnison, I.G. (1966) *Baggara Arabs,* Clarendon Press, Oxford.

Duffield, M. (1981), *Maiurno: capitalism and rural life in Sudan,* Ithaca Press, London.

Duffield, M. (1983) "West African settlers in Northern Sudan," *Review of African Political Economy,* No. 26.

Elhassan, A.M. (1985) "The state and the development of capitalism in agriculture in the Sudan", unpublished Ph.D. thesis, University of East Anglia, Norwich.

Gaitskell, A. (1959) *Gezira: a story of development in Sudan,* Faber and Faber, London.

Haaland, G. (1980a) "Problems of savannah development in Haaland", G. (ed.), *Problems of savannah development: the Sudan case,* Occasional Paper No. 19, Department of Social Anthropology, University of Bergen.

Haaland, G. (1980b) "Social organisation and ecological pressure in Southern Darfur", in Haaland, G., *Problems of savannah development: the Sudan case.*

Hakem, O. (1976) *Revision of agricultural production relations in the Sudan,* Report by the Department of Agricultural Economics, Ministry of Agriculture, Khartoum (in Arabic).

Hill, R. (1959) *Egypt in Sudan* 1820-1881, Oxford University Press, London.

ILO (1976) *Growth, employment and equity — a comprehensive strategy for the Sudan,* ILO, Geneva.

ILO/UNHCR (1984) *Labour markets in the Sudan,* ILO, Geneva.

Lako, G.T. (1983) "Jonglei Canal Project and its impact on the development of the Southern Sudan and on the life of the Dinka people", unpublished Ph.D. thesis, University of Manchester.

Lienhardt, G. (1967) "Western Dinka", in Middleton, J. and Tait, D., *Tribes without rulers: studies in African segmentary systems,* Routledge and Kegan Paul, London.

Mustafa, M.A. (1980) "A comparison of sedentary cultivation and nomadic pastoralists and their market integration in the Radom area of Southern Darfur", in Haaland, G. (ed.).

O'Brien, J. (1980) "Agricultural labour force and development in the Sudan", unpublished Ph.D. thesis, University of Connecticut.

O'Fahey, R.S. (1980) *State and society in Dar Fur,* Hurst, London.

O'Fahey, R.S. and Spaulding, J.L. (1979) *Kingdoms of the Sudan*, Methuen and Co. Ltd., London.

Omer, E.A.B. (1979) "Local traders and agricultural development in Dongola area: a study in rural capitalism from northern Sudan", unpublished Ph.D. thesis, University of Hull.

Purvess, W.D.C.L. (1935) "Some aspects of the northern province", in Hamilton, J.A. de C. (ed.), *The Anglo-Egyptian Sudan,* Faber and Faber Ltd., London.

Shaaeldin, E. (1981) "The development of peripheral capitalism in the Sudan", unpublished Ph.D. thesis, State University of New York.

Shaw, J.D. (1961?) "Labour problems in the Gezira Scheme", manuscript prepared for the Sudan Gezira Board, Sudan Gezira Board Archive Centre, Barakat.

Shaw, J.D. (1966) "The effects of money lending (*shail*) on agricultural development in the Sudan", in Shaw, J.D. (ed.), *Agricultural Development in the Sudan*, University of Khartoum, Khartoum.

Shibeika, M. (1965) *A history of Egypt and the Sudan in the nineteenth century,* Dar-al-Thaghqafah, Beirut (in Arabic).

Spaulding, J.L. (1979) "Farmers, herdsmen and the state in rainland Sennar", *Journal of African History,* Vol. 20, No. 3.

Statistical abstract (n.d. around 1981) Department of Statistics, Khartoum.

Tamin, O.A. (1980) *Labour camps in the Gezira,* report of the Sudan Gezira Board Department of Social Research, Musaad.

10

The Encroachment of Large Scale Mechanised Agriculture: Elements of Differentiation among the Peasantry

Abdalla Mohammed Elhassan

INTRODUCTION

The development of large-scale, rainfed mechanised agriculture was initiated by the British in the 1940s. Expansion along the Savannah belt took place under different political regimes in the post-independence period. The area expanded at a rate of about 200,000 feddans during the period from 1946 to 1968 (ILO 1976). Khalid Affan reported an annual compound growth rate of 20.8% from 1945/6 to 1975/6 (Affan 1982: 25). More recently, this type of agriculture has been growing faster, and "... is currently the most dynamic sub sector in Sudanese agriculture" (ILO 1976). Although such developments are occurring in a number of regions in the Sudan, similar features are exhibited in all of them (Affan 1982; Simpson and Simpson 1978; Dey *et al.*, 1984). Our concern with mechanised farming stems from the fact that rainfed agriculture is by far the most dominant form, in terms of both area and production, within the Sudanese agricultural sector. Thus, the development of large-scale capitalist production is a crucial part of the agricultural transformation of the country at large. This is particularly the case in view of the fact that it is taking place on land which was historically and traditionally used by peasants and nomads.

The importance of rainfed land is reflected in the area that it occupies, amounting to 12 million feddans out of a total cultivated area of 15 million feddans. The national development plan, founded on a policy of horizontal expansion, emphasised the development of this type of agriculture on the Savannah clay plains. The central rainlands of this Savannah extend over an area of 120,000 square miles, and it is for this reason that the Sudan was envisaged as the potential "bread-

These clay plains form a belt extending from Kassala Province, across Blue Nile Province into Southern Kordofan and Darfur. They also include the northern parts of Bahr el Ghazal and Upper Nile in the South. They make up about 51.5% of Sudan's total area, the remainder being either desert (28.2%) or semi-desert (19.6%) (Arab Organisation for Agricultural Development 1978).

Sorghum and sesame are the two main crops grown in these areas, and Table 10.1 gives some idea of the importance of the mechanised sector.

More important, though, is that the mechanised schemes' production

Table 10.1: Production of sorghum and sesame under rainfed mechanised conditions.

Season	Sorghum		Sesame	
	% of total area in in Sudan	% of total production in Sudan	% of total area in in Sudan	% of total production in Sudan
1968/69	24.0	23.7	22.6	24.0
1969/70	37.6	28.9	27.6	33.3
1970/71	41.7	42.7	17.1	16.5
1971/72	44.3	42.8	16.9	19.9
1972/73	67.2	34.0	18.1	29.1
1973/74	44.3	48.6	32.3	41.8
1974/75	52.9	44.7	28.6	24.4
1975/76	49.2	57.6	22.5	19.3
1976/77	49.4	56.1	27.1	36.9
1977/78	44.9	43.2	25.1	29.7

Source: MFC *Agricultural Statistics Bulletin*, No.2, 1979, pp. 77-80.

is primarily directed to the market. According to the Simpsons "the contribution ... as regards the size of saleable surplus is far greater than the share of overall production" (Simpson & Simpson 1978: 20).

In this paper, we shall explore the impact of the encroachment of capitalist farms on the surrounding peasant economies of the Western Savannah. It should be emphasised that what we are considering here is the early stage of a process of social differentiation among the peasantry resulting from this expansion of capitalism. Despite the process being in its early stages, elements of differentiation have started to emerge, and the process is under way. This is not to suggest that this process is explicable solely by the expansion of the large-scale capitalist farms, other factors internal to the peasant communities are also at work. What we are emphasising here is that element of differentiation occurring primarily as a result of the pressure on land as well as access to the use of machinery in farming. Pressure on land has initiated a process of proletarianisation among the peasantry. Small peasants have been driven into the labour market as a result. In the same way, some households which are relatively better-off have started to use agricultural machinery, improving their farming techniques and fundamentally changing their farming activities. It is this group which forms the nucleus of a class of agrarian capitalists.

MECHANISED FARMING AND DIFFERENTIATION: AN OVERVIEW

Planning and demarcation of the mechanised farming areas by government occurred in the late 1960s through the Mechanised Farming Corporation (MFC). This process amounts to nothing short of a massive commercialisation of land administered by the government. This is so because, despite the fact that legally, land is owned by government and leased to individuals, in practice it has developed a commercial character which takes a specific disguised form. In Fayo, one of the four villages discussed in this paper, in 1981 the entire village was encircled by the establishment of a large-scale scheme, and all the villagers – about 500 families – were reported to have lost their initial plots. In the early 1970s, some of the households started to migrate, while the majority put up a struggle against the MFC plan, and took the matter to the central government offices at Khartoum (Affan 1982). Later, the authorities of the MFC allocated nine schemes to the villagers in Fayo. Six of these, with an area of 1000 feddans each, were allocated to the whole village, distributed on the basis of household size and number of dependents. The remaining three schemes, with an area of 1500 feddans each, were allotted to some prominent rich peasants, referred to officially as "small farmers". The most obvious and immediate effect of this encroachment is to restrict land available to the peasant households, disrupting their farming system. The households lost access to their previous rotational areas. All the village land has been affected. Indeed it has been taken away as a result of these changes. Although the peasants have been compensated with new plots within the planned area, their overall position has deteriorated because: (i) the land which was taken away was clean and clear of trees and bushes, whereas the compensation plots were not cleared and incurred clearance costs for which no compensation was given; (ii) the bulk of the peasants lost land due its reallocation to capitalist farmers.

The newly granted plots are far smaller than those which were previously cultivated. Continuous cultivation leads to declining productivity and hence a reduction in household income. With the intensification of farming, the need to use fertiliser arises, an input requiring cash. Evidence suggests that the villagers' schemes are located on poor sites which include drainage areas and hills, contributing further to the decline of productivity (our survey and Affan 1982). Because the area is planned in such a way that the large-scale schemes of the capitalist farmers exist side by side with the village schemes and, also for the safety of the crop, legislation was passed by the MFC preventing the use of *harig* (lit. burning) cultivation. As a result, the households can no longer do the weeding using fire because this would endanger the neighbouring schemes belonging to the large-scale farmers. This has significant implications for household farming practices. It means either that required labour time will increase or the peasants must resort to hired labour, in which case there is a cash cost. However, in a wider sense, peasants' land is further restricted by the clearance of communal forest land. This has imposed limitations on households' ability to expand their cultivated area as population increases. This is likely to result in some labour migration. Even if the remaining common forest land is to be utilised, this can only be done at a cost given its remoteness from the settlements. However, some relatively well-off peasants and certainly the rich peasants, can still manage to reach and cultivate remote forest land.

The disappearance of neighbouring forest and communal land means that the non-agricultural activities of the household, centred around the forest and its products, are also affected. Crafts, building materials, firewood and honey are all becoming increasingly scarce. Since not all households can now have access to them, a large number are likely to start buying these items — once again increasing their need for cash. The combined effects of all these factors indicate that the household has to look for other sources of income to supplement farming. A major response by households is to sell their labour power in the surrounding mechanised farms. This phenomenon is growing in importance. A significant proportion of the peasantry is being marginalised and pushed further towards entering the labour market. The effects fall short of "full" proletarianisation since the peasants retain their plots of land, though these are now smaller. What is significant is that the conditions have been created whereby proletarianisation can occur. The emergence of a class of "allotment-holding wage workers" can be seen to "constitute a rural proletariat in the process of formation" (Bernstein 1982: 170).

On the other hand, the expansion of mechanised farming has benefited a section of the peasantry. This has been achieved through the rent and purchase of agricultural machinery from the large-scale farmers. The significance of the role of mechanisation and its impact on the peasantry has been emphasised by Duffield (1980) in relation to the Central Sudan.

Variations between households in terms of economic resources are not new. These took the form of differences of livestock wealth. Other factors, such as access to large and fertile land as a result of inheritance, access to sources of income other than farming, demographic and climatic factors, contributed to variation between households. This type of inequality does not necessarily indicate socially significant differences at the level of production. However, it does provide the base and the starting point of class differentiation. It is the better-endowed peasants who have been able to take advantage of the opportunities afforded by proximity to the large schemes and profoundly change their techniques and relations of production.

The existence of this class is recognised locally in the rural society, and the MFC refers to them as "small farmers", dealing with them as a separate category distinct from large farmers and the bulk of the peasantry. Initially when the Fayo villagers were dispossessed and later reallocated land, the share of the "small farmers" amounted to 4500 feddan. This was allocated to 45 farmers chosen on the basis of their economic ability and soundness. The World Bank, in accordance with its policy of helping "small farmers", is actually promoting this section of the peasantry by providing finance.

The distinguishing features of these small agrarian capitalists as it emerged from our survey are:

i) they cultivate areas in the range of 100-400 feddans;
ii) they depend upon farming as their main source of income;
iii) they produce for the market;
iv) their production is based on employment of wage labour;
v) they use machinery to cultivate their land;
vi) they are involved in trading activities in addition to farming.

In short, their production is organised on a capitalist basis. Their relationship with the large-scale capitalist farmers is one of conflict.

165

They regard the latter as being favoured by the government in terms of access to large areas, sources of credit and agricultural machinery. The small capitalists view the large capitalists as creating obstacles to their own development and expansion, since the bulk of the land is demarcated for, and allocated to, large farmers with holdings in the range of 1000-1500 feddans. Confronted with this situation, the small agrarian capitalists began to organise and act together and "are now pressing for larger tenancies to give greater scope for their undoubted farming ability". (Simpson and Simpson 1978: 36). Their struggle to acquire the status of large-scale capitalist farmers has involved confrontation with the state authority, the MFC. One of the means used to further their interests and expand their scale of operations is to cultivate outside the areas demarcated by the MFC. Even though this is considered illegal, in the event of the planning and distribution of new areas priority is accorded to those already cultivating in the area. Another response by the petty agrarian capitalists is manifested by their emerging tendency to buy land from those who have failed.

An important feature of the petty agrarian capitalists relates to their involvement in trade. The development of small capitalists from among the peasants appears to follow a general pattern of transition in many parts of the country. The sequence proceeds as follows: rich peasant — petty trader — small agrarian capitalist. The combination of farming and petty trading is an essential stage in this transition. It has considerable advantages insofar as it provides opportunities for gaining the maximum benefit from farming and other related activities which are vertically integrated. Trade also provides an opportunity for appropriating small peasant surplus through *shail*. These small capitalists consider the move into trade as essential for the expansion of their scale of operations.

We now turn to examine the evidence of differentiation as it emerges from our survey of four peasant villages in South Kordofan, namely Fayo, Kurtala, Elfaid and Delami. These villages were chosen to reveal the similarities and differences between those encircled by the expansion of mechanised farming (Fayo and Kurtala) and those which are relatively remote from the new developments (Delami and Elfaid). The results are derived from a 10% sample survey conducted in 1981, as well as from interviews and observation.

FAYO VILLAGE

In this section, we discuss some aspects of class structure. The households in our survey were stratified according to the actual area cultivated so as to allow an examination of the economics of each size category. There are problems associated with stratifying by holding size (Patnaik 1972), but in this case we included other variables such as labour market position, production technique and sources of income. Table 10.2 shows the position of the different strata in relation to the labour market.

Table 10.2: Participation in the labour market in Fayo village

actual area cultivated in feddans	total households		households hiring in labour		households selling labour		contribution of hired/total labour
	N	% of sample	N	% of category	N	% of category	input %
(A)<10	4	9.3	1	25.0	4	100	1.0
(B) 10-<20	12	27.9	8	66.7	10	83.3	31.4
(C) 20-<30	10	23.3	8	80.0	2	20.0	62.8
(D) 30-<60	12	27.9	11	91.7	7	58.3	52.4
(E) 60-<100	-	-	-	-	-	-	-
(F) 100+	2	4.7	2	100	-	-	94.2
Total	40	93.1	30		23		

Source: Own survey, 1981.

Note: Three households did not cultivate their land, thus column three does not sum up to 100%. The total number of observations was 43.

Twenty–five per cent of the households in group (A) hire in labour, but its contribution to their total labour input is negligible, and the labour process is founded on household labour. In the case of group (B), 66.7% of the households hire in labour which accounts for 31.4% of their total labour input. However, the contribution of household labour is still significant for group (B), while the overwhelming majority, 83.3%, sell their labour power. We can observe from Table 10.2, that the percentage of households hiring labour increases with the area cultivated. Thus, 80% of the households in group (C) employ labour to undertake 62.8% of their work, while at the same time a small proportion, 20%, sell their labour power. More than half of the labour requirements of both group (C) and (D) is accounted for by hired labour which is employed by 91.7% of the households in group (D). Whereas all the households in groups (A), (B), (C) and (D) enter the labour market as purchasers and sellers of labour power, group (F) with the largest area cultivated is a net purchaser of labour power. Group (F) is almost entirely dependent on wage labour.

The criterion of hiring and selling labour is insufficient to establish class divisions, since both types of transaction can be undertaken by a considerable number of households. Nevertheless, we note that the hiring in of labour by the small peasants in group (A) is insignificant judging from its percentage contribution to the labour process. In contrast, it is fundamental for the big peasants in group (F). However, we need to consider the range of activities which make up household income. Considering households in group (A), we note that they depend in the main on wage labour — 60 % of their cash income takes this form, coming from migrants' remittances (32%) and local employment (28%). Other income sources include livestock (20.5%) and farming (11.6%). Thus dependence on the sale of labour is more significant for this group than is the hiring in of labour. Households in group (A) can therefore be said to "belong to the poor group, cultivating little land, who cannot cover their needs with their income from farming" (Lenin 1899: 72). It is the existence of this stratum which leads us to consider that there is evidence of the formation of a rural proletariat.

The cash income of group (B) comes from three main sources — farming (36.6%), wage labour (31.3%), and livestock products (30.2%). These diversified sources of income appear to be of more or less equal significance for this group. The households in group (C) are least dependent on farming which makes up only 17.5% of their total income. Rather, their income is generated from craft production and artisanship (36.2%), followed by livestock (24.65), while income from labouring contributes only 21.7% of cash income. As we move to the occupants of the larger cultivated areas, as in group (D), households' dependence on farming becomes pronounced, making up 55% of total cash income. Even here, wage labour still contributes 20.9%. It is noteworthy that these households are involved in petty trade which makes up 7.4% of their income. This is in line with the previously mentioned movement of richer peasants into small trade, and ultimately agrarian capitalism. This is clearer still in the case of group (F) for whom trade accounts for 17% of total income. More important, though, is their significant dependence on farming, almost entirely characterised by capitalist production for the market, and providing 74.4% of their income. Households in group (F) are the typical petty agrarian capitalists of South Kordofan. It is they who have managed to take advantage of the agricultural machinery which can be hired or borrowed from the mechanised farms. In some instances, they have purchased their own.

Table 10.3: Distribution of households by actual area and method of cultivation in 1980 and 1981

actual area cultivated (feddans)	1980 households using tractors		1980 using hoes		1981 households using tractors		1981 using hoes	
	N	%	N	%	N	%	N	%
(A) <10	-	-	2	4.7	1	2.3	3	6.9
(B) 10-<20	6	13.9	7	16.3	8	18.6	8	18.6
(C) 20-<30	4	9.3	8	18.6	2	4.7	5	11.6
(D) 30-<60	9	21.0	8	18.6	11	25.5	7	16.2
(E) 60-<100	-	-	-	-	-	-	-	-
(F) 100+	2	4.7	-	-	2	4.7	-	-

Source: Own survey 1981.

Note: Totals exceed 100% in some cases because respondents used both methods.

Although some households in group (A), (B) and (C) rented tractors for land preparation and sowing, the majority used hoes. The bulk of households in group (D) used tractors, while all households in group (F) used only tractors. Use of tractors increased from 1980 to 1981. The significance of agricultural machinery use is evident from Table 10.4.

The use of tractors has increased the area under cultivation, which has in turn increased the demand for labour. We may also note that in the case of group (C), the proportion of households using tractors and hoes declined in 1981. This was mainly because some of them did not cultivate at all in that year. They did, however, have alternative sources of income.

From what has been said, the following elements of rural class formation can be distinguished: i) a rural proletariat or semi-proletariat; ii) petty agrarian capitalists; iii) some intermediate groups. In what follows, we shall further consider these issues in the light of evidence from three other villages.

Table 10.4: Percentage of farms using tractors in 1980 and 1981

actual area cultivated in feddans		1980 farms using tractors		1981 farms using tractors	
	N	N	%	N	%
(A) <10	-	-	-	-	-
(B) 10-<20	12	6	50.0	8	66.7
(C) 20-<30	10	4	40.0	2	20.0
(D) 30-<60	12	9	75.0	11	91.7
(E) 60-<100	-	-	-	-	-
(F) 100+	2	2	100.0	2	100.0

Source: Own survey 1981.

THE DEVELOPMENT OF A RURAL PROLETARIAT

We have already described the forces leading to proletarianisation. The evidence from Fayo village indicates that the peasants are not homogeneous but differentiated, and that the community is polarised. Evidence from Kurtala, Delami and Elfaid supports this conclusion. Table 10.5 shows the participation in the labour market of households who cultivate small areas of less than 20 feddans in these villages.

The proportion of households belonging to the small size groups (A) and (B) is significant in relation to the total sample of each village, constituting 55.1% in Kurtala, 78.3% in Delami and 83.3% in Elfaid. With the exception of group (A) in Elfaid, most production in these groups is done by household labour. In Kurtala about 15.4% of the households in group (A) hire labour, which contributes 23.2% to family farm labour input. On the other hand, 38.5% of the households in group (A) in Kurtala sell their labour. From this it follows that while the majority of households in group (A) are involved in the labour market, about 46% of this stratum do not enter that market.

As for group (B) in Kurtala, these households rely entirely on family labour. They do not hire labour and about 33.3% work for a wage. In Delami both groups (A) and (B) sell their labour. About 16.7% of the households in group (A) and 50% of group (B) in Delami hire labour, but it contributes little to their total labour input. In this village, the labour process is dominated by household labour, and to a smaller extent, by *nafir* cooperative labour.

The village of Elfaid presents an interesting case which illustrates different strategies adopted by different households in the

Table 10.5: Involvement in the labour market among households in the small size groups

actual area cultivated in feddans	total households		households hiring in labour		households selling labour		contribution of hired/total labour
	N	% of sample	N	% of category	N	% of category	input %
Kurtala							
(A)<10	13	44.8	2	15.4	5	38.5	23.2
(B)10-<20	3	10.3	-	-	1	33.3	-
Delami							
(A)<10	12	52.2	2	16.7	4	33.3	5.2
(B)10-<20	6	26.1	3	50.0	3	50.0	35.5
Elfaid							
(A)<10	2	33.3	1	50.0	1	50.0	63.0
(B)10-<20	3	50.0	1	33.3	2	66.7	18.0

Source: Own survey 1981.

Note: The sample size was 29 households in Kurtala, 23 in Delami, and 6 in Elfaid, representing 10% of each village population.

small size group. The village is located in a relatively remote area. In consequence, the pressure on its land together with the other factors associated with encroachment of mechanised farms, was not particularly strong in 1981 at the time of the research. We may note that half the households in group (A) of this village sell their labour power, while at the same time they hire labour to provide a significant proportion (63%) of their labour input. It is interesting that households in group (A) in Elfaid depend on wage labour for 67.5% of their cash income, while income from farming makes up only 32.5%. This dual dependence on wage labour by the households of group (A) suggests the possibility that they have adopted a strategy which attempts to strike a balance between family farming and wage labouring. This further suggests that labouring may be more rewarding than farming, implying that the price of hired labour in peasant agriculture in these relatively remote areas is low compared to the mechanised farming areas. In Elfaid, 66.7% of the households in group (B) hire labour, but its contribution to total labour input is small at 18%. Thus the households in group (B) in Elfaid depend mainly on household labour. Moreover, they depend for 71.5% of their cash income on farming, while 14.2% comes from labouring. Thus the households in group (B) seem to adopt a different strategy from those in group (A). Households in group (A) in Elfaid are relatively better off than those in group (B) (see Table 10.6). It is unclear why other households do not follow the same strategy as group (A), but it may have to do with knowledge and information about the labour market which is not available to every household.

If we consider the economic activities of the households in Kurtala, we can observe that group (A) is to a large extent dependent on income from labouring, accounting for 39.6% of their cash income, followed by livestock (28.4%) and crafts and artisanship (19.3%). In other words, in Kurtala group (A) is least dependent on farming which provides only 12.7% of their cash income. This group also suffers from indebtedness (see Table 10.6).

Table 10.6: Balance of household budgets in the survey villages.

Actual area cultivated in feddans	Fayo		Kurtala		Delami		Elfaid	
	% of h /h	balance £S.	% of h /h	balance £S.	%of h /h	balance £S.	% of h /h	balance £S.
(A) <10	9.3	-204.9	44.8	-501.8	47.8	-365.2	33.3	+334.4
(B)10-<20	27.9	-591.8	10.3	+4.9	26.1	-183.2	50.0	+43.0
(C) 20-<30	23.3	+492.0	17.2	+347.9	4.3	-877.4	16.7	+415.2
(D) 30-<60	27.9	+515.2	17.2	+1356.7	13.0	-369.6	-	-
(E) 60-<100	-	-	6.9	+1598.9	4.3	-860.3	-	-
(F)100+	4.7	+6658.7	3.4	+2028.8	-	-	-	-

Source: Own survey 1981.

The overall position of the households in the small size groups is very similar to that of the proletariat, with the only difference being that they retain formal control over the means of production. Once more we note income from labouring is very significant for group (B) in Kurtala. It contributes 69.4% of income. This indicates that the smaller the area cultivated, the more peasant households depend on supplementary activities, particularly wage work. An examination of group (B) aggregate family budgets in Kurtala (Table 10.6), reveals that these households experience deficits.

Households in the small size groups (A) and (B) in Delami are dependent on livestock rather than on farming. The sources of income for group (A) in Delami rank as follows: livestock and livestock products 63.3%, wages 16.1%, farming 15.2% and crafts 5.4%. On the other hand, the households of group (B) depend mainly on wage labour (55.6%) followed by livestock (28.8%) and are least dependent on farming (15.5%). However, both groups suffer from budget deficits (Table 10.6).

The general pattern which emerges from this data is in line with our previous discussion of Fayo village. These small size groups represent a rural proletariat in formation, although they may be better described as a semi-proletariat for they are not yet entirely separated from the means of production. We may summarise their position as follows:

i) they cultivate less than 20 feddans using simple tools;

ii) production is, in the main, by household labour and if labour is hired, its contribution is small;

iii) many of them sell their labour power;

iv) in general they are more dependent on wage labour than on farming;

v) where they do depend on farming, their economic position is worse than that of their counterparts who depend on wage labour;

vi) the bulk of their income is in cash rather than kind;

vii) they are significantly involved in commodity relations;

viii) in cases where the proportion of commodities sold appears to be low, the household is dependent on wage labour for its cash income, so that in fact the weight of commodity relations is significant;

ix) these households are often indebted.

THE DEVELOPMENT OF SMALL CAPITALIST FARMERS: EVIDENCE FROM KURTALA

Our earlier discussion of Fayo village indicates the variations in the material conditions of the peasantry. We have seen that the petty capitalists in Fayo are represented by group (F) who cultivate an average of 324 feddans. Development along similar lines is indicated by our data from Kurtala. Table 10.7 shows the position of the large size group in the labour market.

The households in group (D) of Kurtala cultivate relatively large areas, an average of 41 feddans. The majority of these households (80%) hire labour, and this makes up 77.9% of their labour input. They

Table 10.7: Involvement of the households in the larger size groups in the labour market, Kurtala village.

actual area cultivated in feddans	total households		households hiring in labour		households selling labour		contribution of hired/total labour input %
	N	% of sample	N	% of category	N	% of category	
(D) 30-<60	5	17.2	4	80	0.0	0.0	77.9
(F) 100+	1	3.4	1	100	0.0	0.0	95.7

Source: Own survey 1981.

are thus involved in capitalist production. An important characteristic of group (D) is that they do not sell their own labour. In group (F), the capitalist character of production becomes clearer. They cultivate an average of 117.9 feddans using hired labour for 95.7% of their input, and do not sell their labour. Households in both groups (D) and (F) depend upon farming for their livelihood as can be seen from Table 10.8.

Table 10.8: Sources of income of households in the larger size group in Kurtala village

actual area cultivated in feddans	(D) 30-<60		(F) 100+	
no. of households in size group	5		1	
sources of income	income £S.	%	income £S.	%
sale of farm produce	1615.5	59.8	5750.0	98.3
labouring	-	-	-	-
remittances	-	-	-	-
sale of livestock	140.0	5.2	-	-
sale of animal products	48.0	1.7	-	-
trade, business &c.	900.0	33.3	100.0	1.7
Total annual cash income	2703.5	100.0	5850.0	100.0

Source: Own survey 1981.

Sixty per cent of group (D)'s cash income is from agriculture, while trade contributes 33.5%. In these larger groups, farming dominates with trading acquiring an important role. The households in group (F) depend almost entirely on farming (98.3%) while trade contributes only 1.7%. Thus in the large size groups, agriculture becomes the main source of income and production is oriented to the market as indicated in Table 10.9.

Table 10.9: Involvement of the larger size group in the market, Kurtala village

Area cultivated in feddans	% commodities sold / total prodn.	% cash income/ total income	% farms using tractors
(D) 30-<60	67	77	40
(F) 100+	84.5	99	100

Source: Own survey 1981.

In groups (F), production for the market and use of machinery becomes important. The possibilities for accumulation are evident from Table 10.6. Compared to the mechanised farmers, these are petty capitalists, but they contrast sharply with the households in the smaller size groups.

INTERMEDIATE CATEGORY: KURTALA, DELAMI AND ELFAID

This stratum does not correspond to a middle peasantry where the households reproduce themselves by means of household work on their own land. It is merely a statistical artefact. It may include some middle peasants, but also includes elements of the semi-proletariat and the petty capitalists. Their position in the labour market is shown in Table 10.10 .

The intermediate category makes up about 24% of our sample in Kurtala, 21.6% in Delami and 16.7% in Elfaid. In Kurtala, 80% of the households in group (C) employ wage labour to undertake 54.4% of the work. Although 40% of these households sell their labour, their dependence on this income is insignificant (1.4%). In contrast to the semi-proletariat, both wage and household labour are important for this group. Most of their income is derived from agriculture (39.8%) and trade (39.5%). Their production is highly commoditised and 81% of their income is in cash (Elhassan 1985: 424). Thus their position is close to that of the capitalist farmers, with the difference that they

Table 10.10: Involvement in the labour market among households in the intermediate size groups

actual area cultivated in feddans	total households		households hiring in labour		households selling labour		contribution of hired/total labour input %
	N	% of sample	N	% of category	N	% of category	
Kurtala							
(C) 20-<30	5	17.2	4	80.0	2	40.0	54.4
(E) 60-<100	2	6.9	1	50.0	-	-	-
Delami							
(C) 20-<30	1	4.3	1	100.0	-	-	19.4
(D) 30-<60	3	13.0	3	100.0	-	-	78.1
(E) 60-<100	1	4.3	1	100.0	-	-	71.6
Elfaid							
(C) 20-<30	1	16.7	1	100.0	1	100.0	91.0

Source: Own survey 1981.

sometimes work as wage labourers and continue to use household labour on their farms. Their household budgets indicate a surplus (Table 10.6).

The position of group (E) in Kurtala is interesting. About 50% of them hire labour, but its contribution to total labour use is small, only 9%, and these households do not sell their labour. This case shows that the area cultivated is not a sufficient indicator of the presence of capitalist production relations. The households in group (E) in Kurtala depend on the household for over 90% of their labour, using hand tools. This may be explained by the large average family size of eleven members (Elhassan 1985: 409). Farming is important for these people, although in addition they receive substantial remittances. It can be said that their position is akin to that of the middle peasantry.

In Delami village, groups (C), (D) and (E) all employ labour. The households in group (C) and (E) depend on farming as the sole source of their cash income, while it makes up 78% of the total income of group (D). Despite the variation in the area cultivated and in the use of wage labour, the economic performance of the middle groups in Delami as reflected in their aggregate budgets (Table 10.6) is similar. The largest cultivation category in Delami is in the 60-<100 feddan range. The simple tools and the absence of tractors limits the area under cultivation in both Delami and Elfaid. Unlike the large groups in Fayo and Kurtala, there is no possibility of accumulation as all groups are in deficit (Table 10.6). The households of group (C), the largest group in Elfaid, sell their labour, but also rely on hiring labour which accounts for 91% of their total input. It is possible that this group is adopting the same kind of strategy as group (A) described earlier. Group (C) in Elfaid concentrates on livestock which accounts for 86.4% of its total cash income. They are the least related to the market of any group, and their cash income is only 12% of their total income. Presumably they pay their labour in kind or from selling livestock. Their budgets exhibit a surplus.

Thus there are some variations between these villages. There are locational differences in relation to the mechanised farming areas, and the effects of encroachment are more pronounced in Fayo and Kurtala than in Delami and Elfaid. Machinery is in use more widely in Fayo and Kurtala, whereas in the others hand-tools are still the norm. As a result, the area cultivated in Delami and Elfaid is small compared with that in Fayo and Kurtala. There are also differences in economic performance and in the degree of involvement in the market (Elhassan 1985: 332-57).

We can also observe variations in attitudes to surplus utilisation. While large households in Fayo and Kurtala tended to invest in agricultural machinery, in the other villages, livestock was preferred. We believe that an important factor in explaining the major variations is the degree of influence exerted by the mechanised farms and the accompanying changes in production relations. This impact is more apparent in Fayo and Kurtala, where mechanised farming is encircling the villages. As the large schemes spread, so these kinds of changes will affect more remote areas.

CONCLUSION

We can see from the above that large-scale mechanised farming affects adjacent areas through its impact on land and production relations. As a result, rural society is becoming polarised. This is manifested in the appearance of rural proletarians as well as small agrarian capitalists. This tendency has been influenced by unequal access to resources internal to peasant production. In other words "sociological differentiation" is giving way to class differentiation within conditions produced by the development of mechanised farming. These external factors, however, become internalised and form part of a unified process influencing the peasantry.

Over the last decade, a slow process of differentiation has begun. A major factor slowing it down is the character of peasant land which has yet to be commoditised. Historically this has been possible due to abundance of land. Nevertheless, we can see that commoditisation of land has started on a small scale, particularly in Fayo village, as well as in the emerging "partnership" system where small peasants, unable to cultivate their land, lease it to the better-off farmers. All this in addition to some indications of the emergence of a land market. The significance of this latter development lies not in its scale, but in the indication it gives that land is becoming commercialised. This will further intensify commodity relations, the implications of which were summed up by Lenin when he wrote:

> The further the penetration of commodity production into crop cultivation, and consequently, the keener the competition among the agriculturalists, the struggle for land and for economic independence, the more vigorous ... the ousting of the middle and poor peasants by the peasant bourgeoisie (Lenin 1899: 76).

REFERENCES

Affan, K.O. (1982) "Effects on aggregrate peasant labour supply of rural-urban migration to mechanised farming: a case study of South Kordofan, Sudan", unpublished Ph.D. thesis, University of Sussex.

Arab Organisation for Agricultural Development (1978), *A study of the conflicts of interest between the nomadic pastoralists and the sedentary cultivators in Sudan,* Khartoum (in Arabic).

Bernstein, H. (1982) "Notes on capital and the peasantry", in Harriss, J. (ed.), *Rural development,* Hutchinson & Co., London.

Dey, J. *et al.* (1984) "The rural labour market in the rainfed farming areas of Eastern Sudan", in *Labour markets in the Sudan,* ILO/UNHCR, Geneva.

Duffield, M. (1980) *Maiurno: capitalism and rural life in Sudan,* Ithaca Press, London.

Elhassan, A.M. (1985) "The state and the development of capitalism in agriculture in the Sudan: the case of the Western Savannah Rainlands", unpublished Ph.D. thesis, University of East Anglia, Norwich.

Lenin, V.I. (1899) *The development of capitalism in Russia,* Progress Publishers, Moscow, first published 1899, this edition 1977.

Mechanised Farming Corporation (1977), *Agricultural Statistics Bulletin,* MFC, Khartoum.

Patnaik, U. (1972) "The economics of farm size and farm scale: some assumptions re-examined", *Economic and political weekly*, Delhi, special number, August.

Simpson, I.G. & Simpson, M.C. (1978) *Alternative strategies for agricultural development in the central rainlands of the Sudan*, Leeds University Press, Leeds.

11

The Emergence and Expansion of the Urban Wage-Labour Market in Colonial Khartoum

Salah El-Din El-Shazali Ibrahim

INTRODUCTION

The few available studies of urban labour markets in the Sudan focus almost exclusively on Greater Khartoum. With the exception of a few studies (Sa'ad El-Din El Fawzi 1954; 1957; McLoughlin 1965; Ali Ahmed Suleiman 1974), most of the literature has appeared since 1976, after the arrival of the ILO/UNDP Employment Mission which sought to formulate a comprehensive development strategy for the country.

The largest part of the literature consists either of research output conducted and/or funded by that mission (ILO 1976; Kannappan 1977a; Mustafa 1977; 1983; Mustafa and Affan 1977; Affan 1977), or of critiques of the Mission's method or recommendations (Gelal Eldin 1978; 1979; 1980; Kameir 1980a; 1980b). The question of the urban wage-labour market has also been touched on in contributions to the study of Sudanese urbanisation (Elbushra 1971; 1972; 1976; 1980; Salih Elarifi 1971; 1972; 1980).

These contributions are welcome because they fill some gaps in the literature. With the notable exception of the attempts by Mohammed Elawad Gelal Eldin (1980: 425-32) and Elwathig Kameir (1980b; 41-8), the question of how the urban wage-labour market emerged and expanded has been neglected. As a consequence, the connection between that market and the processes of peripheral capitalism, which were imposed on the Sudanese economy at the turn of the century has been mystified. It is worth noting that the pioneering contribution by McLoughlin (1970) adopts what can be called an "historical" approach in the study of the labour market in the Three Towns for the period 1900-1950. The currently popular pre-war/post-war periodisa-

181

tion of the development of the urban labour market was initially formulated in that contribution. However, insofar as McLoughlin focused on the question of wage rates and the balance between supply and demand as described in official reports from the colonial period, his "historical" approach differs very little from the outright synchronic approaches in the recent literature.

The periodisation suggested by McLoughlin, subsequently adopted by Mohammed Elawad (1973; 1974; 1978; 1979; 1980) and Elwathig Kameir (1980b), conceptualises the development of the urban labour market in terms of the destination of rural wage labour migrants. Accordingly, it is argued that prior to the Second World War, labour migration was mainly intra-rural, directed to employment in agriculture, in which pay was higher than in urban areas. In consequence, labour shortages were not uncommon in Sudanese cities in general, and Greater Khartoum in particular. It is asserted that after the end of the war the shortage of urban labour became instead a large surplus, and that the colonial government had to refer migrants in Greater Khartoum to the agricultural regions and/or to their places of origin. Mohammed Elawad Gelal Eldin (1974: 20) explains the emergence of this "labour surplus" by reference to the "revisions and increases" in urban wages in the period 1948-68.

It is important to note in relation to the accepted periodisation that it has in fact distracted the attention of both Elawad and Kameir from pursuing the analysis of the "intra-urban" processes underlying the operation of the urban wage market, even though the basic elements for the construction of such an analysis have tacitly been touched on in the course of their accounts. My aim here is to redress aspects of this omission. Given limitations of space, I concentrate on the colonial period.

The central point is that from their inception, the urban wage-labour markets have been underpinned by the processes of what I term "peripheral capitalist urbanism". This term is meant to describe the pattern of urban life whose primary objective is to fulfil the requirements of colonial capital accumulation in a colonial trade economy created by the internationalisation of the capitalist mode of production.

THE EMERGENCE OF THE URBAN WAGE LABOUR MARKET

The imposition of the colonial trade economy did not only involve the reorientation of production in rural Sudan towards primary exports. It also presupposed the viability and sustainability of domestic agriculture with the household as the production unit. This meant the "petrification" of the domestic form in the so-called "traditional sector".

The significance of the domestic form of agricultural production in the procurement of cheap primary products stems from its so-called "subsistence sphere", through which the small producers satisfy a larger part of their consumption requirements. In the process of capital accumulation, prices for cash crops could be kept as low as possible, precisely because the "traditional" farmers and tenants in the large irrigated schemes are virtually self-reproducing. Even though the large scale mechanised schemes employ wage labour, domestic production plays a critical part in supporting this lucrative means of capital accumulation. The seasonal migrants can only exist because their reproduction is guaranteed by their own farms during the rest of the year.

The "petrification" of domestic production in the "traditional" sector, the inability of the large majority of small producers to develop their forces of production, reflects their inability to initiate and sustain viable accumulation which might lead to mechanisation, because of the monopsonistic position of the commercial bourgeoisie and petit-bourgeoisie (Ibrahim 1980; O'Brien 1980).

In view of the centrality of agricultural production in the process of peripheral capital accumulation, it should hardly surprise us that during both the colonial and post-colonial periods, serious attempts have been made to conserve and sustain (as opposed to "develop") domestic production. In maintaining this position, I do not deny that through processes of monetisation and commercialisation, the long term results of colonial policy were the opposite of their short term objectives. In other words, though the colonial administration attempted to conserve the domestic form of agricultural production, its incorporation into the circuit of capital, through subordination to merchant capital, has in the long run resulted in proletarianisation (if only seasonally) of increasing numbers of small producers. Given the virtual absence of alternative arenas for the extraction of surplus value, the main refuge for the partially proletarianised peasants and pastoralists is wage employment in both the large irrigated and rainfed schemes. It is only recently, with the escalation of the economic crisis and the decline in the real earnings of small producers, that increasing numbers of wage-labour migrants have turned towards urban centres in search of income–generating opportunities. It should be noted that until 1956, wage labourers constituted only a small section of the "economically active" urban population.

The processes of urbanism and urbanisation in contemporary Sudan are founded on the requirements of the colonial trade economy. Thus, the main processes underlying Sudanese urbanisation have been administration and commerce, maintaining primary export production and capital accumulation. Such a pattern of urbanisation not only presupposes the conservation of domestic agricultural production, but also requires a substantial urban wage–labour force. The emergence of such a social category in the Sudan hardly relates to the basic activities underlying the rise and growth of the urban areas. Rather it is the consequence of accelerated proletarianisation in the rural areas and of the increase in opportunities in the so-called "urban informal sector". This last, moreover, is closely related to the rapid urban population growth which is mainly a consequence of the increase in numbers of civil servants, professionals and members of the different factions of the bourgeoisie and their dependents. These latter categories are the elements that control the larger part of the surpluses created in the countryside and transferred to the urban areas, especially to Greater Khartoum. In this connection, it is my central contention that the increase in the size of the urban wage–labour force in recent years reflects the hope by many migrants of having access to a share in the surplus by providing various services to those who control the surplus.

In considering the question of the emergence of an urban wage-labour market, there is some evidence that it existed in a small form for skilled labour in the nineteenth century. The wage earners involved were almost exclusively expatriates, mainly Egyptians, brought to the country by the Turco-Egyptian colonial administration (Stevenson 1966). The small size of this market and its restriction to skilled labour, was mainly the result of the role of slave labour in nineteenth century urban Sudan.

Although slaves were supposed to have made up two-thirds of the population of Khartoum at its evacuation in 1883, by the time the British colonial state was established, virtually no form of urban labour was available. The expatriate skilled workers had left the country during the Mahdist period, while the colonial government abolished slavery in the urban areas. Thus an urban wage-labour force had to be created.

THE EMERGENCE OF THE URBAN WAGE LABOUR MARKET

A prime task facing the British administration was that of urban reconstruction. This process is of prime importance in the emergence of the wage-labour force. In addition to the labour requirements of the government departments, there was also the much greater demand generated by the massive amount of construction which was necessary. In both Khartoum (Abu Salim 1971) and El-Obeid (born 1980), a city had to be rebuilt from scratch. The consolidation of commerce gave rise to a rather smaller demand (Omer 1979; Elmustafa 1983). The virtual absence of a wage-labour force in the Sudan prior to the turn of the century, and the decision of the newly established administration not to use slave labour, meant that the country was virtually devoid of any form of labour which could readily undertake these tasks.

The initial response of the colonial administration to the question of labour was "strongly against the importation of foreign labour on a large scale until every effort has been made locally to adjust supply and demand" (Consul-General 1905: 15). Indeed it was only for skilled tasks that the colonial government relied on imported Egyptian, Greek and Levantine labourers, some of whom were soldiers (Consul-General 1902: 17 et passim).

A Labour Bureau was accordingly established in 1905 in order to register all landless and unemployed persons, especially in the riverain districts where private ownership had been instituted, and in order to "mobilise them to meet the pressing labour demands of government and private contractors" (McLoughlin 1970: 108-9). The pressing nature of that demand, and the determination of the colonial government not to destabilise domestic agricultural production in the course of meeting that demand, was pointed out by the Governor-General (Governor-General 1907: 16), who reported that:

In the present stage of development of Soudan [sic] the building and other construction works are bound to be considerable, and demand an amount of labour which is hard to supply without prejudice to the agricultural expansion of the country, which it is of such paramount importance to develop.

THE EMERGENCE OF THE WAGE LABOUR MARKET IN KHARTOUM

The scale of the building and other infrastructural construction tasks was particularly enormous in the case of Khartoum where by 1900 over 5000 wage labourers were reported as directly employed by the building industry (Kameir 1980: 41). By 1902, moreover, "the majority of the working population" in Khartoum was said to be "engaged in building, quarrying and brick-making" (Consul-General 1902: 22). The reconstruction process was not confined to the building of government offices and houses which were largely completed by 1902 (Elbushra 1976: 35). The construction boom that continued up to around 1910 concerned in addition, the building of houses for the "natives" and business elements, the building of the Military Hospital, the electricity station, market place and roads in the centre of Khartoum, the building of the river wall, and the construction of the Blue Nile Bridge — all completed between 1904 and 1912.

The first unskilled wage labourers in Khartoum were ex-slaves, dispossessed Northern Sudanese and West Africans (McLoughlin 1970: 106) Up to 1908, however, the supply of labour did not meet the demand, and ex-slaves seem to have made up the most significant sections of the unskilled wage-labour force in the Three Towns. As a result of this shortage of labour, wages rose, and to levels that "the native agriculturalist could not afford to pay" (Governor-General 1908: 70).

The "urgent nature" of demand in the construction industry at Khartoum seems to have had detrimental effects on the ability of the various government departments to recruit workers, or to maintain in employment those who had been recruited. This inability was the outcome of the differences in the system of remuneration between the two sectors. Unlike the system of fixed monthly wages adopted in the various government departments, remuneration in the construction industry was based on piece-rates. As it turned out, workers generally preferred the latter not only because they could determine the pace and intensity of their work, but also because when they had earned their target they could cease work for some time. In 1906, the colonial administrators became anxious because numerous workers in government departments were "all leaving permanent employment to take on piece work, for which they [could] get Pt. 6 per diem" (Governor-General 1906: 645).

Though the policy of mobilising local labour did not succeed in inducing increasing numbers of ex-slaves and landless northerners to migrate to Greater Khartoum, the problem of labour shortages continued as a majority of migrants did not wish to work on a permanent basis. This was so because on the one hand "the majority of Northern Sudanese migrants were circulating, rather than permanent labourers" (Kameir 1980: 429). The ex-slaves who seemed to have settled permanently in Greater Khartoum, on the other hand, were content to work for "two or three days in a month to make [their] living" (Governor-General 1909: 72).

In the context of the policy to conserve the domestic form of agricultural production, any attempt to adopt the classical methods of dispossessing farmers was ruled out. Alternative sources of unskilled labour had to be looked for. The alternatives were found in prisoners and imported labour, particularly from West Africa.

Prison labour

The idea of using prison labour was attractive to the colonial state from its inception (Governor-General 1902: 22). Thus it was progressively used to meet the needs of government departments. This aroused the concern of private entrepreneurs, who saw it as a threat to the process of capital accumulation (Governor-General 1906: 451-2).

Through the training of young prisoners under the instruction of Egyptian soldiers, a very small class of Sudanese artisans was created. This partly relieved the shortage of skilled labour. The number of young prisoners was very small. From 1908 onwards, the colonial state started to establish technical schools and to introduce apprenticeships in the workshops of its various mechanical departments. By 1910, the problem of labour supply in government departments seemed to have been solved once and for all. Most of the articles previously furnished by the prison workshops started to be supplied by the Stores and Ordinances department which was established in Khartoum North.

Though prison labour was progressively excluded from skilled tasks, the deployment by the colonial government of prison labour in unskilled tasks continued. In almost all tenders concerning the construction of public buildings in urban areas, the terms were such that the private contractor was to provide the building material and the necessary skilled labour, while the Prisons department was to provide the pool of unskilled labour. Prison labour was also deployed in tasks related to gardens, forests and domestic services (Henderson 1952:54). Nonetheless, prison labour was to provide no ultimate solution to the problem of labour shortage. Owing to the uncertainty involved in securing a regular and stable flow of prisoners, it became imperative to import labour.

Imported labour

It was maintained earlier that the colonial government had to import skilled labourers, especially from Egypt, owing to their virtual absence in the country. Though the colonial government attempted to train young Sudanese, the number of skilled workers and artisans remained a small section of the total skilled labour force up to the 1940s. A major factor contributing to this situation was that in the mid-1920s the Sudan witnessed a "heavy immigration" by skilled workers from Asia Minor, particularly of Greek and Armenians, induced by the collapse of the Ottoman Empire (McLoughlin 1970: 113).

Import of skilled labour meant large wage differentials between skilled and unskilled labour (Fawzi 1954). Not all imported labour was given high wages, and the import of unskilled labour had no such implication. On the contrary, imported unskilled labour not only served the end of conserving domestic agricultural production, but also helped reduce wage rates for unskilled labour in general. This was particularly so because foreign unskilled workers, especially West Africans, were willing to depress the wage rates to their lowest possible level (Duffield 1983: 49).

The colonial policy of encouraging and facilitating Nigerian immigration has recently been exposed (Duffield 1980; 1981; 1983). Prior to 1908, the presence of West Africans — *fellata* — was generally insignificant, but their numbers were steadily increasing (Governor- General 1908: 71). From 1908 onwards, West African immigration increased considerably, and the *fellata* started to emerge as a solid core of the unskilled labour force in the Sudan. The number of West Africans who arrived in greater Khartoum during the last seven months of 1908 alone was in excess of 5,000 (McLoughlin 1970: 110). In view of the fact that the wage-labour force in the whole of Khartoum Province in 1905 was estimated at around 3,500 (Governor-General 1908: 70), while in the early part of 1908 the urban wage labour in the entire country was said to be less than 6,000 (Governor-General 1908: 70), the role of West African immigrants in solving the problem of labour supply in Greater Khartoum hardly needs further elaboration. The labour markets in other towns such as el-Obeid (Duffield 1980; 1983) were likewise affected by the arrival of West African migrants.

Within the span of only one decade of capitalist colonial rule, the Sudan started to experience the emergence of what can be called an urban wage-labour market. The involvement of local labour in the newly established market was initially marginal. This was particularly so because until about 1910 the self-sufficiency of the domestic producers was not yet broken as the colonial government was concerned to stabilise the population in agricultural production. However, by the turn of the second decade of colonial rule, the process of incorporating domestic production into the circuit of capital was well under way. The attendant process of monetisation through taxation was soon to stimulate cash cropping and seasonal labour migration. In the absence of employment opportunities in agriculture in most parts of the country, many rural migrants were progressively to turn for work to the urban areas, especially to Greater Khartoum. In the next section, we shall see that the labour market was very volatile, and the newly created urban wage-labour force was soon to find itself redundant.

THE SATURATION OF THE LABOUR MARKET

The heavy inflow of unskilled labour not only helped meet the demand for urban labour and avoid disruption of domestic agricultural production, but also served to saturate the urban wage-labour market, especially in Greater Khartoum. By 1915, the colonial administration abandoned its initial policy of mobilising local labour, and issued instructions to "government inspectors to try to induce run-away slaves to return to their 'employers' (i.e. masters)" (Gelal Eldin 1980a: 426). Likewise, from 1912 onwards, official reports were hinting at the status of Khartoum as an important source of unskilled workers, and labourers were often sent from there to other regions of the country. These included agricultural districts, the aim being to redress labour shortages and/or help bring down the average daily wage of unskilled workers (McLoughlin 1970: 110 et passim). Indeed, it was not until 1920, with the construction of the Gebel Aulia Dam, that Greater Khartoum needed a flow of unskilled labourers from other parts of the country, as well as from Egypt.

By the time that work on the Gebel Aulia Dam began, the processes of monetisation and commercialisation had become firmly entrenched in most parts of the Sudan. Increasing numbers of Sudanese started to look for wage employment. Owing to the lack of agricultural wage employment in Western and Central Sudan, together with the virtual saturation of the urban labour markets in the west, the inception of the work at Gebel Aulia attracted many migrants from the western provinces. Due to lack of funds, however, work at Gebel Aulia had to be stopped in 1921. In consequence, many of the workers who had been attracted to Greater Khartoum became unemployed. The depression that hit the Sudan in 1930 because of falling cotton prices further aggravated the unemployment problem in the Three Towns (Annual Report of Khartoum Province 1931: 121).

The years 1930-1934 witnessed increasing unemployment of wage labourers as well as of clerical and other employees. The ample supply of wage labourers in Greater Khartoum in 1931/2 brought wages down to three piastres per day (McLoughlin 1970: 115), and gave the colonial administration the "opportunity...to revise rates of pay for servants engaged through the servants' registry and put them on a more reasonable basis" (Henderson 1952: 53). In 1933, moreover, it was reported that in Greater Khartoum there were some 7,000 "unemployed servants" on the register of Khartoum's District Commissioner; "several hundred unemployed effendia [clerks]"; and a "host of detribalised artisans...out of jobs" in addition to "the small but difficult group of axed native officers" (Henderson 1952: 53).

The deterioration in employment opportunities and/or remuneration in Greater Khartoum and other urban areas resulted in a drift by workers from towns to the agricultural districts, especially to the Gezira Scheme where there was work and higher wages (Gelal Eldin 1980: 428). Thus, only three decades following its creation, the unskilled wage-labour force in Greater Khartoum found itself largely redundant.

A VOLATILE REGENERATION

Following four years of unemployment and general hardship for wage earners in the Three Towns, the resumption of work at Gebel Aulia, absorbing between 7,000 and 10,000 workers, heralded a regeneration of the wage-labour market. By June 1934, the administrators of Khartoum were of the opinion that the problem of unemployment was virtually solved.

The outbreak of the Second World War resulted in considerable expansion in employment opportunities, and substantial numbers of workers were attracted to Khartoum. Apart from military service which absorbed around 46,000 Sudanese farmers and pastoralists, public employment in Greater Khartoum increased dramatically. In one government department, an increase of 1200% was reported (File CS/SCR/37.C.1, hereafter "File").

Wartime conditions disrupted sea-borne trade, and severe shortages of imported consumer goods emerged. For this reason, the colonial authorities encouraged private investors to establish a number of import-substituting, consumer-oriented industrial establishments in urban areas (Elmustafa 1983: 264ff; Mahmoud 1984: 53ff). In addition to the expansion in public employment, the war years also witnessed the generation of new employment opportunities in "modern" manufacturing industry. As the largest consumption centre in the country, most of these were located in Greater Khartoum. Despite the substantial increase in employment in both public and private sectors, the labour supply in the Three Towns was still sufficient throughout the war years and wages were maintained at a fairly low and stable level compared to agriculture.

The abundance of wage labour in Greater Khartoum throughout the war was a manifestation of the proletarianisation of increasing numbers of Sudanese farmers and pastoralists who, compared to the conditions at the turn of the century, were more willing to move from their places of original domicile in search of employment. The wartime conditions themselves were, however, factors underlying the intensification of the proletarianisation process. In this regard we should take into consideration the implications of the disruption of foreign trade which adversely affected cash crop earnings and, by extension, the ability of domestic producers to pay their taxes and/or buy goods.

The regeneration of the wage-labour market in Greater Khartoum was short-lived. As soon as the Second World War ended, both public and private employment in the Three Towns was drastically reduced, and rampant unemployment resulted. The resumption of foreign trade resulted in redundancies in manufacturing industry which collapsed owing to its inability to compete on an equal footing with imports. The demobilisation of the Sudan Defence Force accentuated the problem. "Many men were unsettled as a result of having seen military service in more distant places, and headed to the city when they found their farm too small a world for them" (McLoughlin 1970: 116). An abnormal Nile flood in 1946 complicated the situation as it induced an exodus from the devastated districts, especially from the Northern Province and from the Three Towns.

In order to avert the consequences of mass unemployment, the colonial administration started to devise schemes to evict the unemployed from Khartoum. One way was by referral to village of origin (File). Another was by transferring workers to a different region (Khartoum Province 1945: 143; quoted in McLoughlin 1970: 116).

The years 1945-49 witnessed the re-emergence of unemployment in Greater Khartoum. As with the unemployment situation in the 1930s, post-war mass unemployment did not persist, and by 1949 yet another volatile source of demand for labour was to emerge — the construction sector.

In the period 1949-54, Greater Khartoum experienced an unprecedented building boom as attempts were made to build new *deims* ("native lodging areas") (Gelal Eldin 1980: 429; Fawzi 1954b). This required such a large workforce that by 1949 colonial administrators were of the opinion that the "continued building activity ensured that none but the work-shy needed to find himself unemployed" (Governor-General 1949: 165-6).

The scale of both demolition and building operations was massive. By 1954 some 5,855 houses and shops were demolished and around 8,000 new houses were built (Fawzi, 1954b). The enormous demand for unskilled wage workers stimulated the building boom, solved the problem of mass unemployment, and resulted in a shortage of unskilled wage labourers. Prison labour was used once again (Arthur 1954), and there was a flood of migrants, especially from the South and the Nuba mountains (Gelal Eldin 1980: 430).

After the completion of building operations in the new *deims* by 1954, a larger construction labour force found itself redundant. Unlike the previous labour surplus, these unemployed workers were not forced to leave Khartoum. No official reports are available which explain this shift in policy, but an explanation would necessarily touch on the process of rapid political change which was then occurring. The era of formal capitalist colonisation was coming to a close. The transitional national administration, set up in 1953, was being consolidated in preparation for the smooth transfer of power, and the process of "Sudanising" top government positions was well under way. Though these changes hardly affected the peripheral capitalist basis of Sudanese urbanism which persists up to the present, many of the processes that had thereby been set into motion were nevertheless to influence the wage-labour market in urban Sudan in general and in Greater Khartoum in particular. The conditions of the urban wage- labour market in post-colonial Sudan are not addressed in this paper. Instead, in the next section, I will try to expose the peripheral capitalist nature of the wage-labour market in colonial Khartoum.

PERIPHERAL URBANISM AND THE WAGE-LABOUR MARKET

It has been argued above that the handful of studies that have considered the question of the emergence and expansion of the urban wage-labour market have tended to assert that the Second World War constituted the watershed between two epochs in the history of the urban wage-labour market in Sudan. In view of what has been said above, this assertion must be seen as problematic. I should hasten to add that the increase in the urban wage-labour force since independence is not disputed. In this section, I attempt to outline the factors behind my dissatisfaction with the pre-war/post-war dichotomy, and to highlight in retrospect, the interconnectedness of the processes underlying the urban wage-labour market in colonial Khartoum with the structures of peripheral capitalism. These processes and structures have not altered fundamentally in the post-colonial period.

The first point to emphasise concerns the periodisation suggested in the literature. It is important to stress the fact that, throughout the colonial period, the wage-labour market in Greater Khartoum was characterised by oscillation between labour shortage and labour surplus. At the inception of British rule there was an enormous demand for labour, and a wage-labour force was almost non-existent. The colonial government made considerable efforts to mobilise "local labour", and to import labour. By 1910, the problem of labour supply for government departments and commercial enterprises was solved once and for all. By 1912, a labour surplus situation had appeared in Greater Khartoum, and throughout the second decade of colonial rule, the conurbation figured as an important reservoir of labour which could be sent to other parts of the country. In 1920, however, another substantial demand for labour appeared, and a large number of rural Sudanese were attracted to the capital. A year later, the demand abated, unemployment surfaced and once again there was a labour surplus. Until the outbreak of World War Two, moreover, the wage-labour market in Greater Khartoum could not absorb all those seeking employment, and agro-employment in the Gezira Scheme seemed the only alternative available. Increases in government and private employment during the war years not only helped to ease the situation, but also attracted more migrants to the capital. As soon as the war ended, public employment was reduced, and the recently established manufacturing sector collapsed. The result was yet another labour surplus. In short, from the inception of British rule up to 1954 there were frequent oscillations between the two employment poles. Thus, provided that the assertion in the literature concerning the "change" from pre-war shortage to post war surplus can be corroborated (and this seems unlikely given the rampant unemployment in Greater Khartoum in the years immediately preceding the war), such a "change" should be viewed as one instance in a much longer series.

The recurrence of the "feast or famine" situation in colonial Khartoum leads directly to my second point, the question of the "externality" and "volatility" of the larger part of the demand for wage-labour in colonial Khartoum. It should be stressed that the oscillation in the wage-labour market which has been described was not a manifestation of the cycles of full-employment — mass-unemployment inherent in capitalism. The cycles observed in relation to the latter are consequential upon periodic crises of over-production which necessitate redundancies until new or renewed avenues for capital accumulation are found. In all periods of substantial demand for wage labour in colonial Khartoum, as in periods of large scale redundancies, the changes in the demand for labour were external to the basic avenues of capital accumulation, the import-export trade. This point is of such paramount significance to our understanding of the peripheral capitalist nature of Sudanese urbanism in the past and also in the present that it requires careful recapitulation.

Peripheral capitalist urbanism

In defining the concept of peripheral capitalist urbanism, I have maintained that the basic activities underlying the rise of cities in colonial Sudan were commerce and administration, both of which were founded upon primary export production and a colonial trade economy. In the context of progressive intensification of primary export production, and consequent increase in commercial traffic, and the further consolidation of the administration, the demand for labour was not only stable, but also steadily growing. At the inception of colonial rule there was a shortage of labour in both sectors. But within a few years that problem was solved and no difficulties were thereafter encountered in securing the required labour force. The only exceptions to this generalisation are the period of the depression in the 1930s during which commercial employment was apparently affected, and during the Second World War when foreign trade was disrupted, but public employment was temporarily increased owing to external, Imperial considerations.

With the exception of the war years, it was massive building and other infrastructural projects that constituted the main source of demand for labour in Khartoum. Likewise, the largest part of the redundancies resulting in the labour-surplus situations originated in the construction sector. Once the role of construction employment is recognised, and its implications are investigated, a basic contradiction in the operation of that market can readily be seen.

Basic to our understanding of the contradictory operation of the wage-labour market is the recognition of the status of the construction sector in the urban economy. This is not only an essentially auxiliary sector that, in all places and at all times, is intended to service and support other, more "basic", activities (commerce and administration in the case of Sudanese urbanism), but also one which is characterised by frequent and often considerable fluctuations in production schedules. Owing to the particular experiences of 19th century urban Sudan, what ought to have been an auxiliary sector at the beginning of British rule, turned out to be the source of the greater part of the demand for urban unskilled labour. This was so to such an extent that it undermined the flow of labour to the activities it was meant to support. In the initial process of urban reconstruction, as in the construction of the Gebel Aulia Dam and the building of the new *deims*, the construction operations were transient. Each time the operations were completed, massive unemployment ensued, and the colonial regime had to devise ways to evict the unemployed construction workers whom it had previously helped bring to the capital.

The contradiction in the initial emergence and later expansion of the wage-labour market is that while a wage-labour force had to be created, the larger part of it was meant to be temporary, living in the city only as long as was required for the construction. It was this expectation which lay behind the contradiction between, on the one hand, the realities of an urban construction wage-labour force and, on the other, the transience of most of the demand which created that labour force.

The transience of construction employment touches on the particular configuration in Khartoum of two basic features of peripheral capitalism. These are characteristic of the Sudanese economy as a whole. These features are: the disarticulation of sectors in the urban economy, and the severance of the critical link between the capacity of producers to produce and their capacity to consume. A brief discussion of aspects of the position and role of construction employment would illustrate some of the ways in which the disarticulation of sectors at the level of the Sudanese economy have been reproduced at the level of the urban economy.

Generally speaking, the question of disarticulation of sectors in colonial Khartoum can be approached by pointing out the lack of implications and/or linkages between levels of employment in different avenues of capital accumulation in the urban economy. The linkages referred to here are such as those observed in central capitalist economies in which the construction sector could be, and on several occasions was, deliberately used to generate employment, to raise the level of demand in the internal market, stimulating growth in the the wider economy, especially in manufacturing. This is the ABC of Keynesian economics and the basis of its call for public spending. A precondition for the success of this approach is the presence of a "critical link" between the capacity to consume and the capacity to produce. In other words, wages figure as a crucial source of demand in the internal market. Thus expansion of construction employment, with a resultant increase in total wages, should induce an increase in the demand for goods in the internal market. This increase in demand should generate an increase in manufacturing investment and employment, which should boost employment in commerce. All of these increases should feed back by stimulating further construction employment through increased demand for housing, and so on and so forth. This kind of multiplier effect in central capitalist economies is only possible in the short run, precisely because insofar as the orientation of the production process is towards the realisation of surplus-value and capital accumulation, crises of over-production inevitably follow. The point in this discussion is to stress that this kind of multiplier effect cannot happen in the peripheral economies, where wages are treated solely as "costs" to be kept at as low a level as possible in order to sustain the profitability of the colonial trade economy. In all periods of substantial construction employment in colonial Khartoum, there was virtually no implication for employment in those sectors of the urban economy in which the most significant processes of capital accumulation took place.

The basic avenues of capital accumulation in Khartoum were linked to the trade economy. Throughout both the colonial and neo-colonial periods, it has been the export trade which has constituted the primary vehicle for capital accumulation (Mahmoud 1984: 33-8 et passim;

Elmustafa, 1983: 140ff). The export trade, however, has been the most disarticulated sector in the urban economy. Insofar as it deals in primary products from the countryside it remains most insensitive to what takes place in other sectors. In no way could variations in construction employment have had implications for employment in the export trade. In asserting this, however, it is not my wish to deny that export production might have some implications, more often than not detrimental, for the internal market. The increased export of meat, grain and fruit in recent years, and the consequent increase in internal prices is a case in point.

Unlike the case of the export trade, the import trade is sensitive to fluctuations in the level of internal purchasing power. In other words, the increase, or decrease in the size of construction employment of necessity affected the level of demand for imported goods.

We should be careful, however, not to exaggerate the magnitude of these effects as far as employment in the import trade is concerned. Though the precise effects of the increase in construction employment are yet to be investigated and documented, my assertion nevertheless remains plausible when the orientation of the export trade in colonial Sudan, and the position of Greater Khartoum in the national trading hierarchy are considered.

As has been vividly documented (Elmustafa 1983) the consumer-oriented import trade in colonial Sudan had two main lines. The first was concerned with the provision of some basic commodities, the demand for which originated in all strata of the society. It should be noted, though, that in the early years of colonial rule, traders (mainly Greek immigrants) found great difficulty in marketing these commodities, not only because the ordinary Sudanese lacked cash, but also because they had not by then developed a taste for them. The second line was oriented towards the provision of luxury goods to meet the conspicuous consumption needs of a tiny but affluent stratum residing mainly in urban areas. In this regard, construction employment in Khartoum obviously resulted in increased demand for basic commodities, but owing to the low wages of manual workers, it did not touch on the demand for luxury goods.

As far as employment in the import trade is concerned, the increase in the demand for basic commodities could only create a few opportunities in retailing in those neighbourhoods where retail shops had previously been lacking, and in which migrant construction workers came to live. The assumption here is that in those neighbourhoods where retail shops had already been operational, the shopkeepers could easily manage to cope with the increase in demand without expanding employment. At the higher level of the import trade, virtually no increase in employment could have obtained, precisely because Greater Khartoum was the seat for almost all importers and the majority of wholesalers. In other words, as the Three Towns were the main centre from which virtually all imports were distributed to the rest of the country, the increase in demand induced by the expansion in construction employment could constitute no significant increase in the total volume of imports already handled in the city. In this regard, it is worth noting that though the import trade was sensitive to fluctuations in internal purchasing power, and as such was in a sense more articulated than the export trade, it was nonetheless the most accentuated manifestation of the disarticulation of sectors in the colonial economy. This feature can be better appreciated if we consider the fact that an increase in internal demand tended to boost the dependency of the Sudan upon imports, instead of inducing the emergence of a local, "modern" manufacturing industry, which remained virtually absent throughout the colonial period.

Though the expansion in construction employment in colonial Khartoum did not affect employment in those sectors of the economy in which the most significant processes of capital accumulation took place, it ought to have resulted in a relatively significant increase in the opportunities for both waged and self-employment in the small scale, labour intensive, service, manufacturing and repair activities which provide cheap products and services demanded by wage earners. Although I have no figures to support this assertion, given the high labour intensity of these activities there is good reason to believe that such an expansion in the size of employment took place. In other words, the level of employment in these activities which prevailed prior to the expansion in construction employment, and which met the demand by workers in government and commerce, could not cope with the increase in demand owing to difficulties constraining the promotion of productivity. These stemmed not only from the inability of the majority of these petty producers to initiate viable capital accumulation, but also from the fact that even when sufficient capital could be found, the introduction of capital-intensive technology would increase the costs of production to a level beyond what the wage-earners could afford, not to speak of competition from imports. Accordingly, more women could be assumed to have found openings in the market to prepare and sell cheap meals, *merissa* and *aragi* etc., or as in the case of the Ethiopian female migrants, to engage in prostitution. Likewise, more men could engage in petty trade or manufacture and/or repair of traditional articles in demand by the poorer sections of the urban community. To this extent, we may well conceive of a multiplier effect in the interrelations between wages and these so-called informal activities. With the growth of the wage-labour force in post-colonial Greater Khartoum opportunities in "informal employment" were to be accordingly increased.

The contention that the growth in the wage-labour force in post-colonial Khartoum has resulted in a corresponding increase in "informal employment" should not, however, be taken to mean that the whole of the so-called "urban informal sector" is entirely, or even largely, oriented towards wage-earners. Indeed, many of the increased opportunities for employment in secondary and tertiary activities in the "urban informal sector" in present day Khartoum are almost exclusively oriented to meet a demand by elements other than wage-earners (viz. administrators, professionals and the members of different factions of the bourgeoisie). Laundry services, car washing and shoe-shining as well as queue-standing, to mention only a few, are actually undertaken precisely in order to meet the demand originating in these relatively affluent strata. A detailed discussion of the situation in post-colonial Khartoum, however is beyond the aim of this paper; it is taken up elsewhere (Ibrahim 1985).

REFERENCES

Abu Salim, A.I. (1971) *The history of Khartoum*, Dar El-Ershad Press, Khartoum (in Arabic).

Affan, K. (1977) "Wage determination and structure in Sudan", *Sudan Journal of Development Studies*.

Ali, T.M.A. (1982) "The cultivation of hunger: towards the political economy of agricultural development in the Sudan 1956-64", unpublished Ph.D. University of Toronto.

Annual Report of Khartoum Province, Khartoum, 1931.

Arthur, A.J.V. (1954) "Slum clearance in Khartoum", *The Journal of African Administration*, Vol. 6, 1954, reprinted in Pons, V. (ed.) (1980).

Babiker, M. (1984) "The development of peasant commodity production in Dar Hamar: incorporation with immiseration", paper presented to the Sudan Research Workshop, Institute of Social Studies, Den Haag, published with same title in van der Wel, P. and Ahmed, A.G.M. (1986).

Barnett, T. (1975) "The Gezira Scheme: production of cotton and reproduction of underdevelopment", in Oxaal, I., Barnett, T. and Booth, D. (eds) (1975), *Beyond the sociology of development*, Routledge and Kegan Paul, London.

Barnett, T. (1977) *The Gezira Scheme: an illusion of development*, Frank Cass & Co., London.

Born, M. (1980) "Urban development in the Sudan with special reference to El-Obeid, 1968", in Pons, V. (ed.) (1980).

Consul-General, report by His Majesty's Agent and Consul-General on the Finances, Administration and Condition of the Sudan, Cairo, several years.

Duffield, M. (1980) "West African settlement and development in the towns of Northern Sudan", in Pons, V. (ed.) (1980).

Duffield, M. (1981) *Maiurno: capitalism and rural life in Sudan,* Ithaca Press, London.

Duffield, M. (1983) "Change among West African settlers in Northern Sudan", *Review of African Political Economy,* No. 26.

Elarifi, S. (1971), "Urbanisation and the distribution of economic development in the Sudan", in Hale, G. and Hale, S. (eds) (1971).

Elarifi, S. (1972) "Urbanisation and economic development in the Sudan", in Elbushara, E. (1972).

Elarifi, S. (1980) "The Nature and rate of urbanisation in the Sudan", in Pons, V. (ed.) (1980).

Elbushara, Elsayed (1971) "The evolution of the Three Towns", in Hale, G. and Hale, S. (1971)

Elbushara, Elsayed (1972) "Urbanisation in the Sudan", *Proceedings of the 17th Annual Conference of the Philosophical Society of the Sudan,* Khartoum.

Elbushara, Elsayed (1976) *An atlas of Khartoum conurbation,* Khartoum University Press, Khartoum.

Elbushara, Elsayed (1980) "The development of industry in Khartoum", in Pons, V. (ed.) (1980).

Elmustafa, M.Y.A. (1981) *Fertility and migration: a preliminary analysis of the dynamics of urban growth,* Economic and Social Research Council Bulletin, No. 91, Economic and Social Research Council, Khartoum.

Elmustafa, M.Y.A. (1983) "Capital accumulation, 'tribalism' and politics in a Sudanese Town (Hassaheisa): a case study in the political economy of urbanisation", unpublished Ph.D. thesis, University of Hull.

Fawzi, S.E. (1954) "Social aspects of urban housing in the Northern Sudan", *Sudan Notes and Records,* Vol. 35.

Fawzi, S.E. (1955) "The wage structure and wage policy in the Sudan", *Sudan Notes and Records,* Vol. 36.

Fawzi, S.E. (1957) *The labour movement in the Sudan, 1946-55,* Oxford University Press, London.

Gelal Eldin, M.E. (1973) "Internal migration in the Sudan since World War II with special reference to Greater Khartoum", unpublished Ph.D thesis, University of London.

Gelal Eldin, M.E. (1974) "The factors influencing migration to the 'Three Towns' of the Sudan", *Sudan Journal of Economic and Social Studies,* Vol. 1.

Gelal Eldin, M.E. (1978) *Some issues on population and development in the Third World,* DSRC Development Studies Books Series, 1, Khartoum University Press, Khartoum.

Gelal Eldin, M.E. (1980) "The nature and causes of labour migration to the Khartoum Conurbation", in Pons, V. (ed.) (1980).

Governor-General, *Report by the governor-general on the finances, administration and condition of the Sudan,* several years.

Hale, G. and Hale, S. (eds) (1971) *Sudan urban studies* (special issue of *African urban notes,* Vol. 6, No. 2).

Henderson, K.D.D. (ed.) (1952) *The making of the modern Sudan: the life and letters of Sir Douglas Newbold, K.B.E. of the Sudan political service,* Faber and Faber, London.

Ibrahim, Salah E.E. (1980) *Beyond underdevelopment: structural constraints on the development of productive forces among the Jok Gor, Sudan,* African Savannah Studies, Bergen Occasional Papers in Social Anthropology, No. 22, University Printers, Bergen.

Ibrahim, Salah E.E. (1984) 'Theory and ideology in Sudan urban studies: towards a political economy of peripheral capitalist urbanism", paper presented to the Sudan Research Workshop, Institute of Social Studies, Den Haag, July, published in van der Wel, P. and Ahmed, A.G.M. (1986).

Ibrahim, Salah E.E. (1985)"Peripheral urbanism in the Sudan: explorations in the political economy of the urban wage labour market in Greater Khartoum", unpublished Ph.D. thesis, University of Hull.

ILO/UNDP Employment Mission (1976) *Growth, employment and equity: a strategy for the Sudan,* ILO, Geneva.

Kameir, Elwathig (1980a) "Concentration and circulation of labour", in Pons, V. (ed.) (1980).

Kameir, Elwathig (1980b) *Migrant workers in an urban situation: a comparative analysis of factory workers and building site labourers in Khartoum,* unpublished Ph.D. thesis, University of Hull.

Kannappan, S. (1977a) "Urban labour market structure and employment Issues in the Sudan", in Kannappan, S. (ed.).

Kannappan, S. (1977b) *Studies of urban labour market behaviour in developing areas,* International Institute for Labour Studies, Geneva.

Kursani, I. (1983) "Peasants of the Nuba Mountain Region", *Review of African Political Economy,* No. 26.

Mahmoud, F.B. (1980) *The Sudanese bourgeoisie: vanguard of development?,* Zed Press, London.

McLoughlin, P.F. (1973) "Labour market conditions and wages in the Three Towns, 1900-1950", *Sudan Notes and Records,* Vol. 51.

Mustafa, A.M. (1975) *The structural malformation of the Sudanese economy: a historical account of the structural impact of colonial economic policies on the Sudanese economy,* ESRC Bulletin No. 24, Economic and Social Research Council, Khartoum.

Mustafa, M.E. and Affan, K. (1977) 'The Sudanese labour market: an overview of its characteristics and problems with special emphasis on the urban labour market", in Elhassan, A.M. (ed.) (1977), *Growth, Employment and equity: selected papers,* ILO, Geneva.

O'Brien, J.J. (1977) *How "traditional" is traditional agriculture?* ESRC Bulletin No. 62, Economic and Social Research Council, Khartoum.

O'Brien, J.J. (1980) "Agricultural labour and development in the Sudan", unpublished Ph.D. thesis, University of Connecticut.

O'Brien, J.J. (1981) "Sudan: an Arab breadbasket?", *MERIP Reports,* No. 99, London.

O'Brien, J.J. (1983) "The formation of the agricultural labour force in the Sudan", *Review of African Political Economy*, No. 26.

Pons, V.G. (ed.) (1980) *Urbanisation and urban life in the Sudan,* Department of Sociology, University of Hull and Development Studies and Research Centre, University of Khartoum, Khartoum.

Shaaeldin, Elfatih (1981) "The development of peripheral capitalism in the Sudan", unpublished Ph.D. thesis, State University of New York, Buffalo.

van der Wel, P. and Ahmed, G.M.A. (1986) *Perspectives on development in the Sudan,* Institute of Social Studies, Den Haag and Development Studies and Research Centre, Khartoum.

Index